OUTLINES OF MAHAYANA BUDDHISM

OUTLINES
OF
MAHAYANA BUDDHISM

BY

DAISETZ TEITARO SUZUKI

GYAN

Published by

GYAN

Gyan Publishing House
5, Ansari Road
Daryaganj, New Delhi-110002
Phone: 011-47034999, 9811692060
E-mail: books@gyanbooks.com

Distribution Network
gyanbooks.com
India, USA, Canada, UK, Australia, France

ISBN : 978-81-212-1246-5 (PB)
First Published, 1907

2nd Impression 2021

Printed at: Gyan Press, Delhi.

Outlines of Mahayana Buddhism
Author: Daisetz Teitaro Suzuki

OUTLINES

OF

MAHÂYÂNA BUDDHISM

BY

DAISETZ TEITARO SUZUKI

LONDON
LUZAC AND COMPANY
(OPPOSITE THE BRITISH MUSEUM)
PUBLISHERS TO THE UNIVERSITY OF CHICAGO.
1907.

PREFACE.

The object of this book is twofold: (1) To refute the many wrong opinions which are entertained by Western critics concerning the fundamental teachings of Mahâyâna Buddhism; (2) To awake interest among scholars of comparative religion in the development of the religious sentiment and faith as exemplified by the growth of one of the most powerful spiritual forces in the world. The book is therefore at once popular and scholarly. It is popular in the sense that it tries to expose the fallacy of the general attitude assumed by other religionists towards Mahâyânism. It aims to be scholarly, on the other hand, when it endeavors to expound some of the most salient features of the doctrine, historically and systematically.

In attempting the accomplishment of this latter object, however, the author makes no great claim, because it is impossible to present within this prescribed space all the data that are available for a comprehensive and systematic elucidation of the Mahâyâna Buddhism, whose history began in the sixth century before the Christian era and ran through a period of more than two thousand years before it assumed the form in which it is at present taught in the Orient. During this long period, the Mahâyâna doctrine was elaborated by the best minds that India, Tibet, China, and Japan ever produced. It is no wonder then that so many diverse and apparently contradictory teachings are all comprised under the general name of Mahâyâna Buddhism. To expound all these theories even tentatively would be altogether outside the scope of such a work as this. All that I could or hoped to do was to discuss a few of the most general and most essential topics of Mahâyânism, making this a sort of introduction to a more detailed exposition of the system as a whole as well as in particular.

To attain the first object, I have gone occasionally outside the sphere within which I had properly to confine the work. But this deviation seemed imperative for the reason that some critics are so prejudiced that even seemingly self-evident truths are not comprehended by them. I may be prejudiced in my own way, but very frequently I have wondered how completely and how wretchedly some people can be made the prey of self-delusion.

The doctrinal history of Mahâyâna Buddhism is very little known to Occidental scholars. This is mainly due to the inaccessibility of material which is largely written in the Chinese tongue, one of the most difficult of languages for foreigners to master. In this age of liberal culture, it is a great pity that so few of the precious stones contained in the religion of Buddha are obtainable by Western people. Human nature is essentially the same the world over, and whenever and wherever conditions mature we see the same spiritual phenomena; and this fact ever strengthens our faith in the universality of truth and in the ultimate reign of lovingkindness. It is my sincere desire that in so far as my intellectual attainment permits I shall be allowed to pursue my study and to share my findings with my fellow-beings.

In concluding this prelude, the author wishes to say that this little book is presented to the public with a full knowledge of its many defects, to revise which he will not fail to make use of every opportunity offered him.

Daisetz T. Suzuki.

CONTENTS.

SPECULATIVE MAHÂYÂNISM.

Practical Mahâyânism.

INTRODUCTION.

1. THE MAHÂYÂNA AND THE HÎNAYÂNA BUDDHISM.

THE terms "Mahâyâna" and "Hînayâna" may sound unfamiliar to most of our readers, perhaps even to those who have devoted some time to the study of Buddhism. They have hitherto been induced to believe that there is but one form of Buddhism, and that there exists no such distinction as Mahâyânism and Hînayânism. But, as a matter of fact, there are diverse schools in Buddhism just as in other religious systems. It is said that, within a few hundred years after the demise of Buddha, there were more than twenty different schools,[1] all claiming

[1] According to Vasumitra's *Treatise on the Points of Contention by the Different Schools of Buddhism*, of which there are three Chinese translations, the earliest being one by Kumârajîva (who came to China in A. D. 401), the first great schism seems to have broken out about one hundred years after the Buddha. The leader of the dissenters was Mahâdeva, and his school was known as the Mahâsangîka (Great Council), while the orthodox was called the school of Sthaviras (Elders). Since then the two schools subdivided themselves into a number of minor sections, twenty of which are mentioned by Vasumitra. The book is highly interesting as throwing light on the early pages of the history of Buddhism in India.

to be the orthodox teaching of their master. These, however, seem to have vanished into insignificance one after another, when there arose a new school quite different in its general constitution from its predecessors, but far more important in its significance as a religious movement. This new school or rather system made itself so prominent in the meantime as to stand distinctly alone from all the other schools, which latter became a class by itself. Essentially, it taught everything that was considered to be Buddhistic, but it was very comprehensive in its principle and method and scope. And, by reason of this, Buddhism was now split into two great systems, Mahâyânism and Hînayânism, the latter indiscriminately including all the minor schools which preceded Mahâyânism in their formal establishment.

Broadly speaking, the difference between Mahâyânism and Hînayânism is this: Mahâyânism is more liberal and progressive, but in many respects too metaphysical and full of speculative thoughts that frequently reach a dazzling eminence: Hînayânism, on the other hand, is somewhat conservative and may be considered in many points to be a rationalistic ethical system simply.

Mahâyâna literally means "great vehicle" and Hînayâna "small or inferior vehicle," that is, of salvation. This distinction is recognised only by the followers of Mahâyânism, because it was by them that the unwelcome title of Hînayânism was given to their rival brethren, — thinking that they were more progressive and had a more assimilating energy than the latter. The adherents of Hînayânism, as a matter of course, refused to sanction the Mahâyânist doctrine as the genuine teaching of Buddha, and insisted that there could not be any other Buddhism than their own, to them naturally the Mahâyâna system was a sort of heresy.

Geographically, the progressive school of Buddhism found its supporters in Nepal, Tibet, China, Corea, and Japan, while the conservative school established itself in Ceylon,[1] Siam, and Burma. Hence the Mahâyâna and the Hînayâna are also known respectively Northern and Southern Buddhism.

En passant, let me remark that this distinction, however, is not quite correct, for we have some

[1] The Anagârika Dharmapala of Ceylon objects to this geographical distinction. He does not see any reason why the Buddhism of Ceylon should be regarded as Hînayânism, when it teaches a realisation of the Highest Perfect Knowledge (*Anuttara-samyak-sambodhi*) and also of the six Virtues of Perfection (*Pâramitâ*), — these two features, among some others, being considered to be characteristic of Mahâyânism. It is possible that when the so-called Mahâyânism gained great power all over Central India in the times of Nâgârjuna and Âryadeva, it also found its advocates in the Isle of Lion, or at least the followers of Buddha there might have been influenced to such an extent as to modify their conservative views. At the present stage of the study of Buddhism, however, it is not yet perfectly clear to see how this took place. When a thorough comparative review of Pâli, Singhalese, Tibetan, Sanskrit, and Chinese Buddhist documents is effected, we shall be able to understand the history and development of Buddhism to its full extent.

schools in China and Japan, whose equivalent or counterpart cannot be found in the so-called Northern Buddhism, that is, Buddhism flourishing in Northern India. For instance, we do not have in Nepal or in Tibet anything like the Sukhâvatî sects of Japan or China. Of course, the general essential ideas of the Sukhâvatî philosophy are found in the sûtra literature as well as in the writings of such authors as Açvaghoṣa, Asanga, and Nâgârjuna. But those ideas were not developed and made into a new sect as they were in the East. Therefore, it may be more proper to divide Buddhism into three, instead of two, geographical sections: Southern, Northern, and Eastern.

Why the two Doctrines?

In spite of this distinction, the two schools, Hînayânism and Mahâyânism, are no more than two main issues of one original source, which was first discovered by Çâkyamuni; and, as a matter of course, we find many common traits which are essential to both of them. The spirit that animated the innermost heart of Buddha is perceptible in Southern as well as in Northern Buddhism. The difference between them is not radical or qualitative as imagined by some. It is due, on the one hand, to a general unfolding of the religious consciousness and a constant broadening of the intellectual horizon, and, on the other hand, to the conservative efforts to literally preserve the monastic rules and traditions. Both schools started with the same spirit, pursuing the same course. But after a while one did not feel any necessity for broadening the spirit of the master and adhered to his words as literally as possible; whilst the other, actuated by a liberal and comprehensive spirit, has drawn nourishments from all available sources, in order to unfold the germs in the original system that were vigorous and generative. These diverse inclinations among primitive Buddhists naturally led to the dissension af Mahâyânism and Hînayânism.

We cannot here enter into any detailed accounts as to what external and internal forces were acting in the body of Buddhism to produce the Mahâyâna system, or as to how gradually it unfolded itself so as to absorb and assimilate all the discordant thoughts that came in contact with it. Suffice it to state and answer in general terms the question which is frequently asked by the uninitiated: "Why did one Buddhism ever allow itself to be differentiated into two systems, which are apparently in contradiction in more than one point with each other?" In other words, "How can there be two Buddhisms equally representing the true doctrine of the founder?"

The reason is plain enough. The teachings of a great religious founder are as a rule very general, comprehensive, and many-sided: and, therefore, there are great possibilities in them to allow various liberal interpretations by his disciples. And it is on this very account of comprehensiveness that enables followers of diverse needs, characters, and trainings to satisfy their spiritual appetite universally and severally with the teachings of their master. This comprehensiveness, however, is not due to the intentional use by the leader of ambiguous terms, nor is it due to the obscurity and confusion of his own conceptions. The initiator of a movement, spiritual as well as intellectual, has no time to think out all its possible details and consequences. When the principle of the movement is understood by the contemporaries and the foundation of it is solidly laid down, his own part as initiator is accomplished; and the remainder can safely be left over to his successors. The latter will take up the work and carry it out in all its particulars, while making all necessary alterations and ameliorations according to circumstances. Therefore, the rôle to be played by the originator is necessarily indefinite and comprehensive.

Kant, for instance, as promotor of German philosophy, has become the father of such diverse philosophical systems as Jacobi's Fichte's, Hegel's, Schopenhauer's, etc., while each of them endeavored to develop some points indefinitely or covertly or indirectly stated by Kant himself. Jesus of Nazareth, as instigator of a revolutionary movement against Judaism, did not have any stereotyped theological doctrines, such as were established later by Christian doctors. The indefiniteness of his views was so apparent that it caused even among his personal disciples a sort of dissension, while a majority of his disciples cherished a visionary hope for the advent of a divine kingdom on earth. But those externalities which are doomed to pass, do not prevent the spirit of the movement once awakened by a great leader from growing more powerful and noble.

The same thing can be said of the teachings of the Buddha. What he inspired in his followers was the spirit of that religious system which is now known as Buddhism. Guided by this spirit, his followers severally developed his teachings as required by their special needs and circumstances, finally giving birth to the distinction of Mahâyânism and Hînayânism.

The Original Meaning of Mahâyâna.

The term Mahâyâna was first used to designate the highest principle, or being, or knowledge, of which the universe with all its sentient and non-sentient beings is a manifestation, and through which only they can attain final salvation (*mokṣa* or *nirvâna*). Mahâyâna was not the name given to any religious doctrine, nor had it anything to do with doctrinal controversy, though later it was so utilised by the progressive party.

Açvaghoṣa, the first Mahâyâna expounder known to us, — living about the time of Christ, — used the term in his religio-philosophical book called *Discourse on the Awakening of Faith in the Mahâyâna* [1] as synonymous with Bhûtatathâtâ, or Dharmakâyâ, [2] the

[1] Translated into English by the author, 1900. The Open Court Pub. Co. Chicago.

[2] These terms are explained elsewhere.

highest principle of Mahâyânism. He likened the recognition of, and faith in, this highest being and principle into a conveyance which will carry us safely across the tempestuous ocean of birth and death (*samsâra*) to the eternal shore of Nirvâna.

Soon after him, however, the controversy between the two schools of Buddhism, conservatives and progressionists as we might call them, became more and more pronounced; and when it reached its climax which was most probably in the times of Nâgârjuna and Âryadeva, i. e., a few centnries after Açvaghoṣa, the progressive party ingeniously invented the term Hînayâna in contrast to Mahâyâna, the latter having been adopted by them as the watchword of their own school. The Hînayânists and the Tîrthakas [1] then were sweepingly condemned by the Mahâyânists as inadequate to achieve a universal salvation of sentient beings.

An Older Classification of Buddhists.

Before the distinction of Mahâyânists and Hînayânists became definite, that is to say, at the time of Nâgârjuna or even before it, those Buddhists who held a more progressive and broader view tried to distinguish three yânas among the followers of the Buddha, viz., Bodhisattva-yâna, Pratyekabuddha-yâna, and Çrâvaka-yâna; yâna being another name for class.

[1] Followers of any religious sects other than Buddhism. The term is sometimes used in a contemptuous sense, like heathen by Christians.

The Bodhisattva is that class of Buddhists who, believing in the Bodhi (intelligence or wisdom), which is a reflection of the Dharmakâya in the human soul, direct all their spiritual energy toward realising and developing it for the sake of their fellow-creatures.

The Pratyekabuddha is a "solitary thinker" or a philosopher, who, retiring into solitude and calmly contemplating on the evanescence of worldly pleasures, endeavors to attain his own salvation, but remains unconcerned with the sufferings of his fellow-beings. Religiously considered, a Pratyekabuddha is cold, impassive, egotistic, and lacks love for all mankind.

The Çrâvaka which means "hearer" is inferior in the estimate of Mahâyânists even to the Pratyekabuddha, for he does not possess any intellect that enables him to think independently and to find out by himself the way to final salvation. Being endowed, however, with a pious heart, he is willing to listen to the instructions of the Buddha, to believe in him, to observe faithfully all the moral precepts given by him, and rests fully contented within the narrow horizon of his mediocre intellect.

To a further elucidation of Bodhisattvahood and its important bearings in the Mahâyâna Buddhism, we devote a special chapter below. For Mahâyânism is no more than the Buddhism of Bodhisattvas, while the Prayekabuddhas and the Çrâvakas are considered by Mahâyânists to be adherents of Hînayânism.

The Mahâyâna Buddhism Defined.

We can now form a somewhat definite notion as to what the Mahâyâna Buddhism is. It is the Buddhism which, inspired by a progressive spirit, broadened its original scope, so far as it did not contradict the inner significance of the teachings of the Buddha, and which assimilated other religio-philosophical beliefs within itself, whenever it felt that, by so doing, people of more widely different characters and intellectual endowments could be saved. Let us be satisfied at present with this statement, until we enter into a more detailed exposition of its doctrinal peculiarities in the pages that follow.

It may not be out of place, while passing, to remark that the term Mahâyânism is used in this work merely in contradistinction to that form of Buddhism, which is flourishing in Ceylon and Burma and other central Asiatic nations, and whose literature is principally written in the language called Pâli, which comes from the same stock as Sanskrit. The term "Mahâyâna" does not imply, as it is used here, any sense of superiority over the Hînayâna. When the historical aspect of Mahâyânism is treated, it may naturally develop that its over-zealous and one-sided devotees unnecessarily emphasised its controversial and dogmatical phase at the sacrifice of its true spirit; but the reader must not think that this work has anything to do with those complications. In fact, Mahâyânism professes to be a boundless ocean in which all form of thought and faith can find its congenial and welcome home; why then should we make it militate against its own fellow-doctrine, Hînayânism?

2. IS THE MAHÂYÂNA BUDDHISM THE GENUINE TEACHING OF THE BUDDHA?

What is generally known to the Western nations by the name of Buddhism is Hînayânism, whose scriptures as above stated are written in Pâli and studied mostly in Ceylon, Burma, and Siam. It was through this language that the first knowledge of Buddhism was acquired by Orientalists; and naturally they came to regard Hînayânism or Southern Buddhism as the only genuine teachings of the Buddha. They insisted, and some of them still insist, that to have an adequate and thorough knowledge of Buddhism, they must confine themselves solely to the study of the Pâli, that whatever may be learned from other sources, i. e., from the Sanskrit, Tibetan, or Chinese documents should be considered as throwing only a side-light on the reliable information obtained from the Pâli, and further that the knowledge derived from the former should in certain cases be discarded as accounts of a degenerated form of Buddhism. Owing to these unfortunate hypotheses, the significance of Mahâyânism as a living religion has been entirely ignored; and even those who are regarded as best authorities on the subject appear greatly misinformed and, what is worse, altogether prejudiced.

No Life Without Growth.

This is very unfair on the part of the critics, because what religion is there in the whole history of mankind that has not made any development whatever, that has remained the same, like the granite, throughout its entire course? Let us ask whether there is any religion which has shown some signs of vitality and yet retained its primitive form intact and unmodified in every respect. Is not changeableness, that is, susceptibility to irritation the most essential sign of vitality? Every organism grows, which means a change in some way or other. There is no form of life to be found anywhere on earth, that does not grow or change, or that has not any inherent power of adjusting itself to the surrounding conditions.

Take, for example, Christianity. Is Protestantism the genuine teaching of Jesus of Nazareth? or does Catholicism represent his true spirit? Jesus himself did not have any definite notion of Trinity doctrine, nor did he propose any suggestion for ritualism. According to the Synoptics, he appears to have cherished a rather immature conception of the kingdom of God than a purely ideal one as conceived by Paul, and his personal disciples who were just as illiterate philosophically as the master himself were anxiously waiting in all probability for its mundane realisation But what Christians, Catholics or Protestants, in these days of enlightenment, would dare give a literal explanation to this material conception of the coming kingdom?

Again, think of Jesus's view on marriage and social life. Is it not an established fact that he highly advocated celibacy and in the case of married people strict continence, and also that he greatly favored pious poverty and asceticism in general? In these respects, the monks of the Medieval Ages and the Catholic priests of the present day (though I cannot say they are ascetic and poor in their living) must be said to be in more accord with the teaching of the master than their Protestant brethren. But what Protestants would seriously venture to defend all those views of Jesus, in spite of their avowed declaration that they are sincerely following in the steps of their Lord? Taking all in all, these contradictions do not prevent them, Protestants as well as Catholics, from calling themselves Christians and even good, pious, devoted Christians, as long as they are consciously or unconsciously animated by the same spirit, that was burning in the son of the carpenter of Nazareth, an obscure village of Galilee, about two thousand years ago.

The same mode of reasoning holds good in the case of Mahâyânism, and it would be absurd to insist on the genuineness of Hînayânism at the expense of the former. Take for granted that the Mahâyâna school of Buddhism contains some elements absorbed from other Indian religio-philosophical systems; but what of it? Is not Christianity also an amalgamation, so to speak, of Jewish, Greek, Roman, Babylonian, Egyptian, and other pagan thoughts? In fact every healthy and energetic religion is historical, in the sense that, in the course of its development, it has adapted itself to the ever-changing environment, and has assimilated within itself various elements which appeared at first even threatening its own existence. In Christianity, this process of assimilation, adaptation, and modification has been going on from its very beginning. As the result, we see in the Christianity of to-day its original type so metamorphosed, so far as its outward appearance is concerned, that nobody would now take it for a faithful copy of the prototype.

Mahâyânism a Living Faith.

So with Mahâyânism. Whatever changes it has made during its historical evolution, its spirit and central ideas are all those of its founder. The question whether or not it is genuine, entirely depends on our interpretation of the term "genuine." If we take it to mean the lifeless preservation of the original, we should say that Mahâyânism is not the genuine teaching of the Buddha, and we may add that Mahâyânists would be proud of the fact, because being a living religious force it would never condescend to be the corpse of a by-gone faith. The fossils, however faithfully preserved, are nothing but rigid inorganic substances from which life is forever departed.

Mahâyânism is far from this; it is an ever-growing faith and ready in all times to cast off its old garments as soon as they are worn out. But its spirit originally inspired by the "Teacher of Men and Gods" (*çâstadevamanuṣyânam*) is most jealously guarded against pollution and degeneration. Therefore, as far as its spirit is concerned, there is no room left to doubt its genuineness; and those who desire to have a complete survey of Buddhism cannot ignore the significane of Mahâyânism.

It is naught but an idle talk to question the historical value of an organism, which is now full of vitality and active in all its functions, and to treat it like an archeological object, dug out from the depths of the earth, or like a piece of bric-à-brac, discovered in the ruins of an ancient royal palace. Mahâyânism is not an object of historical curiosity. Its vitality and activity concern us in our daily life. It is a great spiritual organism; its moral and religious forces are still exercising an enormous power over millions of souls; and its further development is sure to be a very valuable contribution to the world-progress of the religious consciousness. What does it matter, then, whether or not Mahâyânism is the genuine teaching of the Buddha?

Here is an instance of most flagrant contradictions present in our minds, but of which we are not conscious on account of our preconceived ideas. Christian critics vigorously insist on the genuineness of their own religion, which is no more than a hybrid, at least outwardly; but they want to condemn their rival religion as denegerated, because it went through various stages of development like theirs. It is of no practical use to trouble with this nonsensical question, — the question of the genuineness of Mahâyânism, which by the way is frequently raised by outsiders as well as by some unenlightened Buddhists themselves.

3. SOME MISSTATEMENTS ABOUT THE MAHÂYÂNA DOCTRINES.

Before entering fully into the subject proper of this work, let us glance over some erroneous opinions about the Mahâyâna doctrines, which are held by some Western scholars, and naturally by all uninitiated readers, who are like the blind led by the blind. It may not be altogether a superfluous work to give them a passing review in this chapter and to show broadly what Mahâyânism is not.

Why Injustice is done to Buddhism.

The people who have had their thoughts and sentiments habitually trained by one particular set of religious dogmas, frequently misjudge the value of those thoughts that are strange and unfamiliar to them. We may call this class of people bigots or religious enthusiasts. They may have fine religious and moral sentiments as far as their own religious training goes; but, when examined from a broader point of view, they are to a great extent vitiated with prejudices, superstitions, and fanatical beliefs, which, since childhood, have been pumped into their receptive minds, before they were sufficiently developed and could form independent judgments. This fact so miserably spoils their purityof sentiment and obscures their transparency of intellect, that they are disqualified to perceive and appreciate whatever is good and true and beautiful in the so-called heathen religions. This is the main reason why those Christian missionaries are incapable of rightly understanding the spirit of religion generally—I mean, those missionaries who come to the East to substitute one set of superstitions for another.

This strong general indictment against the Christian missionaries, however, is by no means prompted by any partisan spirit. My desire, on the contrary, is to do justice to those thoughts and sentiments that have been working consciously or unconsciously in the human mind from time immemorial and shall work on till the day of the last judgment, if there ever be such a day. To see what these thoughts and sentiments are, which, by the way, constitute the kernel of every religion, we must without any reluctance throw off all the prejudices we are liable to cherish, though quite unknowingly; and keeping always in view what is most essential in the religious consciousness, we must not confound it with its accessories, which are doomed to die in the course of time.

Examples of Injustice.

As specimen of injustice done to the Mahâyâna Buddhism by Christian critics, we quote the following passages from Monier-William's *Buddhism*, Waddell's *Buddhism in Tibet*, and Samuel Beal's *Buddhism in China*, all of which are representative works each in its own field.

Monier Monier-Williams.

Monier Monier-Williams is a well-known authority on Sanskrit literature, and his works in this department will long remain as a valuable contribution to human knowledge. But, unfortunately, as soon as he attempts to enter the domain of religious controversy, his intellect becomes pitiously obscured by his preconceived ideas. He thinks, for instance, that the principal feature of Mahâyânism consists merely in amplifying the number of Bodhisattvas, who are contented, according to his view, with their "perpetual residence in the heavens, and quite willing to put off all desires for Buddhahood and Parinirvana." (P. 190.)

This remark is so absurd that it will at once be rejected by any one who has a first-hand knowledge of the Mahâyâna system, as even unworthy of refutation, but Monier-Williams takes special pains to give to his characterisation of the Mahâyâna doctrine a show of rational explanation. "Of course," says he, "men instinctively recoiled from utter self-annihilation, and so the Buddha's followers ended in changing the true idea of Nirvana and converting it from a condition of non-existence into a state of lazy beatitude in celestial regions (!), while they encouraged all men — whether monks or laymen — to make a sense of dreamy bliss in Heaven (!), and not total extinction of life, the end of all their efforts." (P. 156.)

This view of the Buddhist heaven as interpreted by Monier-Williams is nothing but the conception of the Christian heaven colored with paganism. Nothing is more foreign to Buddhists than this distinguished Sankritist's interpretation of celestial existence. The life of devas (celestial beings) is just as much subject to the law of birth and death as that of men on earth. What consolation would there be for the Mahâyânists striving after the highest principle of existence, only to find themselves transmigrated to a celestial abode, that is also full of sorrows and sufferings? Always working for the welfare of their fellow-creatures, the Bodhisattvas never desire any earthly or heavenly happiness for themselves. Whatever merits, according to the law of karma, there be stored up for their good work, they do not have any wish to enjoy them by themselves, but they will have all these merits turned over (*parivarta*) to the interests of their fellow-beings. This is the ideal of Bodhisattvas, i. e., of the followers of Mahâyânism.

Beal.

Samuel Beal who is considered by Western scholars to be an authority on Chinese Buddhism, refering to the Mahâyâna conception of Dharmakâya, [1] says in his *Buddhism in China* (p. 156): "We can have little doubt, then, that from early days worship was offered by Buddhists at several spots, consecrated by the presence of the Teacher, to an invisible presence. This presence was formulated by the later Buddhists under the phrase, 'the Body of the Law', Dharmakâya."

Then, alluding to Buddha's instruction that says after his Parinirvana the Law given by him should be regarded as himself, Beal proceeds to say: "Here was the germ from which proceeded the idea or formula of an invisible presence: teaching and power of the Law (*Dharma*) represented the Dharmakâya or Law-Body of Buddha, present with the order, and fit for reverence."

To interpret Dharmakâya as the Body of the Law is quite inadequate and misleading. To the Hînayânists, there is nothing beside the Tripitaka as the object of reverence, and, therefore, the notion of the Body of the Law has no meaning to them. The idea

[1] The conception of Dharmakâya constitutes the central point in the system of Mahâyânism, and the right comprehension of it is of vital importance. The Body of the Law, as it is commonly rendered in English, is not exact and leads frequently to a misconception of the entire system. The point is fully discussed below.

is distinctly Mahâyânistic, but Beal is not well informed about its real significance as understood by the Buddhists. The chief reason of his misinterpretation, as I judge, lies in his rendering *dharma* by "law", while *dharma* here means "that which subsists," or "that which maintains itself even when all the transient modes disappear," in short, "being," or "substance." Dharmakâya, therefore, would be a sort of the Absolute, or Essence-Body of all things. This notion plays such an important rôle in Mahâyânism that an adequate knowledge of it is indispensable to understand the constitution of Mahâyânism as a religious system.

Waddell.

Let us state one more case of misrepresentation by Western scholars of the Mahâyâna Buddhism. Waddell, author of *Buddhism in Tibet*, referring to the point of divergence between the so-called Northern Buddhism and the Southern, says (pp. 10—11): "It was the theistic Mahâyâna doctrine which substituted, for the agnostic idealism and simple morality of Buddha, a speculative theistic system with a mysticism of sophistic nihilism in the background."

And again: "This Mahâyâna meaning Nâgârjuna's Mâdhyamika school] was essentially a sophistic nihilism, or rather Parinirvana, while ceasing to be extinction of life, was converted a mystic state which admitted of no definition."

It may not be wrong to call Mahâyânism a speculative theistic system in a wide sense, but it must be asked on what ground Waddell thinks that it has in its background "a mysticism of sophistic nihilism" Could a religious system be called sophistry when it makes a close inquiry into the science of dialectics, in order to show how futile it is to seek salvation through the intellect alone? Could a religious system be called a nihilism when it endeavors to reach the highest reality which transcends the phenomenality of concrete individual existences? Could a doctrine be called nihilistic when it defines the absolute as neither void (*çûnya*) nor not-void (*açûnya*)?

I could cull some more passages from other Buddhist scholars of the West and show how far Mahâyânism has been made by them a subject of misrepresentation. But since this work is not a polemic, but devoted to a positive exposition of its basic doctrines, I refrain from so doing. Suffice it to state that one of the main causes of the injustice done to Buddhism by the Christian critics comes from their preconceptions, of which they may not be aware, but which all the more vitiate their "impartial" judgments.

4. THE SIGNIFICANCE OF RELIGION.

Those misconceptions about Buddhism as above stated induce me to digress in this introductory part and to say a few words concerning the distinction between the form and the spirit of religion. A clear knowledge of this distinction will greatly facilitate the formation of a correct notion about Mahâyânism and will also help us duly to appreciate its significance as a living religious faith.

By the spirit of religion I mean that element in religion which remains unchanged throughout its successive stages of development and transformation: while the form of it is the external shell which is subject to any modification required by circumstances.

No Revealed Religion.

It admits of no doubt that religion, as everything else under the sun, is subject to the laws of evolution, and that, therefore, there is no such thing as a revealed religion, whose teachings are supposed to have been delivered to us direct from the hands of an anthropomorphic or anthropopsychic supernatural being, and which, like an inorganic substance, remains forever the same, without changing, without growing, without modifying itself in accord with the surrounding conditions. Unless people are so blinded by a belief in this kind of religion as to insist that its dogmas have suffered absolutely no change whatever since its "revelation," they must recognise like every clear-headed person the fact that there are some ephemeral elements in every religion, which must carefully be distinguished from its quintessence which remains eternally the same.

When this discrimination is not observed, prejudice

will at once assert itself, inducing them to imagine that the religion in which they were brought up with all its truths and superstitions is the only orthodox religion in the world, and all the other religions are nothing else than heathenism, idolatry, atheism, apostasy, and the like. This attitude of such religionists, however, serves only to betray their own narrowness of mind and dimness of spiritual insight. No one who desires to penetrate into the innermost recesses of the human heart and who longs to feel the fullest meaning of life, should foster in himself in the least degree a disposition of bigotry.

The Mystery.

Religion is the inmost voice of the human heart that under the yoke of a seemingly finite existence groans and travails in pain. Mankind, from their first appearance on earth, have never been satisfied with the finiteness and impermanency of life. They have always been yearning after something that will liberate them from the slavery of this mortal coil, or from the cursed bondage of metempsychosis, as Hindu thinkers express it. This something, however, on account of its transcending all the principles of separation and individuation, which characterise the phenomena of this mundane existence, has always remained as something indefinite, inadequate, chaotic, and full of mystery. And, according to different degrees of intellectual development in different ages and nations, people have endeavored to invest this mysterious something with all sorts of human feelings and intelligence. Most of modern scientists are now content with the hypothesis that the mystery is unfathomable by the human mind, which is conditioned by the law of relativity, and that our business here, moral as well as intellectual, can be executed without troubling ourselves with this ever-haunting problem of mystery; — this doctrine is called agnosticism.

But this hypothesis can in no wise be considered the final sentence passed on the mystery. From the scientific point of view, the maxim of agnosticism is excellent, as science does not pretend to venture into the realm of non-relativity. Dissatisfaction, however, presents itself, when we attempt to silence by this hypothesis the last demand of the human heart.

Intellect and Imagination.

The human heart is not an intellectual crystal. When the intellect displays itself in its full glory, the heart still aches and struggles to get hold of something beyond. The intellect may sometimes declare that it has at last laid its hand on what is demanded by the heart. Time passes on, and the mystery is examined from the other points that escaped consideration before, and, to the great disappointment of the heart, the supposed solution is found to be wanting. The intellect is baffled. But the human heart never gets tired of its yearnings and demands a satisfaction ever more pressingly. Should they be considered a mere nightmare of imagination? Surely not, for herein lies the field where religion claims supreme authority, and its claim is perfectly right.

But religion cannot fabricate whatever it pleases; it must work in perfect accord with the intellect. As the essential nature of man does not consist solely in intellect, or will, or feeling, but in the coördination of these psychical elements, religion must guard herself against the unrestrained flight of imagination. Most of the superstitions fondly cherished by a pious heart are due to the disregard of the intellectual element in religion.

The imagination creates: the intellect discriminates. Creation without discrimination is wild: discrimination without creation is barren Religion and science, when they do not work with mutual understanding, are sure to be one-sided, The soul makes an abnormal growth at one point, loses its balance, and is finally given up to a collapse of the entire system. Those pious religious enthusiasts who see a natural enemy in science and denounce it with all their energy, are, in my opinion, as purblind and distorted in their view, as those men of science who think that science alone must claim the whole field of soul-activities as well as those of nature. I am not in sympathy with either of them: for one is just as arrogant in its claim as the other. Without a careful examination of both sides of a shield, we are not competent to give a correct opinion upon it.

But the imagination is not the exclusive possession of religion, nor is discrimination or ratiocination the monopoly of science. They are reciprocal and complementary: one cannot do anything without the other. The difference between science and religion is not that between certitude and probability. The difference is rather in their respective fields of activity. Science is solely concerned with things conditional, relative, and finite. When it explains a given phenomenon by some fixed laws which are in turn nothing but a generalisation of particular facts, the task of science is done, and any further attempt to go beyond this, i. e., to make an inquiry into the whence, whither, and why of things, is beyond its realm. But the human soul does not remain satisfied here, it asks for the ultimate principle underlying all so-called scientific laws and hypotheses. Science is indifferent to the teleology of things: a mechanical explanation of them appeases its intellectual curiosity. But in religion teleology is of paramount importance, it is one of the most fundamental problems, and a system which does not give any definite conception on this point is no religion. Science, again, does not care if there is something beyond or outside its manifold laws and theories; but a religion which does not possess a God or anything corresponding to it, ceases to be so, for it fails to give consolation to the human heart.

The Contents of Faith vary.

The solution of religious problems, as far as they fall within the sphere of relative experience, is largely a matter of personal conviction, determined by one's intellectual development, external circumstances, education, disposition, etc. The conceptions of faith thus formulated are naturally infinitely diversified; even among the followers of a certain definite set of dogmas, each will understand them in his own way, owing to individual peculiarities. If we could subject their conceptions of faith to a strict analysis as a chemist does his materials, we should detect in them all the possible forms of differentiation. But all these things belong to the exterior of religion and have nothing to do with the essentials which underlie them.

The abiding elements of religion come from within, and consist mainly in the mysterious sentiment that lies hidden in the deepest depths of the human heart, and that, when awakened, shakes the whole structure of personality and brings about a great spiritual revolution, which results in a complete change of one's world-conception. When this mysterious sentiment finds expression and formulates its conceptions in the terms of intellect, it becomes a definite system of beliefs, which is popularly called religion, but which should properly be termed dogmatism, that is, an intellectualised form of religion. On the other hand, the outward forms of religion consist of those changing elements that are mainly determined by the intellectual and moral development of the times as well as by individual esthetical feelings.

True Christians and enlightened Buddhists may, therefore, find their point of agreement in the recognition of the inmost religious sentiment that constitutes the basis of our being, though this agreement does by no means prevent them from retaining their individuality in the conceptions and expressions of faith. My conviction is: If the Buddha and the Christ changed their accidental places of birth, Gautama might have been a Christ rising against the Jewish traditionalism, and Jesus a Buddha, perhaps propounding the doctrine of non-ego and Nirvâna and Dharmakâya.

However great a man may be, he cannot but be an echo of the spirit of the times. He never stands, as is supposed by some, so aloof and towering above the masses as to be practically by himself. On the contrary, "he," as Emerson says, "finds himself in the river of the thoughts and events, forced onward by the ideas and necessities of his contemporaries." So it was with the Buddha, and so with the Christ. They were nothing but the concrete representatives of the ideas and feelings that were struggling in those times against the established institutions, which were degenerating fast and menaced the progress of humanity. But at the same time those ideas and sentiments were the outburst of the Eternal Soul, which occasionally makes a solemn announcement of its will, through great historical figures or through great worldevents.

* * *

Believing that a bit of religio-philosophical exposition as above indulged will prepare the minds of my Christian readers sincerely to take up the study of a religious system other than their own, I now proceed to a systematical elucidation of the Mahâyâna Buddhism, as it is believed at present in the Far East.

CHAPTER I.

A GENERAL CHARACTERISATION OF BUDDHISM.

No God and no Soul.

BUDDHISM is considered by some to be a religion without a God and without a soul. The statement is true and untrue according to what meaning we give to those terms.

Buddhism does not recognise the existence of a being, who stands aloof from his "creations," and who meddles occasionally with human affairs when his capricious will pleases him. This conception of a supreme being is very offensive to Buddhists They are unable to perceive any truth in the hypotheses, that a being like ourselves created the universe out of nothing and first peopled it with a pair of sentient beings; that, owing to a crime commited by them, which, however, could have been avoided if the creator so desired, they were condemned by him to eternal damnation; that the creator in the meantime feeling pity for the cursed, or suffering the bite of remorse for his somewhat rash deed, despatched his only beloved son to the earth for the purpose of rescuing mankind from universal misery, etc., etc. If Buddhism is called atheism on account of its refusal to take poetry for actual fact, its followers would have no objection to the designation.

Next, if we understand by soul âtman, which, secretly hiding itself behind all mental activities, direct them after the fashion of an organist striking different notes as he pleases, Buddhists outspokenly deny the existence of such a fabulous being. To postulate an independent âtman outside a combination of the five Skandhas [1], of which an individual being is supposed by Buddhists to consist, is to unreservedly welcome egoism with all its pernicious corollaries. And what distinguishes Buddhism most characteristically and emphatically from all other religions is the doctrine of non-âtman or non-ego, exactly opposite to the postulate of a soul-substance which is cherished by most of religious enthusiasts. In this sense, Buddhism is undoubtedly a religion without the soul.

To make these points clearer in a general way, let us briefly treat in this chapter of such principal tenets of Buddhism as Karma, Âtman, Avidyâ, Nirvâna, Dharmakâya, etc. Some of these doctrines being the common property of the two schools of Buddhism, Hînayânism and Mahâyânism, their brief, comprehensive exposition here will furnish our readers with a general notion about the constitution of Buddhism, and will also prepare them to pursue a further specific exposition of the Mahâyâna doctrine which follows.

[1] They are: (1) form or materiality (*rûpa*), (2) sensation (*vedanâ*), (3) conception (*samjnâ*), (4) action or deeds (*samkâra*), and (5) consciousness (*vijnâna*). These terms are explained elsewhere.

Karma.

One of the most fundamental doctrines established by Buddha is that nothing in this world comes from a single cause, that the existence of a universe is the result of a combination of several causes *(hetu)* and conditions *(pratyaya)*, and is at the same time an active force contributing to the production of an effect in the future. As far as phenomenal existences are concerned, this law of cause and effect holds universally valid. Nothing, even God, can interfere with the course of things thus regulated, materially as well as morally. If a God really exists and has some concern about our worldly affairs, he must first conform himself to the law of causation. Because the principle of karma, which is the Buddhist term for causation morally conceived, holds supreme everywhere and all the time.

The conception of karma plays the most important rôle in Buddhist ethics. Karma is the formative principle of the universe. It determines the course of events and the destiny of our existence. The reason why we cannot change our present state of things as we may will, is that it has already been determined by the karma that was performed in our previous lives, not only individually but collectively. But, for this same reason, we shall be able to work out our destiny in the future, which is nothing but the resultant of several factors that are working and that are being worked by ourselves in this life.

Therefore, says Buddha:

"By self alone is evil done,
By self is one disgraced;
By self is evil left undone,
By self alone is he purified;
Purity and impurity belong to self:
No one can purify another." [1]

Again,

"Not in the sky
Nor in the midst of the sea,
Nor entering a cleft of the mountains,
Is found that realm on earth
Where one may stand and be
From an evil deed absolved." [2]

This doctrine of karma may be regarded as an application in our ethical realm of the theory of the conservation of energy. Everything done is done once for all; its footprints on the sand of our moral and social evolution are forever left; nay, more than left, they are generative, good or evil, and waiting for further development under favorable conditions. In the physical world, even the slightest possible movement of our limbs cannot but affect the general cosmic motion of the earth, however infinitesimal it be; and if we had a proper instrument, we could surely measure its precise extent of effect. So is it even with our deeds. A deed once performed, together with its subjective motives, can never vanish without leaving some impressions either on the individual

[1] *The Dhammapada*, v. 165. Tr. by A. J. Edmunds.

[2] *The Dhammapada*, v. 127.

consciousness or on the supra-individual, i. e., social consciousness.

We need not further state that the conception of karma in its general aspect is scientifically verified. In our moral and material life, where the law of relativity rules supreme, the doctrine of karma must be considered thoroughly valid. And as long as its validity is admitted in this field, we can live our phenomenal life without resorting to the hypothesis of a personal God, as declared by Lamarck when his significant work on evolution was presented to Emperor Napoleon.

But it will do injustice to Buddhism if we designate it agnosticism or naturalism, denying or ignoring the existence of the ultimate, unifying principle, in which all contradictions are obliterated. Dharmakâya is the name given by Buddhists to this highest principle, viewed not only from the philosophical but also from the religious standpoint. In the Dharmakâya, Buddhists find the ultimate significance of life, which, when seen from its phenomenal aspect, cannot escape the bondage of karma and its irrefragable laws.

Avidyâ.

What claims our attention next, is the problem of nescience, which is one of the most essential features of Buddhism. Buddhists think, nescience (in Sanskrit *avidyâ*) is the subjective aspect of karma, involving us in a series of rebirths. Rebirth, considered by itself, is no moral evil, but rather a necessary condition of progress toward perfection, if perfection ever be attainable here. It is an evil only when it is the outcome of ignorance, — ignorance as to the true meaning of our earthly existence.

Ignorant are they who do not recognise the evanescence of wordly things and who tenaciously cleave to them as final realities; who madly struggle to shun the misery brought about by their own folly; who savagely cling to the self against the will of God, as Christians would say; who take particulars as final existences and ignore one pervading reality which underlies them all; who build up an adamantine wall between the mine and thine: in a word, ignorant are those who do not understand that there is no such thing as an ego-soul, and that all individual existences are unified in the system of Dharmakâya. Buddhism, therefore, most emphatically maintains that to attain the bliss of Nirvana we must radically dispel this illusion, this ignorance, this root of all evil and suffering in this life.

The dotrine of nescience or ignorance is technically expressed in the following formula, which is commonly called the Twelve Nidânas or Pratyayasamutpada, that is to say Chains of Dependence:

(1) There is Ignorance (*avidyâ*) in the beginning; (2) from Ignorance Action (*sanskâra*) comes forth; (3) from Action Consciousness (*vijñâna*) comes forth; (4) from Consciousness Name-and-Form (*nâmarûpa*) comes forth; (5) from Name-and-Form the Six Organs (*ṣadâyâtana*) come forth; (6) from the Six Organs

Touch (*sparça*) comes forth; (7) from Touch Sensation (*vedanâ*) comes forth; (8) from Sensation Desire (*tṛṣnâ*) comes forth; (9) from Desire Clinging (*upâdâna*) comes forth; (10) from Clinging Being (*bhâva*) comes forth; (11) from Being Birth (*jati*) comes forth; and (12) from Birth Pain (*duḥkha*) comes forth.

According to Vasubandhu's *Abhidharmakoça*, the formula is explained as follows: Being ignorant in our previous life as to the significance of our existence, we let loose our desires and act wantonly. Owing to this karma, we are destined in the present life to be endowed with consciousness (*vijñâna*), name-and-form (*nâmarûpa*), the six organs of sense (*ṣadâyâtana*), and sensation (*vedanâ*). By the exercise of these faculties, we now desire for, hanker after, cling to, these illusive existences which have no ultimate reality whatever. In consequence of this "Will to Live" we potentially accumulate or make up the karma that will lead us to further metempsychosis of birth and death.

The formula is by no means logical, nor is it exhaustive, but the fundamental notion that life started in ignorance or blind will remains veritable.

Non-Atman.

The problem of nescience naturally leads to the doctrine usually known as that of non-Atman, i. e., non-ego, to which allusion was made at the beginning of this chapter. This doctrine of Buddhism is one of the subjects that have caused much criticism by Christian scholars. Its thesis runs: There is no such thing as ego-soul, which, according to the vulgar interpretation, is the agent of our mental activities. And this is the reason why Buddhism is sometimes called a religion without the soul, as aforesaid.

This Buddhist negation of the ego-soul is perhaps startling to the people, who, having no speculative power, blindly accept the traditional, materialistic view of the soul. They think, they are very spiritual in endorsing the dualism of soul and flesh, and in making the soul something like a corporeal entity, though far more ethereal than an ordinary object of the senses. They think of the soul as being more in the form of an angel, when they teach that it ascends to heaven immediately after its release from the material imprisonment.

They further imagine that the soul, because of its imprisonment in the body, groans in pain for its liberty, not being able to bear its mundane limitations. The immortality of the soul is a continuation after the dismemberment of material elements of this ethereal, astral, ghost-like entity,—very much resembling the Samkhyan *Lingham* or the Vedantic *sûkṣama-çârîra.* Self-consciousness will not a whit suffer in its continued activity, as it is the essential function of the soul. Brothers and sisters, parents and sons and daughters, wives aud husbands, all transfigured and sublimated, will meet again in the celestial abode, and perpetuate their home life much after the manner of their earthly one. People who take this view of the soul and its immortality must feel a great disappointment or even resentment, when they are asked to recognise the Buddhist theory of non-âtman.

The absurdity of ascribing to the soul a sort of astral existence taught by some theosophists is due to the confusion of the name and the object corresponding to it. The soul, or what is tantamount according to the vulgar notion, the ego, is a name given to a certain coördination of mental activities. Abstract names are invented by us to economise our intellectual labors, and of course have no corresponding realities as particular presences in the concrete objective world. Vulgar minds have forgotten the history of the formation of abstract names. Being accustomed always to find certain objective realities or concrete individuals answering to certain names, they—those naïve realists—imagine that all names, irrespective of their nature, must have their concrete individual equivalents in the sensual world. Their idealism or spiritualism, so called, is in fact a gross form of materialism, in spite of their unfounded fear for the latter as atheistic and even immoral;—curse of ignorance!

The non-âtman theory does not deny that there is a coördination or unification of various mental operations. Buddhism calls this system of coördination vijñâna, not âtman. Vijñâna is consciousness, while âtman is the ego conceived as a concrete entity,—a hypostatic agent which, abiding in the deepest recess of the mind, directs all subjective activities according to its own discretion. This view is radically rejected by Buddhism.

A familiar analogy illustrating the doctrine of non-âtman is the notion of a wheel or that of a house. Wheel is the name given to a combination in a fixed form of the spokes, axle, tire, hub, rim, etc.; house is that given to a combination of roofs, pillars, windows, floors, walls, etc., after a certain model and for a certain purpose. Now, take all these parts independently, and where is the house or the wheel to be found? House or wheel is merely the name designating a certain form in which parts are systematically and definitely disposed. What an absurdity, then, it must be to insist on the independent existence of the wheel or of the house as an agent behind the combination of certain parts thus definitely arranged!

It is wonderful that Buddhism clearly anticipated the outcome of modern psychological researches at the time when all other religious and philosophical systems were eagerly cherishing dogmatic superstitions concerning the nature of the ego. The refusal of modern psychology to have soul mean anything more than the sum-total of all mental experiences, such as sensations, ideas, feelings, decisions, etc., is precisely a rehearsal of the Buddhist doctrine of non-âtman. It does not deny that there is a unity of consciousness, for to deny this is to doubt our everyday experiences, but it refuses to assert that this unity is absolute, unconditioned, and independent. Everything in this phenomenal phase of existence, is a combination of certain causes *(hetu)* and conditions *(pratyaya)* brought together according to the principle of karma; and everything that is compound is finite and subject to dissolution, and, therefore, always limited by something else. Even the soul-life, as far as its phenomenality goes, is no exception to this universal law. To maintain the existence of a soul-substance which is supposed to lie hidden behind the phenomena of consciousness, is not only misleading, but harmful and productive of some morally dangerous conclusions. The supposition that there is something where there is really nothing, makes us cling to this chimerical form, with no other result than subjecting ourselves to an eternal series of sufferings. So we read in the *Lankâvatâra Sûtra*, III:

> "A flower in the air, or a hare with horns,
> Or a pregnant maid of stone:
> To take what is not for what is,
> 'Tis called a judgment false.
>
> "In a combination of causes,
> The vulgar seek the reality of self.
> As truth they understand not,
> From birth to birth they transmigrate."

The Non-Atman-ness of Things.

Mahâyânism has gone a step further than Hînayânism in the development of the doctrine of non-âtman, for it expressly disavows, besides the denial of the existence of the ego-substance, a noumenal conception of things, i. e., the conception of particulars as having something absolute in them. Hînayânism, indeed, also disfavors this conception of thinginess, but it does so only implicitly. It is Mahâyânism that definitely insists on the non-existence of a personal (*pudgala*) as well as a thingish (*dharma*) ego.

According to the vulgar view, particular existences are real, they have permanent substantial entities, remaining forever as such. They think, therefore, that organic matter remains forever organic just as much as inorganic matter remains inorganic; that, as they are essentially different, there is no mutual transformation between them. The human soul is different from that of the lower animals and sentient beings from non-sentient beings; the difference being well-defined and permanent, there is no bridge over which one can cross to the other. We may call this view naturalistic egoism.

Mahâyânism, against this egoistic conception of the world, extends its theory of non-âtman to the realm lying outside us. It maintains that there is no irreducible reality in particular existences, so long as they are combinations of several causes and conditions brought together by the principle of karma. Things are here because they are sustained by karma. As soon as its force is exhausted, the conditions that made their existence possible lose efficience and dissolve, and in their places will follow other conditions and existences. Therefore, what is organic to-day, may be inorganic to-morrow, and *vice versa*. Carbon, for instance, which is stored within the earth appears in the form of coal or graphite or diamond; but that which exists on its surface is found sometimes combined with other elements in the form of an animal or a vegetable, sometimes in its free elementary state. It is the same carbon everywhere; it becomes inorganic or organic, according to its karma, it has no âtman in itself which directs its transformation by its own self-determining will. Mutual transformation is everywhere observable; there is a constant shifting of forces, an eternal transmigration of the elements,—all of which tend to show the transitoriness and non-âtman-ness of individual existences. The universe is moving like a whirl-wind, nothing in it proving to be stationary, nothing in it rigidly adhering to its own form of existence.

Suppose, on the other hand, there were an âtman behind every particular being; suppose, too, it were absolute and permanent and self-acting; and this phenomenal world would then come to a standstill, and life be forever gone. For is not changeability the most essential feature and condition of life, and also the strongest evidence for the non-existence of individual things as realities? The physical sciences recognise this universal fact of mutual transformation in its positive aspect and call it the law of the conservation of energy and of matter. Mahâyânism, recognising its negative side, proposes the doctrine of the non-âtman-ness of things, that is to say, the impermanency of all particular existences. Therefore, it is said, "*Sarvam anityam, sarvam çûnyam, sarvam anâtman.*" (All is transitory, all is void, all is without ego.)

Mahâyânists condemn the vulgar view that denies the consubstantiality and reciprocal transformation of all beings, not only because it is scientifically untenable, but mainly because, ethically and religiously considered, it is fraught with extremely dangerous ideas, — ideas which finally may lead a "brother to deliver up the brother to death and the father the child," and, again, it may constrain "the children to rise up against their parents and cause them to be put to death." Why? Because this view, born of egoism, would dry up the well of human love and sympathy, and transform us into creatures of bestial selfishness; because this view is not capable of inspiring us with the sense of mutuality and commiseration and of making us disinterestedly feel for our fellow-beings. Then, all fine religious and humane sentiments would depart from our hearts, and we should be nothing less than rigid, lifeless corpses, no pulse beating, no blood running. And how many victims are offered every day on this altar of egoism! They are not necessarily immoral by nature, but blindly led by the false conception of life and the world, they have been rendered incapable of seeing their own spiritual doubles in their neighbors. Being ever controlled by their sensual impulses, they sin against humanity, against nature, and against themselves.

We read in the *Mahâyâna-abhisamaya Sûtra* (Nanjo, no. 196):

"Empty and calm and devoid of ego
Is the nature of all things:
There is no individual being
That in reality exists.

"Nor end nor beginning having
Nor any middle course,
All is a sham, here's no reality whatever:
It is like unto a vision and a dream.

"It is like unto clouds and lightning,
It is like unto gossamer or bubbles floating
It is like unto fiery revolving wheel,
It is like unto water-splashing.

"Because of causes and conditions things are here:
In them there's no self-nature [i. e., âtman]:
All things that move and work,
Know them as such.

"Ignorance and thirsty desire,
The source of birth and death they are:
Right contemplation and discipline by heart,
Desire and ignorance obliterate.

"All beings in the world,
Beyond words they are and expressions:
Their ultimate nature, pure and true,
Is like unto vacuity of space." [1]

The Dharmakâya.

The Dharmakâya, which literally means "body or system of being," is, according to the Mahâyânists,

[1] This last passage should not be understood in the sense of a total abnegation of existence. It means simply the transcendentality of the highest principle.

the ultimate reality that underlies all particular phenomena; it is that which makes the existence of individuals possible; it is the *raison d'être* of the universe; it is the norm of being, which regulates the course of events and thoughts. The conception of Dharmakâya is peculiarly Mahâyânistic, for the Hînayâna school did not go so far as to formulate the ultimate principle of the universe; its adherents stopped short at a positivistic interpretation of Buddhism. The Dharmakâya remained for them to be the Body of the Law, or the Buddha's personality as embodied in the truth taught by him.

The Dharmakâya may be compared in one sense to the God of Christianity and in another sense to the Brahman or Paramâtman of Vedantism. It is different, however, from the former in that it does not stand transcendentally above the universe, which, according to the Christian view, was created by God, but which is, according to Mahâyânism, a manifestation of the Dharmakâya himself. It is also different from Brahman in that it is not absolutely impersonal, nor is it a mere being. The Dharmakâya, on the contrary, is capable of willing and reflecting, or, to use Buddhist phraseology, it is *Karunâ* (love) and *Bodhi* (intelligence), and not the mere state of being.

This pantheistic and at the same time entheistic Dharmakâya is working in every sentient being, for sentient beings are nothing but a self-manifestation of the Dharmakâya. Individuals are not isolated existences, as imagined by most people. If isolated, they are nothing, they are so many soap-bubbles which vanish one after another in the vacuity of space. All particular existences acquire their meaning only when they are thought of in their oneness in the Dharmakâya. The veil of Mâya, i. e., subjective ignorance may temporally throw an obstacle to our perceiving the universal light of Dharmakâya, in which we are all one. But when our Bodhi or intellect, which is by the way a reflection of the Dharmakâya in the human mind, is so fully enlightened, we no more build the artificial barrier of egoism before our spiritual eye; the distinction between the *meum* and *teum* is obliterated, no dualism throws the nets of entanglement over us; I recognise myself in you and you recognise yourself in me; *tat tvam asi.* Or,

> "What is here, that is there;
> What is there, that is here:
> Who sees duality here,
> From death to death goes he."[1]

This state of enlightenment may be called the spiritual expansion of the ego, or, negatively, the ideal annihilation of the ego. A never-drying stream of sympathy and love which is the life of religion will now spontaneously flow out of the fountain-head of Dharmakâya.

The doctrine of non-ego teaches us that there is no reality in individual existences, that we do not have any transcendental entity called ego-substance.

---

[1] *The Kathopaniṣad*, IV. 10.

The doctrine of Dharmakâya, to supplement this, teaches us that we all are one in the System of Being and only as such are immortal. The one shows us the folly of clinging to individual existences and of coveting the immortality of the ego-soul; the other convinces us of the truth that we are saved by living into the unity of Dharmakâya. The doctrine of non-âtman liberates us from the shackle of unfounded egoism; but as mere liberation does not mean anything positive and may perchance lead us to asceticism, we apply the energy thus released to the execution of the will of Dharmakâya.

The questions: "Why have we to love our neighbors as ourselves? Why have we to do to others all things whatsoever we would that they should do to us?" are answered thus by Buddhists: "It is because we are all one in the Dharmakâya, because when the clouds of ignorance and egoism are totally dispersed, the light of universal love and intelligence cannot help but shine in all its glory. And, enveloped in this glory, we do not see any enemy, nor neighbor, we are not even conscious of whether we are one in the Dharmakâya. There is no 'my will' here, but only 'thy will,' the will of Dharmakâya, in which we live and move and have our being."

The Apostle Paul says: "For as in Adam all die, even so in Christ shall all be made alive." Why? Buddhists would answer, "because Adam asserted his egoism in giving himself up to ignorance, (the tree of knowledge is in truth the tree of ignorance, for from it comes the duality of me and thee); while Christ on the contrary surrendered his egoistic assertion to the intelligence of the universal Dharmakâya. That is why we die in the former and are made alive in the latter."

Nirvâna.

The meaning of Nirvâna has been variously interpreted by non-Buddhist students from the philological and the historical standpoint; but it matters little what conclusions they have reached, as we are not going to recapitulate them here; nor do they at all affect our presentation of the Buddhists' own view as below. For it is the latter that concerns us here most and constitutes the all-important part of the problem We have had too much of non-Buddhist speculation on the question at issue. The majority of the critics, while claiming to be fair and impartial, have, by some preconceived ideas, been led to a conclusion, which is not at all acceptable to intelligent Buddhists. Further, the fact has escaped their notice that Pâli literature from which they chiefly derive their information on the subject represents the views of one of the many sects that arose soon after the demise of the Master and were constantly branching off at and after the time of King Açoka. The probability is, that Buddha himself did not have any stereotyped conception of Nirvana, and, as most great minds do, expressed his ideas outright as formed under various circumstances; though of course they could not be in contradiction with his central beliefs, which must have remained the same throughout the course of his religious life. Therefore, to understand a problem in all its apparently contradictory aspects, it is very necessary to grasp at the start the spirit of the author of the problem, and when this is done the rest will be understood comparatively much easier. Non-Buddhist critics lack in this most important qualification; therefore, it is no wonder that Buddhists themselves are always reluctant to accede to their interpretations.

Enough for apology. Nirvâna, according to Buddhists, does not signify an annihilation of consciousness nor a temporal or permanent suppression of mentation [1], as imagined by some; but it is the

[1] Guyau, a French sociologist, refers to the Buddhist conception of Nirvâna in his *Non-Religion of the Future* I take his interpretation as typical of those non-Buddhist critics who are very little acquainted with the subject but pretend to know much. (English translation, pp 472—474.)

"Granted the wretchedness of life, the remedy that pessimists propose is the new religious salvation that modern Buddhists are to make fashionable. . . The conception is that of Nirvâna. To sever all the ties which attach you to the external world; to prune away all the young offshoots of desire, and recognise that to be rid of them is a deliverance; to practise a sort of complete psychial circumcision; to recoil upon yourself and to believe that by so doing you enter into the society of the great totality of things (the mystic would say, of God); to create an inner vacuum, and to feel dizzy in the void and, nevertheless, to believe that the void is plenitude supreme, pleroma, these have always constituted temptations to mankind. Mankind has been tempted to meddle with them, as it has been tempted to creep up to annihilation of the notion of ego-substance and of all the desires that arise from this erroneous conception. But this represents the negative side of the doctrine, and its positive side consists in universal love or sympathy (*karunâ*) for all beings.

These two aspects of Nirvâna, i. e., negatively, the destruction of evil passions, and, positively, the practice of sympathy, are complementary to each other; and when we have one we have the other. Because, as soon as the heart is freed from the cangue of egoism, the same heart, hitherto so cold and hard, undergoes a complete change, shows animation, and, joyously escaping from self-imprisonment, finds its freedom in the bosom of Dharmakâya. In this latter sense, Nirvâna is the "humanisation" of Dharmakâya, that is to say, "God's will done in earth as it is in heaven." If we make use of the

the verge of dizzy precipices and look over... Nirvâna leads, in fact, to the annihilation of the individual and of the race, and to the logical absurdity that the vanquished are the victors over the trials and miseries of life"

Then, the author recites the case of one of his acquaintances, who made a practical experiment of Nirvâna, rejecting variety in his diet, giving up meat, wine, every kind of ragout, every form of condiment, and reducing to its lowest possible terms the desire that is most fundamental in every living being—the desire of food, and substituting a certain number of cups of pure milk. "Having thus blunted his sense of taste and the grosser of his appetites, having abandoned all physical activity, he thought to find a recompense in the pleasure of abstract meditation and of esthetic contemplation. He entered to a state which was not that of dreamland, but neither was it that of real life, with its definite details."

terms, subjective and objective. Nirvâna is the former, and the Dharmakâya is the latter, phase of one and the same principle. Again, psychologically, Nirvâna is enlightenment, the actualisation of the Bodhiçitta [1] (Heart of Intelligence).

The gospel of love and the doctrine of Nirvâna may appear to some to contradict each other, for they think that the former is the source of energy and activity, while the latter is a lifeless, inhuman, ascetic quietism. But the truth is, love is the emotional aspect and Nirvâna the intellectual aspect of the inmost religious consciousness which constitutes the essence of the Buddhist life.

That Nirvâna is the destruction of selfish desires is plainly shown in this stanza:

> "To the giver merit is increased;
> When the senses are controlled anger arises not,
> The wise forsake evil,
> By the destruction of desire, sin, and infatuation,
> A man attains to Nirvâna." [2]

The following which was breathed forth by Buddha against a certain class of monks, testifies that when Nirvâna is understood in the sense of quietism or pessimism, he vigorously repudiated it:

> "Fearing an endless chain of birth and death,
> And the misery of transmigration,
> Their heart is filled with worry,
> But they desire their safety only.

[1] For detailed explanation of this term see Chapter XI.

[2] *The Udâna*, Ch. VIII, p. 118. Translation by General Strong

"Quietly sitting and reckoning the breaths,
They're bent on the Anâpânam. [1]
They contemplate on the filthiness of the body, —
Thinking how impure it is!

"They shun the dust of the triple world,
And in ascetic practise their safety they seek:
Incapable of love and sympathy are they,
For on Nirvâna abides their thought." [2]

Against this ascetic practise of some monks, the Buddha sets forth what might be called the ideal of the Buddhist life:

"Arouse thy will, supreme and great,
Practise love and sympathy, give joy and protection;
Thy love like unto space,
Be it without discrimination, without limitation.

Merits establish, not for thy own sake,
But for charity universal;
Save and deliver all beings,
Let them attain the wisdom of the Great Way."

It is apparent that the ethical application of the doctrine of Nirvâna is naught else than the Golden

[1] This is a peculiarly Indian religious practice, which consists in counting one's exhaling and inhaling breaths. When a man is intensely bent on the practise, he gradually passes to a state of trance, forgetting everything that is going on around and within himself. The practise may have the merit of alleviating nervousness and giving to the mind the bliss of relaxation, but it oftentimes leads the mind to a self-hypnotic state.

[2] Here Nirvâna is evidently understood to mean self-abnegation or world-flight or quietism, which is not in accord with the true Buddhist interpretation of the term.

Rule,[1] so called. The Golden Rule, however, does not give any reason why we should so act, it is a mere command whose authority is ascribed to a certain superhuman being. This does not satisfy an intellectually disposed mind, which refuses to accept anything on mere authority, for it wants to go to the bottom of things and see on what ground they are standing. Buddhism has solved this problem by finding the oneness of things in Dharmakâya, from which flows the eternal stream of love and sympathy. As we have seen before, when the cursed barrier of egoism is broken down, there remains nothing that can prevent us from loving others as ourselves.

Those who wish to see nothing but an utter barrenness of heart after the annihilation of egoism, are much mistaken in their estimation of human nature. For they think its animation comes from selfishness, and that all forms of activity in our life are propelled simply by the desire to preserve self and the race. They, therefore, naturally shrink from the doctrine that teaches that all things worldly are empty, and that there is no such thing as ego-substance whose

[1] The sentiment of the Golden Rule is not the monopoly of Christianity; it has been expressed by most of the leaders of thought, thus, for instance: "Requite hatred with virtue" (Lao-tze). "Hate is only appeased by love" (Buddha). "Do not do to others what ye would not have done to you by others" (Confucius). "One must neither return evil, nor do any evil to any one among men, not even if one has to suffer from them" (Plato, *Crito*, 49).

immortality is so much coveted by most people. But the truth is, the spring of love does not lie in the idea of self, but in its removal. For the human heart, being a reflection of the Dharmakâya which is love and intelligence, recovers its intrinsic power and goodness, only when the veil of ignorance and egoism is cast aside. The animation, energy, strenuousness, which were shown by a self-centered will, and which therefore were utterly desplicable, will not surely die out with the removal of their odious atmosphere in which egoism had enveloped them. But they will gain an ever nobler interpretation, ever more elevating and satisfying significance; for they have gone through a baptism of fire, by which the last trace of egoism has been thoroughly consumed. The old evil master is eternally buried, but the willing servants are still here and ever ready to do their service, now more efficiently, for their new legitimate and more authoritative lord.

Destruction is in common parlance closely associated with nothingness, hence Nirvâna, the destruction of egoism, is ordinarily understood as a synonym of nihilism. But the removal of darkness does not bring desolation, but means enlightenment and order and peace. It is the same chamber, all the furniture is left there as it was before. In darkness chaos reigned, goblins walked wild; in enlightenment everything is in its proper place. And did we not state plainly that Nirvâna was enlightenment?

The Intellectual Tendency of Buddhism.

One thing which in this connection I wish to refer to, is what makes Buddhism appear somehow cold and impassive. By this I mean its intellectuality.

The fact is that anything coming from India greatly savors of philosophy. In ancient India everybody of the higher castes seems to have indulged in intellectual and speculative exercises. Being rich in natural resources and thus the struggle for existence being reduced to a minimum, the Brahmans and the Kṣatriyas gathered themselves under most luxuriously growing trees, or retired to the mountain-grottoes undisturbed by the hurly-burly of the world, and there they devoted all their leisure hours to metaphysical speculations and discussions. Buddhism, as a product of these people, is naturally deeply imbued with intellectualism.

Further, in India there was no distinction between religion and philosophy. Every philosophical system was at the same time a religion, and *vice versa.* Philosophy with the Hindus was not an idle display of logical subtlety which generally ends in entangling itself in the meshes of sophistry. Their aim of philosophising was to have an intellectual insight into the significance of existence and the destiny of humanity. They did not believe in anything blindly nor accept anything on mere tradition. Buddha most characteristically echoes this sentiment when he says, "Follow my teachings not as taught by a Buddha, but as being in accord with truth." This spirit of self-reliance and self-salvation later became singularly Buddhistic. Even when Buddha was still merely an enthusiastic aspirant for Nirvâna, he seems to have been strongly possessed of this spirit, for he most emphatically declared the following famous passage, in response to the pathetic persuation of his father's ministers, who wanted him to come home with them: "The doubt whether there exists anything or not, is not to be settled for me by another's words. Arriving at the truth either by mortification or by tranquilisation, I will grasp myself whatever is ascertainable about it. It is not mine to receive a view which is full of conflicts, uncertainties, and contradictions. What enlightened men would go by other's faith? The multitudes are like the blind led in the darkness by the blind." [1]

To say simply, "Love your enemy," was not satisfactory to the Hindu mind, it wanted to see the reason why. And as soon as the people were convinced intellectually, they went even so far as to defend the faith with their lives. It was not an uncommon event that before a party of Hindu philosophers entered into a discussion they made an agreement that the penalty of defeats should be the sacrifice of the life. They were, above all, a people of intellect, though of course not lacking in religious sentiment.

It is no wonder, then, that Buddha did not make the first proclamation of his message by "Repent, for

[1] *The Buddhacarita*, Book IX; 63–64.

the kingdom of heaven is at hand," but by the establishment of the Four Noble Truths.[1] One appeals to the feeling, and the other to the intellect. That which appeals to the intellect naturally seems to be less passionate, but the truth is, feeling without the support of intellect leads to fanaticism and is always ready to yield itself to bigotry and superstition.

The doctrine of Nirvâna is doubtless more intellectual than the Christian gospel of love. It first recognises the wretchedness of human life as is proved by our daily experiences; it then finds its cause in our subjective ignorance as to the true meaning of existence, and in our egocentric desires which, obscuring our spiritual insight, make us tenaciously cling to things chimerical; it then proposes the complete annihilation of egoism, the root of all evil, by which, subjectively, tranquillity of heart is restored, and, objectively, the realisation of universal love becomes possible. Buddhism, thus, proceeds most logically in the development of its doctrine of Nirvâna and universal love.

Says Victor Hugo (*Les Misérables*, vol. II): "The reduction of the universe to a single being, the expansion of a single being even to God, this is love." When a man clings to the self and does not want

[1] According to one Northern Buddhist tradition, Buddha is recorded to have exclaimed at the time of his supreme spiritual beatitude: "Wonderful! All sentient beings are universally endowed with the intelligence and virtue of the Tathâgata!"

to identify himself with other fellow-selves, he cannot expand his being to God. When he shuts himself in the narrow shell of ego and keeps all the world outside, he cannot reduce the universe to his innermost self. To love, therefore, one must first enter Nirvâna.

The truth is everywhere the same and is attained through the removal of ignorance. But as individual disposition differs according to the previous karma, some are more prone to intellectualism, while the others to sentimentality (in its psychological sense). Let us then follow our own inclination conscientiously and not speak evil of others. This is called the Doctrine of Middle Path.

CHAPTER II.

HISTORICAL CHARACTERISATION OF MAHÂYÂNISM.

WE are now in a position to enter into a specific exposition of the Mahâyâna doctrine. But, before doing so, it will be well for us first to consider the views that were held by the Hindu Buddhist thinkers concerning its characteristic features; in other words, to make an historical survey of its peculiarities.

As stated in the Introduction, the term Mahâyâna was invented in the times of Nâgârjuna and Âryadeva (about the third or fourth century after Christ), when doctrinal struggles between the Çrâvaka and the Bodhisattva classes reached a climax. The progressive Hindu Buddhists, desiring to announce the essential features of their doctrine, did so naturally at the expense of their rival and by pointing out why theirs was greater than, or superior to, Hînayânism. Their views were thus necessarily vitiated by a partisan spirit, and instead of impartially and critically enumerating the principal characteristics of Mahâyânism, they placed rather too much stress upon those points that do not in these latter days appear to be very essential, but that were then considered by them to be of paramount importance. These points, nevertheless, throw some light on the nature of Mahâyâna Buddhism as historically distinguished from its consanguineous rival and fellow-doctrine.

Sthiramati's Conception of Mahâyânism.

Sthiramati [1] in his *Indroduction to Mahâyânism* states that Mahâyânism is a special doctrine for the Bodhisattvas, who are to be distinguished from the other two classes, viz, the Çrâvakas and the Pratyekabuddhas. The essential difference of the doctrine consists in the belief that objects of the senses are merely phenomenal and have no absolute reality, that the indestructible Dharmakâya which is all-pervading constitutes the norm of existence,. that all Bodhisattvas [2] are incarnations of the Dharmakâya, who not by their evil karma previously accumulated, but by their boundless love for all mankind, assume

[1] His date is not known, but judging from the contents of his works, of which we have at present two or three among the Chinese Tripitaka, it seems that he lived later than Açvaghoṣa, but prior to, or simultaneously with, Nâgârjuna. This little book occupies a very important position in the development of Mahâyânism in India. Next to Açvaghoṣa's *Awakening of Faith*, the work must be carefully studied by scholars who want to grasp every phase of the history of Mahâyâna school as far as it can be learned through the Chinese documents.

[2] Be it remarked here that a Bodhisattva is not a particularly favored man in the sense of chosen people or elect. We are all in a way Bodhisattvas, that is, when we recognise the truth that we are equally in possession of the Samyaksambodhi, Highest True Intelligence, and through which everybody without exception can attain final enlightenment.

corporeal existences, and that persons who thus appear in the flesh, as avatars of the Buddha supreme, associate themselves with the masses in all possible social relations, in order that they might thus lead them to a state of enlightenment.

While this is a very summary statement of the Mahâyâna doctrine, a more elaborate and extended enumeration of its peculiar features in contradistinction to those of Hînayânism, is made in the *Miscellanea on Mahâyâna Metaphysics*, [1] *The Spiritual Stages of the Yogâcâra*, [2] *An Exposition of the Holy Doctrine*, [3] *A Comprehensive Treatise on Mahâyânism*, [4] and others. Let us first explain the "Seven General Characteristics" as described in the first three works here mentioned.

Seven Principal Features of Mahâyânism.

According to Asanga, who lived a little later than Nâgârjuna, that is, at the time when Mahâyânism was further divided into the Yogâcârya and the Mâdhyamika school, the seven features peculiar to Mahâyânism as distinguished from Hînayânism, are as follows:

(1) *Its Comprehensiveness*. Mahâyânism does not confine itself to the teachings of one Buddha alone;

[1] *Mahâyâna-abhidharma-sangîti-çâstra*, by Asanga. Nanjo, No. 1199.

[2] *Yogâcârya-bhûmi-çâstra*, Nanjo, No. 1170. The work is supposed to have been dictated to Asanga by a mythical Bodhisattva.

[3] By Asanga. Nanjo, 1177.

[4] *Mahâyâna-samparigraha-çâstra*, by Asanga. Nanjo, 1183.

but wherever and whenever truth is found, even under the disguise of most absurd superstitions, it makes no hesitation to winnow the grain from the husk and assimilate it in its own system. Innumerable good laws taught by Buddhas [1] of all ages and localities are all taken up in the coherent body of Mahâyânism.

(2) *Universal love for All Sentient Beings.* Hînayânism confines itself to the salvation of individuals only; it does not extend its bliss universally, as each person must achieve his own deliverance. Mahâyânism, on the other hand, aims at general salvation; it endeavors to save us not only individually, but universally. All the motives, efforts, and actions of the Bodhisattvas pivot on the furtherance of universal welfare.

(3) *Its Greatness in Intellectual Comprehension.* Mahâyânism maintains the theory of non-âtman not only in regard to sentient beings but in regard to things in general. While it denies the hypothesis of a metaphysical agent directing our mental operations, it also rejects the view that insists on the noumenal or thingish reality of existences as they appear to our senses.

(4) *Its Marvelous Spiritual Energy.* The Bodhisattvas never become tired of working for universal salvation,

[1] Perceiving an incarnation of the Dharmakâya in every spiritual leader regardless of his nationality and professed creed, Mahâyânists recognise a Buddha in Socrates, Mohammed, Jesus, Francis of Assisi, Confucius, Laotze, and many others.

nor do they despair because of the long time required to accomplish this momentous object. To try to attain enlightenment in the shortest possible period and to be self-sufficient without paying any attention to the welfare of the masses, is not the teaching of Mahâyânism.

(5) *Its Greatness in the Exercise of the Upâya.* The term *upâya* literally means expediency. The great fatherly sympathetic heart of the Bodhisattva has inexhaustible resources at his command in order that he might lead the masses to final enlightenment, each according to his disposition and environment. Mahâyânism does not ask its followers to escape the metempsychosis of birth and death for the sake of entering into the lethargic tranquillity of Nirvâna; for metempsychosis in itself is no evil, and Nirvâna in its coma is not productive of any good. And as long as there are souls groaning in pain, the Bodhisattva cannot rest in Nirvâna; there is no rest for his unselfish heart, so full of love and sympathy, until he leads all his fellow-beings to the eternal bliss of Buddhahood. To reach this end he employs innumerable means (*upâya*) suggested by his disinterested lovingkindness.

(6) *Its Higher Spiritual Attainment.* In Hînayânism the highest bliss attainable does not go beyond Arhatship which is ascetic saintliness. But the followers of Mahâyânism attain even to Buddhahood with all its spiritual powers.

(7) *Its Greater Activity.* When the Bodhisattva

reaches the stage of Buddhahood, he is able to manifest himself everywhere in the ten quarters of the universe [1] and to minister to the spiritual needs of all sentient beings.

These seven peculiarities are enumerated to be the reasons why the doctrine defended by the progressive Buddhists is to be called Mahâyânism, or the doctrine of great vehicle, in contradistinction to Hînayânism, the doctrine of small vehicle. In each case, therefore, Asanga takes pains to draw the line of demarcation distinctly between the two schools of Buddhism and not between Buddhism and all other religious doctrines which existed at his time.

The Ten Essential Features of Buddhism.

The following statement of the ten essential features of Mahâyânism as presented in the *Comprehensive Treatise on Mahâyânism*, is made from a different standpoint from the preceding one, for it is the pronunciamento of the Yogâcâra school of Asanga

[1] Ancient Hindu Buddhists, with their fellow-philosophers, believed in the existence of spiritually transfigured beings, who, not hampered by the limitations of space and time, can manifest themselves everywhere for the benefit of all sentient beings. We notice some mysterious figures in almost all Mahâyâna sûtras, who are very often described as shedding innumerable rays of light from the forehead and illuminating all the three thousand worlds simultaneously. This may merely be a poetic exaggeration. But this Sambhogakâya or Body of Bliss (see Açvaghoṣa's *Awakening of Faith*, p. 101) is very difficult for us to comprehend as it is literally described. For a fuller treatment see the chapter on "Trikâya."

and Vasubandhu rather than that of Mahâyânism generally. This school together with the Mâdhyamika school of Nâgârjuna constitute the two divisions of Hindu Mahâyânism.[1]

The points enumerated by Asanga and Vasubandhu as most essential in their system are ten.

(1) It teaches an immanent existence of all things in the *Âlayavijñâna* or All-Conserving Soul. The conception of an All-Conserving Soul, it is claimed, was suggested by Buddha in the so-called Hînayâna sûtras; but on account of its deep meaning and of the liability of its being confounded with the ego-soul conception, he did not disclose its full significance in their sûtras; but made it known only in the Mahâyâna sûtras.

According to the Yogâcâra school, the Âlaya is not an universal, but an individual mind or soul, whatever we may term it, in which the "germs" of all things exist in their ideality.[2] The objective world in reality does not exist, but by dint of sub-

[1] Though I am very much tempted to digress and to enter into a specific treatment concerning these two Hindu Mahâyâna doctrines, I reluctantly refrain from so doing, as it requires a somewhat lengthy treatment and does not entirely fall within the scope of the present work.

[2] That Açvaghoṣa's conception of the Âlaya varies with the view here presented may be familiar to readers of his *Awakening of Faith.* This is one of the most abstruse problems in the philosophy of Mahâyâna Buddhism, and there are several divergent theories concerning its nature, attributes, activities, etc. In a work like this, it is impossible to give even a general statement of those controversies, however

jective illusion that is created by ignorance, we project all these "germs" in the Âlayavijñâna to the outside world, and imagine that they are there really as they are; while the Manovijñâna (ego-consciousness) which is too a product of illusion, tenaciously clinging to the Âlayavijñâna as the real self, never abandons its egoism. The Âlayavijñâna, however, is indifferent to, and irresponsible for, all these errors on the part of the Manovijñâna. [1]

(2) The Yogâcâra school distinguishes three kinds of knowledge: 1. Illusion (*parikalpita*), 2. Discriminative or Relative Knowledge (*paratantra*), and 3. Perfect Knowledge (*pariniṣpanna*).

The distinction may best be illustrated by the well-known analogy of a rope and a snake. Deceived by a similarity in appearance, men frequently take a rope lying on the ground for a poisonous snake and

interesting they may be to students of the history of intellectual development in India.

The Âlayavijñâna, to use the phraseology of Samkhya philosophy, is a composition, so to speak, of the Soul (*puruṣa*) and Primordial Matter (*prakṛti*). It is the Soul, so far as it is neutral and indifferent to all those phenomenal manifestations, that are going on within as well as without us. It is Primordial Matter, inasmuch as it is the reservoir of everything, whose lid being lifted by the hands of Ignorance, there instantly springs up this universe of limitation and relativity. Enlightenment or Nirvâna, therefore, consists in recognising the error of Ignorance and not in clinging to the products of imagination.

[1] For a more detailed explanation of the ideal philosophy of the Yogâcâra, see my article on the subject in *Le Muséon*, 1905.

are terribly shocked on that account. But when they approach and carefully examine it, they become at once convinced of the groundlessness of this apprehension, which was the natural sequence of illusion. This may be considered to correspond to what Kant calls *Schein*.

Most people, however, do not go any further in their inquiry. They are contented with the sensual, empirical knowledge of an object with which they come in contact. When they understand that the thing they mistook for a snake was really nothing but a yard of innocent rope, they think their knowledge of the object is complete, and do not trouble themselves with a philosophical investigation as to whether the rope which to them is just what it appears to be, has any real existence in itself. They do not stop a moment to reflect that their knowledge is merely relative, for it does not go beyond the phenomenal significance of the things they perceive.

But is an object in reality such as it appears to be to our senses? Are particular phenomena as such really actual? What is the value of our knowledge concerning those so-called realities? When we make an investigation into such problems as these, the Yogâcâra school says, we find that their existence is only relative and has no absolute value whatever independent of the perceiving subject. They are the "ejection" of our ideas into the outside world, which are centred and conserved in our Âlayavijñâna and which are awakened into activity by subjective ignorance. This clear insight into the nature of things, i.e., into their non-realness as âtman, constitutes perfect knowledge.

(3) When we attain to the perfect knowledge, we recognise the ideality of the universe. There is no such thing as an objective world, which is really an illusive manifestation of the mind called Âlayavijñâna, But even this supposedly real existence of the Âlayavijñâna is a product of particularisation called forth by the ignorant Manovijñâna. The Manovijñâna, or empirical ego, as it might be called, having no adequate knowledge as to the true nature of the Âlaya, takes the latter for a metaphysical agent, that like the master of a puppet-show manages all mental operations according to its humour. As the silkworm imprisons itself in the cacoon created by itself, the Manovijñâna, entangling itself in ignorance and confusion, takes its own illusory creations for real realities.

(4) For the regulation of moral life, the Yogâcâra with the other Mahâyâna schools, proposes the practising of the six Pâramitâs (virtues of perfection), which are: 1. *Dana* (giving), 2. *Çîla* (moral precept), 3. *Kṣânti* (meekness), 4. *Vîrya* (energy), 5. *Dhyâna* (meditation), 6. *Prajñâ* (knowledge or wisdom). In way of explanation, says Asanga: "By not clinging to wealth or pleasures (1), by not cherishing any thoughts to violate the precepts (2), by not feeling dejected in the face of evils (3), by not awakening any thought of indolence while practising goodness (4),

by maintaining serenity of mind in the midst of disturbance and confusion of this world (5), and finally by always practising *ekacitta*[1] and by truthfully comprehending the nature of things (6), the Bodhisattvas recognise the truth of *vijñânamâtra*, — the truth that there is nothing that is not of ideal or subjective creation.

(5) Mahâyânism teaches that there are ten spiritual stages of Bodhisattvahood, viz., 1. Pramuditâ, 2. Vimalâ, 3. Prabhâkarî, 4. Arcismatî, 5. Sudurjayâ, 6. Abhimukhî, 7. Dûrangamâ, 8. Acalâ, 9. Sâdhumatî, 10. Dharmameghâ[2]. By passing through all these stages one after another, we are believed to reach the oneness of Dharmakâya.

(6) The Yogâcârists claim that the precepts that are practised by the followers of Mahâyânism are far superior to those of Hînayânists. The latter tend to externalism and formalism, and do not go deep into our spiritual, subjective motives. Now, there are physical, verbal, and spiritual precepts observed by the Buddha. The Hînayânists observe the first two neglecting the last which is by far more important than the rest. For instance, the Çrâvaka's interpretation of the ten Çikṣas[3] is literal and not spiritual;

[1] "One mind" or "one heart" meaning the mental attitude which is in harmony with the monistic view of nature in its broadest sense.

[2] These ten stages of spiritual development are somewhat minutely explained below. See Chapter XII.

[3] The ten moral precepts of the Buddha are: (1) Kill no living being; (2) Take nothing that is not given; (3) Keep

further, they follow these precepts because they wish to attain Nirvâna for their own sake, and not for others'. The Bodhisattva, on the other hand, does not wish to be bound within the narrow circle of moral restriction. Aiming at an universal emancipation of mankind, he ventures even violating the ten çikṣas, if necessary. The first çikṣa, for instance, forbids the killing of any living being; but the Bodhisattva does not hesitate to go to war, in case the cause he espouses is right and beneficient to humanity at large.

(7) As Mahâyânism insists on the purification of the inner life, its teaching applies not to things outward, its principles are not of the ascetic and exclusive kind. The Mahâyânists do not shun to commingle themselves with the "dust of worldliness"; they aim at the realisation of the Bodhi; they are not afraid of being thrown into the whirlpool of metempsychosis; they endeavor to impart spiritual benefits to all sentient beings without regard to their attitude, whether hostile or friendly, towards themselves; having immovable faith in the Mahâyâna, they never become contaminated by vanity and worldly pleasures with which they may constantly be in touch; they have a clear insight into the doctrine of non-âtman; being free from all spiritual faults, they live in perfect accord with the laws of Suchness and discharge their duties without the

matrimonial sanctity; (4) Do not lie; (5) Do not slander; (6) Do not insult; (7) Do not chatter; (8) Be not greedy; (9) Bear no malice; (10) Harbor no scepticism.

least conceit or self-assertion: in a word, their inner life is a realisation of the Dharmakâya.

(8) The intellectual superiority of the Bodhisattva is shown by his possession of knowledge of non-particularisation (*anânârtha*).[1] This knowledge, philosophically considered, is the knowledge of the absolute, or the knowledge of the universal. The Bodhisattva's mind is free from the dualism of samsâra (birth-and-death) and nirvâna, of positivism and negativism, of being and non-being, of object and subject, of ego and non-ego. His knowledge, in short, transcends the limits of final realities, soaring high to the realm of the absolute and the abode of non-particurality.

(9) In consequence of this intellectual elevation, the Bodhisattva perceives the working of birth and death in nirvâna, and nirvâna in the transmigration of birth and death. He sees the "ever-changing many" in the "never-changing one," and the "never-

[1] Mahâyânism recognises two "entrances" through which a comprehensive knowledge of the universe is obtained. One is called the "entrance of sameness" *(samatâ)* and the other the "entrance of diversity" (*nânâtva*). The first entrance introduces us to the universality of things and suggests a pantheistic interpretation of existence. The second leads us to the particularity of things culminating in monotheism or polytheism, as it is viewed from different standpoints. The Buddhists declare that neither entrance alone can lead us to the sanctum sanctorum of existence; and in order to obtain a sound, well-balanced knowledge of things in general, we must go through both the entrances of universality and particularity.

changing one" in the "ever-changing many." His inward life is in accord at once with the laws of transitory phenomena and with those of transcendental Suchness. According to the former, he does not recoil as ascetics do when he comes in contact with the world of the senses; he is not afraid of suffering the ills that the flesh is heir to; but, according to the latter, he never clings to things evanescent, his inmost consciousness forever dwells in the serenity of eternal Suchness.

(10) The final characteristic to be mentioned as distinctly Mahâyânistic is the doctrine of Trikâya. There is, it is asserted, the highest being which is the ultimate cause of the universe and in which all existences find their essential origin and significance. This is called by the Mahâyânists Dharmakâya. The Dharmakâya, however, does not remain in its absoluteness, it reveals itself in the realm of cause and effect. It then takes a particular form. It becomes a devil, or a god, or a deva, or a human being, or an animal of lower grade, adapting itself to the degrees of the intellectual development of the people. For it is the people's inner needs which necessitate the special forms of manifestation. This is called Nirmânakâya, that is, the body of transformation. The Buddha who manifested himself in the person of Gautama, the son of King of Çuddhodâna about two thousand five hundred years ago on the Ganges, is a form of Nirmânakâya. The third one is called Sambhogakâya, or body of bliss. This is the spiri-

tual body of a Buddha, invested with all possible grandeur in form and in possession of all imaginable psychic powers. The conception of Sambhogakâya is full of wild imaginations which are not easy of comprehension by modern minds.[1]

These characteristics enumerated at seven or ten as peculiarly Mahâyânistic are what the Hindu Buddhist philosophers of the first century down to the fifth or sixth century of the Christian era thought to be the most essential points of their faith and what they thought entitled it to be called the "Great Vehicle" (*Mahâyâna*) of salvation, in contradistinction to the faith embraced by their conservative brethren. But, as we view them now, the points here specified are to a great extent saturated with a partisan spirit, and besides they are more or less scattered and unconnected statements of the so-called salient features of Mahâyânism. Nor do they furnish much information concerning the nature of Mahâyânism as a coherent system of religious teachings. They give but a general and somewhat obscure delineation of it, and that in opposition to Hînayânism. In point of fact, Mahâyânism is a school of Buddhism and has many characteristics in common with Hînayânism. Indeed, the spirit of the former is also that of the latter, and as far as the general trend of Buddhism is concerned there is no need of em-

[1] The doctrine of Trikâya will be given further elucidation in the chapter bearing the same title.

phasising the significance of one school over the other. On the following pages I shall try to present a more comprehensive and impartial exposition of the Buddhism, which has been persistently designated by its followers as Mahâyânism.

SPECULATIVE MAHÂYÂNISM.

CHAPTER III.

PRACTISE AND SPECULATION.

MAHÂYÂNISM perhaps can best be treated in two main divisions, as it has distinctly two principal features in its doctrinal development. I may call one the speculative phase of Mahâyânism and the other practical. The first part is essentially a sort of Buddhist metaphysics, where the mind is engaged solely in ratiocination and abstraction. Here the intellect plays a very prominent part, and some of the most abstruse problems of philosophy are freely discussed. Speculative followers of Buddhism have taken great interest in the discussion of them and have written many volumes on various subjects. [1]

[1] No efforts have yet been made systematically to trace the history of the development of the Mahâyâna thoughts in India as well as in China and Japan. We have enough material at least to follow the general course it has taken, as far as the Chinese and Tibetan collections of Tripitaka are concerned. When a thorough comparison by impartial, unprejudiced scholars of these documents has been made with the Pali and Sanskrit literature, then we shall be able to write a comprehensive history of the human thoughts that

The second or practical phase of Mahâyânism deals with such religious beliefs that constitute the life and essence of the system. Mahâyânists might have reasoned wrongfully to explain their practical faith, but the faith itself is the outburst of the religious sentiment which is inherent in human nature. This practical part, therefore, is by far more important, and in fact it can be said that the speculative part is merely a preparatory step toward it. Inasmuch as Mahâyânism is a religion and not a philosophical system, it must be practical, that is, it must directly appeal to the inmost life of the human heart.

Relation of Feeling and Intellect in Religion.

So much has been said about the relation between philosophy and religion; and there are many scholars who so firmly believe in the identity of religion either with superstitions or with supernatural revelation, that the denial of this assertion is considered by them practically to be the disavowal of all religions. For, according to them, there is no midway in religion. A religion which is rational and yet practical is no religion. Now, Buddhism is neither a vagary of imagination nor a revelation from above, and on this account it has been declared by some to be a philosophy. The title "Speculative Mahâyânism" thus, is apt to

have governed the Oriental people during the last two thousand years. When this is done, the result can further be compared with the history of other religious systems, thus throwing much light on the general evolution of humanity be taken as a confirmation of such opinion. To remove all the misconceptions, therefore, which might be entertained concerning the religious nature of Mahâyânism and its attitude toward intellectualism, I have deemed it wise here to say a few words about the relation between feeling and intellect in religion.

There is no doubt that religion is essentially practical; it does not necessarily require theorisation. The latter, properly speaking, is the business of philosophy. If religion was a product of the intellect solely, it could not give satisfaction to the needs of man's whole being. Reason constitutes but a part of the organised totality of an individual being. Abstraction however high, and speculation however deep, do not as such satisfy the inmost yearings of the human heart. But this they can do when they enter into one's inner life and constitution; that is, when abstraction becomes a concrete fact and speculation a living principle in one's existence; in short, when philosophy becomes religion.

Philosophy as such, therefore, is generally distinguished from religion. But we must not suppose that religion as the deepest expression of a human being can eliminate altogether from it the intellectual element. The most predominant rôle in religion may be played by the imagination and feeling, but ratiocination must not fail to assert its legitimate right in the co-ordination of beliefs. When this right is denied, religion becomes fanaticism, superstition, fata morgana, and even a menace to the progress of humanity.

The intellect is critical, objective, and always tries to stand apart from the things that are taken up for examination. This alienation or keeping itself aloof from concrete facts on the part of the intellect, constantly tends to disregard the real significance of life, of which it is also a manifestation. Therefore, the conflict between feeling and reason, religion and science, instinct and knowledge, has been going on since the awakening of consciousness.

Seeing this fact, intellectual people are generally prone to condemn religion as barring the freedom and obstructing the progress of scientific investigations. It is true that religion went frequently to the other extreme and tried to suppress the just claim of reason; it is true that this was especially the case with Christianity, whose history abounds with regretable incidents resulting from its violent encroachments upon the domain of reason. It is also true that the feeling and the intellect are sometimes at variance, that what the feeling esteems as the most valuable treasure is at times relentlessly crushed by the reason, while the feeling looks with utmost contempt at the results that have been reached by the intellect after much lucubration. But this fatal conflict is no better than the fight which takes place between the head and the tail of a hydra when it is cut in twain; it always results in self-destruction.

We cannot live under such a miserable condition forever; when we know that it is altogether due to a myopia on the part of our understanding. The truth is that feeling and reason "cannot do without one another, and must work together inseparably in the process of human development, since reason without feeling could have nothing to act for and would be impotent to act, while feeling without reason would act tyrannically and blindly — that is to say, if either could exist and act at all without the other; for in the end it is not feeling nor reason, which acts, but it is the man who acts according as he feels and reasons". (H. Maudsley's *Natural Causes and Supernatural Seemings,* p. VII). If it is thus admitted that feeling and reason must co-ordinate and co-operate in the realisation of human ideals, religion, though essentially a phenomenon of the emotional life, cannot be indifferent to the significance of the intellect. Indeed, religion, as much as philosophy, has ever been speculating on the problems that are of the most vital importance to human life. In Christianity speculation has been carried on under the name of theology, though it claims to be fundamentally a religion of faith. In India, however, as mentioned elsewhere, there was no dividing line between philosophy and religion; and every teaching, every system, and every doctrine, however abstract and speculative it might appear to the Western mind, was at bottom religious and always aimed at the deliverance of the soul. There was no philosophical system that did not have some practical purpose.

Indian thinkers could not separate religion from

philosophy, practice from theory. Their philosophy flowed out of the very spring of the human heart and was not a mere display of fine intellectuation. If their thinking were not in the right direction and led to a fallacy which made life more miserable, they were ever ready to surrender themselves to a superior doctrine as soon as it was discovered. But when they thought they were in the right track, they did not hesitate to sacrifice their life for it. Their philosophy had as much fire as religion.

Buddhism and Speculation.

Owing to this fact, Buddhism as much as Hinduism is full of abstract speculations and philosophical reflections so much so that some Christian critics are inclined to deny the religiosity of Buddhism. But no student of the science of comparative religion would indorse such a view nowadays. Buddhism, in spite of its predominant intellectualism, is really a religious system. There is no doubt that it emphasises the rational element of religion more than any other religious teachings, but on that account we cannot say that it altogether disregards the importance of the part to be played by the feeling. Its speculative, philosophical phase is really a preparation for fully appreciating the subjective significance of religion, for religion is ultimately subjective, that is to say, the essence of religion is love and faith, or, to use Buddhist phraseology, it is the expression of the Bodhi which consists in *prajñâ*[1] (intelligence or wisdom) and *karunâ* (love or compassion). Mere knowledge (not *prajñâ*) has very little value in human life. When not guided by love and faith, it readily turns out to be the most obedient servant of egoism and sensualism. What Tennyson says in the following verses is perfectly true with Buddhism:

"Who loves not knowledge? Who shall rail
Against her beauty? May she mix
With men and prosper! Who shall fix
Her pillars? Let her work prevail.

"But on her forehead sits a fire;
She sets her forward countenance
And leaps into the future chance,
Submitting all things to desire.

"Half grown as yet, a child, and vain—
She cannot fight the fear of death.
What is she, cut from love and faith,
But some wild Pallas from the brain

"Of demons? fiery-hot to burst
All barriers in her onward race
For power. Let her know her place;
She is the second, not the first.

"A higher hand must make her mild,
If all be not in vain, and guide
Her footsteps, moving side by side
With Wisdom, like the younger child."

[1] *Prajñâ*, *bodhi*, *buddhi*, *vidyâ* and *jñâ* or *jñâna* are all synonymous and in many cases interchangeable. But they allow a finer discrimination. Speaking in a general way, *prajñâ* is reason, *bodhi* wisdom or intelligence, *buddhi* enlightenment, *vidyâ* ideality or knowledge, and *jñâ* or *jñâna* intellect. Of these five terms, *prajñâ* and *bodhi* are essentially Buddhistic

But it must be remembered that Buddhism never ignores the part which is played by the intellect in the purification of faith. For it is by the judicious exercise of the intellect, that all religious superstitions and prejudices are finally destroyed.

The intellect is so far of great consequence, and we must respect it as the thunderbolt of Vajrapani, which crushes everything that is mere sham and false. But at the same time we must also remember that the quintessence of religion like the house built on the solid rock never suffers on account of this destruction. Its foundation lies too deeply buried in human

and have acquired technical meaning. In this work both *prajñâ* and *bodhi* are mostly translated by intelligence, for their extent of meaning closely overlaps each other. But this is rather vague, and wherever I thought the term intelligence alone to be misleading, I either left the originals untranslated, or inserted them in parentheses. To be more exact, *prajñâ* in many cases can safely be rendered by faith, not a belief in revealed truths, but a sort of immediate knowledge gained by intuitive intelligence. *Prajñâ* corresponds in some respects to wisdom, meaning the foundation of all reasonings and experiences. It may also be considered an equivalent for Greek *sophia*. Bodhi, on the other hand, has a decidedly religious and moral significance. Besides being *prajñâ* itself, it is also love (*karunâ*): for, according to Buddhism, these two, *prajñâ* and *karunâ*, constitute the essence of Bodhi. May Bodhi be considered in some respects synonymous with the divine wisdom as understood by Christian dogmatists? But there is something in the Buddhist notion of Bodhi that cannot properly be expressed by wisdom or intelligence. This seems to be due to the difference of philosophical interpretation by Buddhists and Christians of the conception of God. It will become clearer as we proceed farther.

heart to be damaged by knowledge or science. So long as there is a human heart warm with blood and burning with the fire of life, the intellect however powerful will never be able to trample it under foot. Indeed, the more severely the religious sentiment is tested in the crucible of the intellect, the more glorious and illuminating becomes its intrinsic virtue. The true religion is, therefore, never reluctant to appear before the tribunal of scientific investigation. In fact by ignoring the ultimate significance of the religious consciousness, science is digging its own grave. For what purpose has science other than the unravelling of the mysteries of nature and reading into the meaning of existence? And is this not what constitutes the foundation of religion? Science cannot be final, it must find its reason in religion; as a mere intellectual exercise it is not worthy of our serious consideration.

Religion and Metaphysics.

The French sociologist, M. Guyau, says in his *Irreligion of the Future* (English translation p. 10):

"Every positive and historical religion presents three distinctive and essential elements: (1) An attempt at a mythical and non-scientific explanation of natural phenomena (divine intervention, miracles, efficacious prayers, etc.), or of historical facts (incarnation of Jesus Christ or of Buddha, revelation, and so forth); (2) A system of dogmas, that is to say, of symbolic ideas, of imaginative beliefs, forcibly imposed upon one's faith as absolute verities, even though they are susceptible of no scientific demonstration or philosophical justification; (3) A cult and a system of rites, that is to say, of more or less immutable practices regarded as possessing a marvelous efficacy upon the course of things, a propitiatory virtue. A religion without myth, without dogma, without cult, without rite, is no more than that somewhat bastard product, 'natural religion,' which is resolvable to a system of metaphysical hypotheses."

M. Guyau seems to think that what will be left in religion, when severed from its superstitions and imaginary beliefs and mysterious rites, is a system of metaphysical speculations, and that, therefore, it is not a religion. But in my opinion the French sociologist shares the error that is very prevalent among the scientific men of to-day. He is perfectly right in trying to strip religion of all its ephemeral elements and external integuments, but he is entirely wrong when he does this at the expense of its very essence, which consists of the inmost yearings of the human heart. And this essence has no affinity with the superstitions which grow round it like excrescences as the results of insufficient or abnormal nourishment. Nor does it concern itself with mere philosophising and constructing hypotheses about metaphysical problems. Far from it. Religion is a cry from the abysmal depths of the human heart, that can never be silenced, until it finds that something and identifies itself with it, which reveals the teleological significance of life and the universe. But this something has a subjective value only, as Goethe makes Faust exclaim, "Feeling is all in all, name for it I have none." Why? Because it cannot objectively or intellectually be demonstrated, as in the case with those laws which govern phenomenal existences, — the proper objects of the discursive human understanding. And this subjectivity of religion is what makes "all righteousnesses as filthy garments." If religion deprived of its dogmas and cults is to be considered, as M. Guyau thinks, nothing but a system of metaphysics, we utterly lose sight of its subjective significance or its emotional element, which indeed constitutes its *raison d'être.*

* * *

Having this in view we proceed to see first on what metaphysical hypothesis speculative Mahâyâna Buddhism is built up; but the reader must remember that this phase of Mahâyânism is merely a preliminary to its more essential part, which we expound later under the heading of "Practical Mahâyânism," in contradistinction to "Speculative Mahâyânism."

CHAPTER IV.

CLASSIFICATION OF KNOWLEDGE.

Three Forms of Knowledge.

MAHÂYÂNISM generally distinguishes two or three forms of knowledge. This classification is a sort of epistemology, inasmuch as it proposes to ascertain the extent and nature of human knowledge, from a religious point of view. Its object is to see what kind of human knowledge is most reliable and valuable for the annihilation of ignorance and the attainment of enlightenment. The Mahâyâna school which has given most attention to this division of Buddhist philosophy is the Yogâcâra of Asanga and Vasubandhu. The *Lankâvatarâ* and the *Sandhinirmocana* and some other Sûtras, on which the school claims to have its doctrinal foundation, teach three forms of knowledge. The sûtra literature, however, as a rule does not enter into any detailed exposition of the subject; it merely classifies knowledge and points out what form of knowledge is most desirable by the Buddhists. To obtain a fuller and more discursive elucidation, we must come to the Abhidharma Pitaka of that school. Of the text books most generally studied of the

Yogâcâra, we may mention Vasubandhu's *Vijñânamâtra* with its commentaries and Asanga's *Comprehensive Treatise on Mahâyânism* The following statements are abstracted mainly from these documents.

The three forms of knowledge as classified by the Yogâcâra are: (1) Illusion *(parikalpita)*, (2) Relative Knowledge *(paratantra)*, and (3) Absolute Knowledge *(parinispanna)*.

Illusion.

Illusion *(parikalpita)*, to use Kantian phraseology, is a sense-perception not co-ordinated by the categories of the understanding; that is to say, it is a purely subjective elaboration, not verified by objective reality and critical judgment. So long as we make no practical application of it, it will harbor no danger; there is no evil in it, at least religiously. Perceptual illusion is a psychical fact, and as such it is justified. A straight rod in water appears crooked on account of the refraction of light; a sensation is often felt in the limb after it has been amputated, for the nervous system has not yet adjusted itself to the new condition. They are all illusions, however. They are doubtless the correct interpretation of the sense-impressions in question, but they are not confirmed by other sense-impressions whose coördination is necessary to establish an objective reality. The moral involved in this is: all sound inferences and correct behavior must be based on critical knowledge and not on illusory premises.

Reasoning in this wise, the Mahâyânists declare that the egoism fostered by vulgar minds belongs to this class of knowledge, though of a different order, and that those who tenaciously cling to egoism as their final stronghold are believers in an intellectual fata morgana, and are like the thirsty deer that madly after the visionary water in the desert, or like the crafty monkey that tries to catch the lunar reflection in the water. Because the belief in the existence of a metaphysical agent behind our mental phenomena is not confirmed by experience and sound judgment, it being merely a product of unenlightened subjectivity.

Besides this ethical and philosophical egoism, all forms of world-conception which is founded on the sandy basis of subjective illusion, such as fetichism, idolatry, anthropomorphism, anthropopsychism, and the like, must be classed under the *parikalpita-lakṣana* as doctrines having illusionary premises.

Relative Knowledge.

Next comes the *paratantra-lakṣana*, a *welt-anschauung* based upon relative knowledge, or better, upon the knowledge of the law of relativity. According to this view, everything in the world has a relative and conditional existence, and nothing can claim an absolute reality free from all limitations. This closely corresponds to the theory advanced by most of modern scientists, whose agnosticism denies our intellectual capability of transcending the law of relativity.

The *paratantra-lakṣana*, therefore, consists in the knowledge derived from our daily intercourse with the outward world. It deals with the highest abstractions we can make out of our sensuous experiences. It is positivistic in its strictest sense. It says: The universe has only a relative existence, and our knowledge is necessarily limited. Even the highest generalisation cannot go beyond the law of relativity. It is impossible for us to know the first cause and the ultimate end of existence; nor have we any need to go thus beyond the sphere of existence, which would inevitably involve us in the maze of mystic imagination.

The *paratantra-lakṣana*, therefore, is a positivism, agnosticism, or empiricism in its spirit. Though the Yogâcâra Buddhists do not use all these modern philosophical terms, the interpretation here given is really what they intended to mean by the second form of knowledge. A world-conception based on this view, it is declared by the Mahâyânists, is sound as far as our perceptual knowledge is concerned; but it does not exhaust the entire field of human experience, for it does not take into account our spiritual life and our inmost consciousness. There is something in the human heart that refuses to be satisfied with merely systematising under the so-called laws of nature those multitudinous impressions which we receive from the outside world. There is a singular feeling, or sentiment, or yearning, whatever we may call it, in our inmost heart, which defies any plainer description than a mere suggestion or an indirect statement. This somewhat mystic consciousness seems despite its obscureness to contain the meaning of our existence as well as that of the universe. The intellect may try to persuade us with all its subtle reasonings to subdue this disquieting feeling and to remain contented with the systematising of natural laws, so called. But it is deceiving itself by so doing; because the intellect is but a servant to the heart, and so far as it is not forced to self-contradiction, it must accommodate itself to the needs of the heart. That is to say, we must transcend the narrow limits of conditionality and see what indispensable postulates are underlying our life and experiences. The recognition of these indispensable postulates of life constitutes the Yogâcâra's third form of knowledge called *parinişpanna-lakṣana*.

Absolute Knowledge.

Parinişpanna-lakṣana literally means the world-view founded on the most perfect knowledge. According to this view, the universe is a monistico-pantheistic system. While phenomenal existences are regulated by natural laws characterised by conditionality and individuation, they by no means exhaust all our experiences which are stored in our inmost consciousness. There must be something, — this is the absolute demand of humanity, the ultimate postulate of experience, — be it Will, or Intelligence, which, underlying and animating all existences, forms the basis of cosmic, ethical, and religious life. This highest Will, or Intelligence, or both may be termed God, but the Mahâyânists call it religiously Dharmakâya, ontologically Bhûtatathâtâ, and psychologically Bodhi or Sambodhi. And they think it must be immanent in the universe manifesting itself in all places and times; it must be the cause of perpetual creation; it must be the principle of morality. This being so, how do we come to the recognition of its presence? The Buddhists say that when our minds are clear of illusions, prejudices, and egotistic assumptions, they become transparent and reflect the truth like a dust-free mirror. The illumination thus gained in our consciousness constitutes the so-called *pariniṣpanna*, the most perfect knowledge, that leads to Nirvâna, final salvation, and eternal bliss.

World-views Founded on the Three Froms of Knowledge.

The reason will be obvious to the reader why the Yogâcâra school distinguishes three classes of world-conception founded on the three kinds of knowledge. The *parikalpita-lakṣana* is most primitive and most puerile. However, in these days of enlightenment, what is believed by the masses is naught else than a *parikalpita* conception of the world. The material existence as it appears to our senses is to them all in all. They seem to be unable to shake off the yoke of egoistic illusion and naïve realism. Their God must be transcendent and anthropopathic, and always willing to meddle with worldly affairs as his whim pleases. How different the world is, in which the multitudes of unreflecting minds are living, from that which is conceived by Buddhas and Bodhisattvas! Hartmann, a German thinker, is right, when he says that the masses are at least a century behind in their intellectual culture. But the most strange thing in the world is that, in spite of all their ignorance and superstitious beliefs, the waves of universal transformation are ever carrying them onward to a destination, of which, perhaps, they have not the slightest suspicion.

The *paratantra-lakṣana* advances a step further, but the fundamental error involved in it is its persistent self-contradictory disregard for what our inmost consciousness is constantly revealing to us. The intellect alone can by no means unravel the mystery of our entire existence. In order to reach the highest truth, we must boldly plunge with our whole being into a region where absolute darkness defying the light of intellect is supposed to prevail. This region which is no more nor less than the field of religious consciousness is shunned by most of the intellectual people on the plea that the intellect by its very nature is unable to fathom it. But the only way that leads us to the final pacification of the heart-yearnings is to go beyond the horizons of limiting reason and to resort to the faith that has been planted in the heart as the *sine qua non* of its own existence and vitality. And by faith I mean *Prajñâ* (wisdom), transcendental knowledge, that comes direct from the intelligence-essence of the Dharmakâya. A miṇd, so tired in vainly searching after truth and bliss in the verbiage of philoṣophy and the nonsense of ritualism, finds itself here completely rested bathing in the rays of divine effulgence, — whence this is, it does not question, being so filled with supramundane blessings which alone are felt. Buddhism calls this exalted spiritual state Nirvâna or Mokṣa; and *pariniṣpanna-lakṣana* is a world-conception which naturally follows from this subjective, ideal enlightenment. [1]

Two Forms of Knowledge.

The other Hindu Mahâyânism, the Mâdhyamika school of Nâgârjuna, distinguishes two, instead of three, orders of knowledge, but practically the Yogâcâra and the Mâdhyamika come to the same conclusion. [2]

[1] For detailed exposition of the three forms of knowledge, the reader is requested to peruse Asanga's *Comprehensive Treatise on Mahâyânism* (Nanjo's Catalogue, No. 1183), Vasubandhu's work on Mahâyâna idealism (*Vijnânamâtra Çâstra*, Nanjo, No. 1215), the *Sûtra on the Mystery of Deliverance* (*Sandhinirmocana-sûtra*, Nanjo. Nos. 246 aud 247), etc.

[2] When the eminent representatives of both parties, such as Dharmapala and Bhavaviveka, were at the height of their literary activity in India about the fifth or sixth century after Christ, their partisan spirit incited them bitterly to denounce each other, forgetting the common ground on which their principles were laid down. Their disagreement in fact on which they put an undue emphasis was of a very trifling nature. It was merely a quarrel over phraseology, for one insisted on using certain words just in the sense which the other negated.

The two kinds of knowledge or truth distinguished by the Mâdhyamika philosophy are *Samvṛtti-satya* and *Paramârtha-satya*, that is, conditional truth and transcendental truth. We read in Nâgârjuna's *Mâdhyamika Çâstra* (Buddhist Text Society edition, pp. 180, 181):

> "On two truths is founded
> The holy doctrine of Buddhas:
> Truth conditional,
> And truth transcendental.
>
> "Those who verily know not
> The distinction of the two truths.
> Know not the essence
> Of Buddhism which is meaningful." [1]

The conditional truth includes illusion and relative knowledge of the Yogâcâra school, while the transcendental truth corresponds to the absolute knowledge.

In explaining these two truths, the Mâdhyamika philosophers have made a constant use of the terms, *çûnya* and *açûnya*, void and not-void, which unfortunately became a cause of the misunderstanding by Christian scholars of Nâgârjuna's transcendental philosophy. Absolute truth is void in its ultimate nature, for it contains nothing concrete or real or individual that makes it an object of particularisation. But this must not be understood, as is done by some superficial critics, in the sense of absolute

[1] Dve satye samupâçritya buddhânâm dhardeçanâ
Lokasamvṛttisatyañ ca satyañ ca paramârthataḥ.
Ye ca anayor na jânanti vibhâgam satyayor dvayoḥ,
Te tatvam na vijânanti gambhîrabuddhaçâsane."

nothingness. The Mâdhyamika philosophers make the *satya* (transcendental truth) empty when contrasted with the realness of phenomenal existences. Because it is not real in the sense a particular being is real; but it is empty since it transcends the principle of individuation. When considered absolutely, it can neither be empty nor not-empty, neither *çûnya* nor *açûnya*, neither *asti* nor *nâsti*, neither *abhâva* nor *bhâva*, neither real nor unreal. All these terms imply relation and contrast, while the *Paramârtha Satya* is above them, or better, it unifies all contrasts and antitheses in its absolute oneness. Therefore, even to designate it at all may lead to the misunderstanding of the true nature of the *Satya*, for naming is particularising. It is not, as such, an object of intellectuation or of demonstrative knowledge. It underlies everything conditional and phenomenal, and does not permit itself to be a particular object of discrimination.

Transcendental Truth and Relative Understanding.

One may say: If transcendental truth is of such an abstract nature, beyond the reach of the understanding, how can we ever hope to attain it and enjoy its blessings? But Nâgârjuna says that it is not absolutely out of the ken of the understanding; it is, on the contrary, through the understanding that we become acquainted with the quarter towards which our spiritual efforts should be directed, only let us not cling to the means by which we grasp the final reality. A finger is needed to point at the moon, but when we have recognised the moon, let us no more trouble ourselves with the finger. The fisherman carries a basket to take the fish home, but what need has he to worry about the basket when the contents are safely on the table? Only so long as we are not yet aware of the way to enlightenment, let us not ignore the value of relative knowledge or conditional truth or *lokasamvṛttisatya* as Nâgârjuna terms it.

> "If not by worldly knowledge,
> The truth is not understood;
> When the truth is not approached,
> Nirvâna is not attained." [1]

From this, it is to be infered that Buddhism never discourages the scientific, critical investigation of religious beliefs. For it is one of the functions of science that it should purify the contents of a belief and that it should point out in which direction our final spiritual truth and consolation have to be sought. Science alone which is built on relative knowledge is not able to satisfy all our religious cravings, but it is certainly able to direct us to the path of enlightenment. When this path is at last revealed, we shall know how to avail ourselves of the discovery, as then Prajñâ (or Sambodhi, or Wisdom) becomes the

[1] Vyavahâram anâçritya paramârtho na deçyate,
Paramârtham anâgamya nirvâṇam na adhigamyata.
The Mâdhyamika, p. 181.

guide of life. Here we enter into the region of the unknowable. The spiritual facts we experience are not demonstrable, for they are so direct and immediate that the uninitiated are altogether at a loss to get a glimpse of them.

CHAPTER V.

BHÛTATATHÂTÂ (SUCHNESS).

FROM the ontological point of view, Paramârtha-satya or Parinișpanna (transcendental truth) is called Bhûtatathâtâ, which literally means "suchness of existence." As Buddhism does not separate being from thought nor thought from being, what is suchness in the objective world, is transcendental truth in the subjective world, and *vice versa*. Bhûtatathâtâ, then, is the Godhead of Buddhism, and it marks the consummation of all our mental efforts to reach the highest principle, which unifies all possible contradictions and spontaneously directs the course of world-events. In short, it is the ultimate postulate of existence. Like Paramârtha-satya, as above stated, it does not belong to the domain of demonstrative knowledge or sensuous experience; it is unknowable by the ordinary processes of intellectuation, which the natural sciences use in the formulation of general laws; and it is grasped, declare the Buddhists, only by the minds that are capable of exercising what might be called religious intuition.

Açvaghoșa argues, in his *Awakening of Faith* for the indefinability of this first principle. When we say it is çûnya or empty, on account of its being independent of all the thinkable qualities, which we attribute to things relative and conditional, people would take it for the nothingness of absolute void But when we define it as a real reality, as it stands above the evanescence of phenomena, they would imagine that there is something individual and existing outside the pale of this universe, which, though as concrete as we ourselves are, lives an eternal life. It is like describing to the blind what an elephant looks like; each one of them gets but a very indistinct and imperfect conception of the huge creature, yet every one of them thinks he has a true and most comprehensive idea of it.[1] Açvaghoṣa, thus, wishes to eschew all definite statements concerning the ultimate nature of being, but as language is the only mode with which we mortals can express our ideas and communicate them to others, he thinks the best expression that can be given to it is Bhûtatathâtâ, i. e., "suchness of existence," or simply, "suchness."

Bhûtatathâtâ (suchness), thus absolutely viewed, does not fall under the category of being and non-being; and minds which are kept within the narrow circle of contrasts, must be said to be incapable of grasping it as it truly is. Says Nâgârjuna in his Çâstra (Ch. XV.):

> "Between thisness (*svabhâva*) and thatness (*parabhâva*),
> Between being and non-being,
> Who discriminates,
> The truth of Buddhism he perceives not."[2]

[1] Cf. *The Udâna*, chapter VI.

[2] Svabhâvam parabhâvanca, bhâvancâbhâvameva ca,
Ye paçyanti, na paçyante tatvam hi buddhaçâsane.

Or,

"To think 'it is', is eternalism,
To think 'it is not', is nihilism:
Being and non-being,
The wise cling not to either."[1]

Again,

"The dualism of 'to be' and 'not to be,'
The dualism of pure and not-pure:
Such dualism having abandoned,
The wise stand not even in the middle."[2]

To quote, again, from the *Awakening of Faith* (pp. 58—59): "In its metaphysical origin, Bhûtatathâtâ has nothing to do with things defiled, i. e., conditional: it is free from all signs of individualisation, such as exist in phenomenal objects: it is independent of an unreal, particularising consciousness."

Indefinability.

Absolute Suchness from its very nature thus defies all definitions. We cannot even say that it is, for everything that is presupposes that which is not: existence and non-existence are relative terms as much as subject and object, mind and matter, this and that, one and other: one cannot be conceived

[1] Astîti çâçvatagrâho, nâstîtyucchedadarçanam:
Tasmâdastitvanâstitve nâçriyeta vicaksanah

[2] Astiti nâstiti ubhe 'pi antâ
Çuddhî açuddhîti ime 'pi antâ;
Tasmâdubhe anta vivarjayitvâ
Madhye 'pi syânam na karoti panditah.

without the other. "It is not so (*na iti*) [1]," therefore, may be the only way our imperfect human tongue can express it. So the Mahâyânists generally designate absolute Suchness as Çûnyatâ or void.

But when this most significant word, çûnyatâ, is to be more fully interpreted, we would say with Açvaghoṣa that "Suchness is neither that which is existence nor that which is non-existence; neither that which is at once existence and non-existence, nor that which is not at once existence and non-existence; it is neither that which is unity nor that which is plurality; neither that which is at once unity and plurality, nor that which is not at once unity and plurality." [2]

[1] This is the famous phrase in the *Brhadaranyaka Upanisad* occurring in several places (II, 3, 6; III, 9, 26; IV, 2, 4; IV, 4, 22; IV, 5, 5). The Atman or Brahman, it says, "is to be described by No, No! He is incomprehensible, for he cannot be comprehended; he is imperishable, for he cannot perish; he is unattached, for he does not attach himself; unfettered, he does not suffer, he does not fail. Him (who knows), these two do not overcome, whether he says that for some reason he has done evil, or for some reason he has done good—he overcomes both, and neither what he has done, nor what he has omitted to do, affects him."

[2] *The Awakening of Faith*, p. 59. Cf. this with the utterances of Dionysius the Areopagite, as quoted by Prof. W. James in his *Varieties of Religious Experience*, pp. 416—417: "The cause of all things is neither soul nor intellect; nor has it imagination, opinion, or reason, or intelligence; nor is it spoken or thought. It is neither number, nor order, nor magnitude, nor littleness, nor equality, nor inequality, nor similarity, nor dissimilarity. It neither stands, nor moves, nor rests.... It is neither essence, nor eternity, nor time.

Nâgârjana's famous doctrine of "The Middle Path of Eight No's" breathes the same spirit, which declares:

"There is no death, no birth, no destruction, no persistence,
No oneness, no manyness, no coming, no departing, [1]

Elsewhere, he expresses the same idea in a somewhat paradoxical manner, making the historical Buddha a real concrete manifestation of Suchness:

"After his passing, deem not thus:
'The Buddha still is here,'
He is above all contrasts,
To be and not to be.

"While living, deem not thus:
'The Buddha is now here.'
He is above all contrasts,
To be and not to be." [2]

This view of Suchness as no-ness abounds in the literature of the Dhyâna school of Mahâyânism. To cite one instance: When Bodhi-Dharma [3], the founder

Even intellectual contact does not belong to it. It is neither science nor truth. It is not even royalty nor wisdom; not one; not unity; not divinity or goodness; nor even spirit as we know it.".... *ad libitum.*

[1] Anirodham anutpâdam anucchedam açâçvatam,
Anekârtham anânârtham anâgamam anirgamam.
(*Mâdhyamika Çâstra*, first stanza.)

[2] Param nirodhâdbhagavân bhavatîtyeva nohyate,
Na bhavatyubhayam ceti nobhayam ceti nohyate:
Atisthamâno 'pi bhagavân bhavatîtyeva nohyate,
Na bhavatyubhayam ceti nobhayam ceti nohyate.
(*Mâdhyamika*, p. 199).

[3] He was the third son of king of Kâçi (?) in southern India. He came to China A. D. 527 and after a vain attempt to convert Emperor Wu to his own view, he retired to a monastery, where, it is reported, he spent all day in gazing at the wall

of the Dhyâna sect, saw Emperor Wu of Liang dynasty (A D. 502—556), he was asked what the first principle of the Holy Doctrine was, he did not give any lengthy, periphrastic statement after the manner of a philosopher, but laconically replied, "Vast emptiness and nothing holy." The Emperor was bewildered and did not know how to take the words of his holy adviser. Naturally, he did not expect such an abrupt answer, and, being greatly disappointed, ventured another question: "Who is he, then, that stands before me?" By this he meant to repudiate the doctrine of absolute Suchness. His line of argument being this: If there is nothing in the ultimate nature of things that distinguishes between holiness and sinfulness, why this world of contrasts, where some are revered as holy, for instance, Bodhi-Dharma who is at this very moment standing in front of him with the mission of propagating the holy teachings of Buddha? Bodhi-Dharma, however, was a mystic and was fully convinced of the insufficiency of the human tongue to express the highest truth which is revealed only

without making any further venture to propagate his mysticism. But finally he found a most devoted disciple in the person of Shen Kuang, who was once a Confucian, and through whom the Dhyâna school became one of the most powerful Mahâyâna sect in China as well as in Japan. Dharma died in the year 535. Besides the one here mentioned, he had another audience with the Emperor. At that time, the Emperor said to Dharma: "I have dedicated so many monasteries, copied so many sacred books, and converted so many bhiksus and bhiksunis: what do you think my merits are or ought to be?" To this, however, Dharma replied curtly, "No merit whatever."

intuitively to the religious consciousness. His conclusive answer was, "I do not know" [1]

This "I do not know" is not to be understood in the spirit of agnosticism, but in the sense of "God when understood is no God," for *in se est et per se conceptur*. This way of describing Suchness by negative terms only, excluding all differences of name and form (*nâmarûpa*) to reach a higher kind of affirmation, seems to be the most appropriate one, inasmuch as the human understanding is limited in so many respects; but, nevertheless, it has caused much misinterpretation even among Buddhists themselves, not to mention those Christian Buddhist scholars of to-day, who sometimes appear almost wilfully to misconstrue the significance of the çûnyatâ philosophy. It was to avoid these unfortunate misinterpretations that the Mahâyânists frequently made the paradoxical assertion that absolute Suchness is empty and not empty, çûnya and açunya, being and non-being, sat and asat, one and many, this and that.

The "Thundrous Silence."

There yet remains another mode of explaining absolute Suchness, which though most practical and most effective for the religiously disposed minds, may prove very inadequate to a sceptical intellect.

[1] Another interesting utterance by a Chinese Buddhist, who, earnestly pondering over the absoluteness of Suchness for several years, understood it one day all of a sudden, is: "The very instant you say it is something (or a nothing), you miss the mark."

It is the "thundrous silence" of Vimalakîrti in response to an inquiry concerning the nature of Suchness or the "Dharma of Non-duality," as it is termed in the Sûtra [1]

Bodhisattva Vimalakîrti once asked a host of Bodhisattvas led by Mañjuçri, who came to visit him, to express their views as to how to enter into the Dharma of Non-duality. Some replied, "Birth and death are two, but the Dharma itself was never born and will never die. Those who understand this are said to enter into the Dharma of Non-duality." Some said, "'I' and 'mine' are two. Because I think 'I am' there are things called 'mine.' But as there is no 'I am' where shall we look for things 'mine'? By thus reflecting we enter into the Dharma of Non-duality." Some replied, "Samsâra and Nirvâna are two. But when we understand the ultimate nature of Samsâra, Samsâra vanishes from our consciousness, and there is neither bondage nor release, neither birth nor death. By thus reflecting we enter into the Dharma of Non-duality." Others said, "Ignorance and enlightenment are two. No ignorance, no enlightenment, and there is no dualism. Why? Because those who have entered a meditation in which there is no sense-impression, no cogitation, are free from ignorance as well as from enlightenment. This holds true with all the other dualistic categories. Those who enter thus into the thought of sameness are

[1] *The Vimalakîrti Sûtra*, Kumârajîva's translation, Part II, Chapter 5.

said to enter into the Dharma of Non-duality." Still others answered, "To long for Nirvâna and to shun worldliness are of dualism. Long not for Nirvâna, shun not worldliness, and we are free from dualism. Why? Because bondage and release are relative terms, and when there is no bondage from the beginning, who wishes to be released? No bondage, no release, and therefore no longing, no shunning: this is called the entering into the Dharma of Non-duality."

Many more answers of similar nature came forth from all the Bodhisattvas in the assembly except the leader Mañjuçri. Vimalakîrti now requested him to give his own view, and to this Mañjuçri responded, "What I think may be stated thus: That which is in all beings wordless, speechless, shows no signs, is not possible of cognisance, and is above all questionings and answerings, — to know this is said to enter into the Dharma of Non-duality."

Finally, the host Vimalakîrti himself was demanded by Mañjuçri to express his idea of Non-duality, but he kept completely silent and uttered not a word. Thereupon, Mañjuçri admiringly exclaimed, "Well done, well done! The Dharma of Non-duality is truly above letters and words!" [1]

[1] Deussen relates, in his address delivered before the Bombay Branch of the Royal Asiatic Society, 1893, a similar attitude of a Vedantist mystic in regard to the highest Brahma. "The Bhava, therefore, when asked by the king Vaksalin, to explain the Brahman, kept silence. And when the king repeated his request again and again, the rishi broke out into the answer: 'I tell it you, but you don't understand it; *çânto 'yam âtmâ*, this âtmâ is silence!"

Now, of this Suchness, the Mahâyânists distinguish two aspects, as it is comprehended by our consciousness, which are conditional and non-conditional, or the phenomenal world of causality and the transcendental realm of absolute freedom. This distinction corresponds to that, in the field of knowledge, of relative truth and transcendental truth. [1]

[1] It is a well-known fact that the Vedanta philosophy, too, makes a similar distinction between Brahman as sagunam (qualified) and Brahman as nirgunam (unqualified). The former is relative, phenomenal, and has characteristics of its own; but the latter is absolute, having no qualification whatever to speak of, it is absolute Suchness. (See Max Mueller's *The Six Systems of Indian Philosophy*, p. 220 et seq.)

Here, a very interesting question suggests itself: Which is the original and which is the copy, Mahâyânism or Vedantism? Most of European Sanskrit scholars would fain wish to dispose of it at once by declaring that Buddhism must be the borrower. But I am strongly inclined to the opposite view, for there is reliable evidence in favor of it. In a writing of Açvaghoṣa, who dates much earlier than Çankara or Badarayana we notice this distinction of absolute Suchness and relative Suchness. He writes in his *Awakening of Faith* (p. 55 et seq.) that though Suchness is free from all modes of limitation and conditionality, and therefore it cannot be thought of by our finite consciousness, yet on account of Avidyâ inherent in the human mind absolute Suchness manifests itself in the phenomenal world, thereby subjecting itself to the law of causality and relativity and proceeds to say that there is a twofold aspect in Suchness from the point of view of its explicability. The first aspect is trueness as negation *(çûnyatâ)* in the sense that it is completely set apart from the attributes of all things unreal, that it is a veritable reality The second aspect is trueness as affirmation (*açûnyatâ*), in the sense that it contains infinite merits, that it is self-existent. Considering the fact that Açvaghoṣa comes

Suchness Conditioned.

Absolute transcendental Suchness defying all means of characterisation does not, as long as it so remains, have any direct significance in the phenomenal world and human life. When it does, it must become conditional Suchness as *Gesetzmässigkeit* in nature and as ethical order in our practical life. Suchness as absolute is too remote, too abstract, and may have only a metaphysical value. Its existence or non-existence seems not to affect us in our daily social life, inasmuch as it is transcendental. In order to enter into our limited consciousness, to become the norm of our conscious activities, to regulate the course of the evolutionary tide in nature, Suchness must surrender its "splendid isolation," must abandon its absoluteness.

When Suchness thus comes down from its sovereign-seat in the realm of unthinkability, we have this universe unfolded before our eyes in all its diversity and magnificence. Twinkling stars inlaid in the vaulted sky; the planet elaborately decorated with verdant meadows, towering mountains, and rolling waves; the birds cheerfully singing in the woods; the beasts wildly running through the thickets; the summer heavens ornamented with white fleecy clouds and on

earlier than any Vedanta philosophers, it stands to reason to say that the latter might have borrowed the idea of distinguishing the two aspects of Brahma from their Buddhist predecessors.

Çankara also makes a distinction between *saguna* and *nirguna vidya*, whose parallel we find in the Mahâyânist *samvṛtti* and *paramârtha satya*.

earth all branches and leaves growing in abundant luxury; the winter prairie destitute of all animation, only with naked trees here and there trembling in the dreary north winds; all these manifestations, not varying a hair's breadth of deviation from their mathematical, astronomical, physical, chemical, and biological laws, are naught else than the work of conditional Suchness in nature.

When we turn to human life and history, we have the work of conditional Suchness manifested in all forms of activity as passions, aspirations, imaginations, intellectual efforts, etc. It makes us desire to eat when hungry, and to drink when thirsty; it makes the man long for the woman, and the woman for the man; it keeps children in merriment and frolic; it braces men and women bravely to carry the burden of life. When we are oppressed, it causes us to cry, "Let us have liberty or die"; when we are treated with injustice, it leads us even to murder and fire and revolution; when our noble sentiments are aroused to the highest pitch, it makes us ready to sacrifice all that is most dear to us. In brief, all the kaleidoscopic changes of this phenomenal world, subjective as well as objective, come from the playing hands of conditional Suchness. It not only constitutes the goodness and blessings of life, but the sins, crimes, and misery which the flesh is heir to.[1]

[1] While passing, I cannot help digressing and entering on a polemic in this footnote. The fact is, Western Buddhist critics stubbornly refuse to understand correctly what is

Açvaghoṣa in his *Awakening of Faith* speaks of the Heart (*hṛdaya*) of Suchness and of the Heart of Birth-and-Death. By the Heart of Suchness he means the absolute and by the Heart of Birth-and-Death a manifestation of the absolute in this world of particulars. "They are not separate," however, says he, but they are one, for the Heart of

insisted by Buddhists themselves. Even scholars who are supposed to be well informed about the subject, go astray and make false charges against Buddhism. Max Mueller, for example, declares in his *Six Systems of Indian Philosophy* (p. 242) that "An important distinction between Buddhists and Vedantists is that the former holds the world to have arisen from what is not, the latter from what is, the Sat or Brahman." The reader who has carefully followed my exposition above will at once detect in this Max Mueller's conclusion an incorrect statement of Buddhist doctrine As I have repeatedly said, Suchness, though described in negative terms, is not a state of nothingness, but the highest possible synthesis that the human intellect can reach. The world did not come from the void of Suchness, but from its fulness of reality. If it were not so, to where does Buddhism want us to go after deliverance from the evanescence and nothingness of the phenomenal world?

Max Mueller in another place (op. cit. p. 210) speaks of the Vedantists' assertion of the reality of the objective world for practical purposes (*vyavahârârtham*) and of their antagonistic attitude toward "the nihilism of the Buddhists." "The Buddhists" this seems to refer to the followers of the Mâdhyamika school, but a careful perusal of their texts will reveal that what they denied was not the realness of the world as a manifestation of conditional Suchness, but its independent realness and our attachment to it as such. The Mâdhyamika school was not in any sense a nihilistic system. True, its advocates used many negative terms, but what they meant by them was obvious enough to any careful reader.

Suchness is the Heart of Birth-and-Death. It is on account of our limited senses and finite mind that we have a world of particulars, which, as it is, is no more than a fragment of the absoulte Bhûtatathâtâ. And yet it is through this fragmentary manifestation that we are finally enabled to reach the fundamental nature of being in its entirety. Says Açvaghoṣa, "Depending on the Tathâgata-garbha, there evolves the Heart of Birth-and-Death. What is immortal and what is mortal are harmoniously blended, for they are not one, nor are they separate. . . . . Herein all things are organised. Hereby all things are created."

The above is from the ontological standpoint. When viewed psychologically, the Heart of Suchness is enlightenment, for Buddhism makes no distinction between being and thought, world and mind. The ultimate nature of the two is considered to be absolutely one. Now, speaking of the nature of enlightenment, Açvaghoṣa says: "It is like the emptiness of space and the brightness of the mirror in that it is true, and real, and great. It completes and perfects all things. It is free from the condition of destructibility. In it is reflected every phase of life and activity in the world. Nothing goes out of it, nothing enters into it, nothing is annihilated, nothing is destroyed. It is one eternal soul, no forms of defilement can defile it. It is the essence of intelligence. By reason of its numerous immaculate virtues which inhere in it, it perfumes the hearts of all beings." Thus, the Heart of Suchness, which is enlightenment and the essence of intelligence, constantly works in and through the hearts of all human beings, that is, in and through our finite minds. In this sense, Buddhism declares that truth is not to be sought in highly abstract philosophical formulæ, but in the phenomena of our everyday life such as eating, dressing, walking, sleeping, etc. The Heart of Suchness acts and does not abstract; it synthesises and does not "dissect to murder."

Questions Defying Solution.

Speaking of the world as a manifestation of Suchness, we are here beset with the most puzzling questions that have baffled the best minds ever since the dawn of intellect. They are: Why did Suchness ever leave its abode in the mysterious realm of transcendentality and descend on earth where every form of misery greets us on all sides? What inherent necessity was there for it to mingle in the dust of worldliness while it could enjoy the unspeakable bliss of its own absoluteness? In other words, why did absolute Suchness ever become conditional Suchness? To dispose of these questions as not concerning human interests is the creed of agnosticism and positivism; but the fact is, they are not questions whimsically framed by the human mind when it was in the mood of playing with itself. They are queries of the most vital importance ever put to us, and the significance of life entirely hangs on our interpretation of them.

Buddhism confesses that the mystery is unsolvable purely by the human mind, for it is absolutely beyond the region of finite intellect and the power of a logical demonstrability. The mystery can only be solved in a practical way when we attain the highest spiritual enlightenment of Buddhahood, in which the Bodhi with its unimpeded supernatural light directly looks into the very abyss of Suchness. The Bodhi or Intelligence which constitutes the kernel of our being, is a partial realisation in us of Suchness. When this intelligence is merged and expands in the Body of Suchness, as the water in a vessel poured into the waters of the boundless ocean, it at once perceives and realises its nature, its destiny, and its significance in life.

Buddhism is a religion and leaves many topics of metaphysics unsolved, at least logically. Though it is more intellectual and philosophical than any other religion, it does not pretend to build a complete system of speculation. As far as theorisation is concerned, Buddhism is dogmatic and assumes many propositions without revealing their dialectical processes. But they are all necessary and fundamental hypotheses of the religious consciousness; they are the ultimate demands of the human soul. Religion has no positive obligation to prove its propositions after the fashion of the natural sciences. It is enough for religion to state the facts as they are, and the intellect, though hampered by limitations inherent in it, has to try her best to put them together in a coherent system.

The solution, then, by Buddhism of those queries stated above cannot be said to be very logical and free from serious dufficulties, but practically it serves all required purposes and is conducive to religious discipline. By this I mean the Buddhist theory of Nescience or Ignorance (*avidyâ*).

Theory of Ignorance.

The theory of nescience or ignorance (*avidyâ*) is an attempt by Buddhists to solve the relation between the one and the many, between absolute Suchness and conditional Suchness, between Dharmakâya and Sarvasattva, between wisdom (*bodhi*) and sin (*kleça*), between Nirvâna and Samsâra. But Buddhism does not give us any systematic exposition of the doctrine. What it says is categorical and dogmatic. "This universe is really the Dharmadhâtu;[1] it is characterised by sameness (*samatâ*); there is no differentiation (*visama*) in it; it is even emptiness itself (*çûnyatâ*); all things have no *pudgala* (self). But, because of nescience, there are four or six *mahâbhûta* (elements), five *skandha* (aggregates), six (or eight) *vijñâna* (senses), and twelve *nidâna* (chains of causation). All these names and forms (*nâmarûpa*) are of nescience or ignorance." Or, according to Açvaghoṣa, "The Heart of Suchness is the vast All of one Dharmadhâtu; it is the essence of all doctrines. The ultimate nature does not perish, nor does it

[1] Dharmadhâtu is the world as seen by an enlightened mind, where all forms of particularity do not contradict one another, but make one harmonious whole.

decay. All particular objects exist because of confused subjectivity (*smṛti*).[1] Independent of confused subjectivity, there is no outside world to be perceived and discriminated." "Everything that is subject to the law of birth and death exists only because of ignorance and karma." Such statements as these are found almost everywhere in the Buddhist literature; but as to the question how and why this negative principle of ignorance came to assert itself in the body of Suchness, we are at a loss where to find an authoritative and definite answer to it.

One thing, however, is certain, which is this: Ignorance (*avidyâ*) is principium individium, that creates the multitudinousness of phenomena in the absolute oneness of being, that tosses up the roaring billows of existence in the eternal ocean of Suchness, that breaks the silence of Nirvâna and starts the wheel of metempsychosis perpetually rolling, that, veiling the transpicuous mirror of Bodhi, affects the reflection of Suchness therein, that transforms the sameness (*samatâ*) of Suchness to the duality of thisness and thatness and leads many confused minds to egoism with all its pernicious corollaries.

Perhaps, the best way to attack the problem of ignorance is to understand that Buddhism is a thoroughly idealistic doctrine as every true religion should be, and that psychologically, and not ontologic-

[1] The word literally means recollection or memory. Açvaghoṣa uses it as a synonym of ignorance, and so do many other Buddhist philosophers.

ally, should Suchness be conceived, and further, that nescience is inherent in Suchness, though only hypothetically, illusively, apparently, and not really in any sense.

According to Brahmanism, there was in the beginning only one being; and this being willed to be two; which naturally resulted in the differentiation of subject and object, mind and nature. In Buddhism, however, Suchness is not explicitly stated as having had any desire to be other than itself, at least when it is purely metaphysically conceived. But as Buddhism interprets this world of particularisation as a manifestation of Suchness conditioned by the principle of ignorance, ignorance must be considered, however illusory in its ultimate nature, to have potentially or rather negatively existed in the being of Suchness; and when Suchness, by its transcendental freedom of will, affirmed itself, it did so by negating itself, that is, by permitting itself to be conditioned by the principle of ignorance or individuation. The latter, as is expressly stated everywhere in Buddhist sûtras and çâstras, is no more than an illusion and a negative quantity, it is merely the veil of Mâya. This chimerical nature of ignorance preserves the essential absoluteness of the first principle and makes the monism of the Mahâyâna doctrine thoroughly consistent. What is to be noted here, however, is this: Buddhism does not necessarily regard this world of particulars as altogether evanescent and dream-like. When ignorance alone is taken notice of and the presence of Suchness in all this multitudinousness of things is denied, this existence is positively declared to be void. But when an enlightened mind perceives Suchness even in the midst of the utter darkness of ignorance, this life assumes an entirely new aspect, and we come to realise the illusiveness of all evils.

To return to the subject, ignorance or nescience is defined by Açvaghoṣa as a spark of consciousness[1] that spontaneously flashes from the unfathomable depths of Suchness. According to this, ignorance and consciousness are interchangeable terms, though with different shades of meaning. Ignorance is, so to speak, the *raison d'être* of consciousness, is that which makes the appearance of the latter possible, while ignorance itself is in turn an illusive emanation of Suchness. It is then evident that the awakening of consciousness marks the first step toward the rising of this universe from the abyss of the self-identity of Suchness. For the unfolding of consciousness implies the separation of the perceiving and the perceived, the *viṣayin* and the *viṣaya*, of subject and object, mind and nature.

The eternal abyss of Suchness, so called, is the point where subjectivity and objectivity are merged in absolute oneness. It is the time, though strictly

[1] *Smṛti* or *citta* or *vijñāna*. They are all used by Açvaghoṣa and other Buddhist authors as synonymous. *Smṛti* literally means memory; *citta*, thought or mentation; and *vijñāna* is generally rendered by consciousness, though not very accurately.

speaking chronology does not apply here, when all "the ten thousand things" of the world have not yet been differentiated and even when the God who "created the heaven and earth" has not yet made his debut. To use psychological terms, it is a state of transcendental or transmarginal consciousness, where all sense-perceptions and conceptual images vanish, and where we are in a state of absolute unconsciousness. This sounds mystical; but it is an established fact that in the field of our mental activities there is an abyss where consciousness sometimes suddenly disappears. This region beyond the threshold of awaredness, though often a trysting place for psychical abnormalities, has a great religious significance, which cannot be ignored by superficial scientific arguments. Here is the region where the consciousness of subject and object is completely annihilated, but here we do not have the silence and darkness of a grave, nor is it a state of absolute nothingness. The self is here lost in the presence of something indescribable, or better, it expands so as to embrace the world-all within itself, and is not conscious of any egoistic elation or arrogance; but it merely feels the fulness of reality and a touch of celestial joy that cannot be imparted to others by anything human. The most convincing spiritual insight into the nature of being comes from this source. Enlightenment is the name given by Buddhists to the actual gaining of this insight. Bodhi or Prajñâ or intelligence is the term for the spiritual power that brings about this enlightenment

When the mind emerges from this state of sameness, consciousness spontaneously comes back as it vanished before, retaining the memory of the experience so unique and now confronting the world of contrasts and mutual dependence, in which our empirical ego moves. The transition from one state to the other is like a flash of lightning scintilating from behind the clouds; though the two, the subliminal and the superficial consciousness, seem to be one continuous form of activity, permitting no hiatus between them. At any rate, this awakening of subjectivity and the leaving behind of transmarginal consciousness marks the start of ignorance. Therefore, psychologically speaking, ignorance must be considered synonymous with the awakening of consciousness in a sentient being.

Here we have the most mysterious fact that baffles all our intellectual efforts to unravel, which is: How and why has ignorance, or what is tantamount, consciousness, ever been awakened from the absolute calmness *(çānti)* of being? How and why have the waves of mentation ever been stirred up in the ocean of eternal tranquillity? Açvaghoṣa simply says, "spontaneously." This by no means explains anything, or at least it is not in the line with our so-called scientific interpretations, nor does it give us any reason why. Nevertheless, religiously and practically viewed, "spontaneous" is the most graphic and vigorous term there is for describing the actual state of things as they pass before our mental eye. In fact, there is always something vague and indefinite in all our psychological experiences. With whatever scientific accuracy, with whatever objective precision we may describe the phenomena that take place in the mind, there is always something that eludes our scrutiny, is too slippery, as it were, to take hold of; so that after all our strenuous intellectual efforts to be exact and perspicuous in our expositions, we are still compelled to leave much to the imagination of the reader. In case he happens to be lacking in the experience which we have endeavored to describe we shall vainly hope to awaken in him the said impression with the same degree of intensity and realness

It is for this reason that Açvaghoṣa and other Mahâyânists declare that the rising of consciousness out of the abysmal depths of Suchness is *felt* by Buddhas and other enlightened minds only that have actually gone through the experience. The why of ignorance nobody can explain as much as the why of Suchness But when we personally experience this spiritual fact, we no more feel the need of harboring any doubt about how or why. Everything becomes transparent, and the rays of supernatural enlightenment shine like a halo round our spiritual personality. We move as dictated by the behest of Suchness, i. e., by the Dharmakâya, and in which we feel infinite bliss and satisfaction. This religious experience is the most unique phenomenon in the life of a sentient being.

Dualism and Moral Evil.

As we cannot think that the essence of the external world to be other than that of our own mind, that is to say, as we cannot think subject and object to be different in their ultimate nature, our conclusion naturally is that the same principle of Ignorance which gathers the clouds of subjectivity, calls up the multitudinousness of phenomena in the world-mind of Suchness The universe in its entirety is an infinite mind, and our limited mind with its transmarginal consciousness is a microcosm. What the finite mind feels in its inmost self, must also be what the cosmic mind feels; nay, we can go one step further, and say that when the human mind enters the region lying beyond the border of subjectivity and objectivity, it is in communion with the heart of the universe, whose secrets are revealed here without reserve. Therefore, Buddhism does not make any distinction between knowing and being, enlightenment and Suchness. When the mind is free from ignorance and no more clings to „things particular, it is said to be in harmony and even one with Suchness.

We must, however, remember that ignorance as the principle of individuation and a spontaneous expression of Suchness, is no moral evil. The awakening of subjectivity or the dawn of consciousness forms part of the necessary cosmic process. The separation of subject and object, or the appearance of a phenomenal world, is nothing but a realisation of the cosmic mind (Dharmakâya). As such Ignorance performs an essential function in the evolution of the world-totality. Ignorance is inherent in Buddhas as well as in all sentient beings. Every one of us cannot help perceiving an external world (*viṣaya*) and forming conceptions and reasoning and feeling and willing. We do not see any moral fault here. If there is really anything morally wrong, then we cannot do anything with it, we are utterly helpless before it, for it is not our fault, but that of the cosmic soul from which and in which we have our being.

Ignorance has produced everywhere a state of relativity and reciprocal dependence. Birth is inseparably linked with death, congregation with segregation, evolution with involution, attraction with repulsion, the centripetal with the centrifugal force, the spring with the fall, the tide with the ebb, joy with sorrow, God with Satan, Adam with Eve, Buddha with Devadatta, etc., ect., *ad infinitum*. These are necessary conditions of existence; and if existence is an evil, they must be abolished, and with their abolition the very reason of existence is abolished, which means absolute nothingness, — an impossibility as long as we exist. The work of ignorance in the world of conditional Suchness is quite innocent, and Buddhists do not recognise any fault in its existence, if not contaminated by confused subjectivity. Those who speak of the curse of existence, or those who conceive Nirvâna to be the abode of non-existence and the happiness of absolute annihilation, are considered by Buddhists to be unable to understand the significance of Ignorance.

Is there then no fault to be found with Ignorance? Not in Ignorance itself, but in our defiled attachment to it, that is, when we are ignorant of Ignorance. It is wrong to cling to the dualism of subject and object as final and act accordingly. It is wrong to take the work of ignorance as ultimate and to forget the foundation on which it stands. It is wrong, thinking that the awakening of consciousness reveals the whole world, to ignore the existence of unseen realities. In short, evils quickly follow our steps when we try to realise the conclusions of ignorance without knowing its true relation to Suchness. Egoism is the most fundamental of all errors and evils.

When we speak of ignorance as hindering the light of intelligence from penetrating to the bottom of reality, we usually understand the term ignorance not in the philosophical sense of principium individuum, but in the sense of confused subjectivity, which conceives the work of Ignorance as the final reality culminating in egoism. So, we might say that while the principle of Ignorance is philosophically justified, its unenlightened actualisation in our practical life is altogether unwarranted and brings on us a series of dire calamities.

CHAPTER VI.

THE TATHÂGATA-GARBHA AND THE ÂLAYA-VIJÑÂNA.

SUCHNESS (*Bhûtatathâtâ*), the ultimate principle of existence, is known by so many different names, as it is viewed in so many different phases of its manifestation. Suchness is the Essence of Buddhas, as it constitutes the reason of Buddhahood; it is the Dharma, when it is considered the norm of existence; it is the Bodhi when it is the source of intelligence; Nirvana, when it brings eternal peace to a heart troubled with egoism and its vile passions; Prajñâ (wisdom), when it intelligently directs the course of nature; the Dharmakâya, when it is religiously considered as the fountain-head of love and wisdom; the Bodhicitta (intelligence-heart), when it is the awakener of religious consciousness; Çûnyatâ (vacuity), when viewed as transcending all particular forms; the summum bonum (*kuçalam*), when its ethical phase is emphasised; the Highest Truth (*paramârtha*), when its epistemological feature is put forward; the Middle Path (*mâdhyamârga*), when it is considered above the onesidedness and limitation of individual existences; the Essence of Being (*bhûtakoti*), when its ontological aspect is taken into account; the Tathagata-garbha (the Womb of Tathâgata), when it is thought of in analogy to mother earth, where all the germs of life are stored, and where all precious stones and metals are concealed under the cover of filth. And it is of this last aspect of Suchness that I here propose to consider at some length.

The Tathâgata-Garbha and Ignorance.

Tathâgata-Garbha literally means Tathâgata's womb[1] or treasure or store, in which the essence of Tathâgatahood remains concealed under the veil of Ignorance. It may rightly be called the womb of universe, from which issues forth the multitudinousness of things, mental as well as physical.

The Tathâgata-Garbha, therefore, may be explained ontologically as a state of Suchness quickened by Ignorance and ready to be realised in the world of particulars, that is, when it is about to transform itself to the duality of subject and object, though there is yet no perceptible manifestation of motility in any form. Psychologically, it is the transcendental soul of man just coming under the bondage of the law of karmaic causation Though pure and free in its nature as the expression of Suchness in man, the transcen-

[1] Cf. the *Bhagavadgîtâ* (*S. B E.* Vol. VIII, chap. XIV, p. 107): "The Brahman is a womb for me, in which I cast the seed. From that, O descendant of Bharata! is the birth of all things. Of the bodies, O son of Kunti! which are born from all wombs, the main womb is the great Brahman, and I am the father, the giver of the seed."

dental soul or pure intelligence is now influenced by the principle of birth-and-death and subjects itself to organic determinations. As it is, it is yet devoid of differentiation and limitation, save that there is a bare possibility of them. It will, however, as soon as it is actualised in a special form, unfold all its particularities subject to their own laws; it will hunger, desire, strive, and even be annoyed by its material bonds, and then, beginning to long for liberation, will struggle inwardly. Here is then no more of the absolute freedom of Suchness, as long as its phenomenal phase alone is considered, since the Garbha works under the constraint of particularisation. The essence of Tathâgatahood, however, is here preserved intact, and, whenever it is possible, our finite minds are able to feel its presence and power. Hypothetically, therefore, the Garbha is always in association with passions and desires that are of Ignorance.

We read in the *Çrimâlâ-Sûtra:* "With the storage of passions attached we find the Tathâgata-Garbha," or, "The Dharmakâya of the Tathâgata not detached from the storage of passions is called Tathâgata-Garbha." In Buddhism, passion or desire or sin *(kleça)* is generally used in contrast to intelligence or Bodhi or Nirvâna. As the latter, religiously considered, represents a particular manifestation in the human mind of the Dharmakâya or Bhûtatathâtâ, so the former is a reflection of universal Ignorance in the microcosm. Therefore, the human soul in which, according to Buddhism, intelligence and desire are merged, should be regarded as an individuation of the Tathâgata-Garbha. And it is in this capacity that the Garbha is called *Âlayavijñâna*.

The Âlayavijñâna and its Evolution.

As we have seen, the Âlayavijñâna or All-Conserving Soul is a particularised expression in the human mind of the Tathâgata-Garbha. It is an individual, ideal reflex of the cosmic Garbha. It is this "psychic germ," as the Âlaya is often designated, that stores all the mental possibilities, which are set in motion by the impetus of an external world, which works on the Âlaya through the six senses (*vijñâna*).

Mahâyânism is essentially idealistic and does not make a radical, qualitative distinction between subject and object, thought and being, mind and nature, consciousness and energy. Therefore, the being and activity of the Âlaya are essentially those of the Garbha; and again, as the Garbha is the joint creation of universal Ignorance and Suchness, so is the Âlaya the product of desire (*kleça*) and wisdom (*bodhi*). The Garbha and the Âlaya, however, are each in itself innocent and absolutely irresponsible for the existing state of affairs. And let it be remarked here that Buddhism does not condemn this life and universe for their wickedness as was done by some religious teachers and philosophers. The so-called wickedness is not radical in nature and life. It is merely superficial. It is the work of ignorance and desire, and when they are converted to do service for the

Bodhi, they cease to be wicked or sinful or evil. Buddhists, therefore, strongly insist on the innate and intrinsic goodness of the Âlaya and the Garbha

Says Açvaghoṣa in his *Awakening of Faith* (p. 75): "In the All-Conserving Soul (*Âlaya*) Ignorance obtains, and from non-enlightenment [thus produced] starts that which sees, that which represents, that which apprehends an objective world, and that which constantly particularises." Here we have the evolution of the Garbha in its psychological manifestation; in other words, we have here the evolution of the Âlayavijñâna. When the Garbha or Âlaya comes under the influence of birth-and-death (*samsâra*), it no longer retains its primeval indifference or sameness (*samatâ*); but there come to exist that which sees (*viṣayin*) and that which is seen (*viṣaya*), a mind and an objective world. From the interaction of these two forms of existence, we have now before our eyes the entire panorama of the universe swiftly and noiselessly moving with its never-tiring steps A most favorite simile with Buddhists to illustrate these incessant activities of the phenomenal world, is to compare them to the waves that are seen forever rolling in a boundless ocean, while the body of waters which make up the ocean is compared to Suchness, and the wind that stirs up the waves to the principle of birth-and-death or ignorance which is the same thing So we read in the *Lankâvatâra Sûtra*:

"Like unto the ocean-waves,
Which by a raging storm maddened
Against the rugged precipice strike
Without interruption;
Even so in the Alaya-sea
Stirred by the objectivity-wind
All kinds of mentation-waves
Arise a-dancing, a-rolling." [1]

But all the psychical activities thus brought into full view, should not be conceived as different from the Mind (*citta*) itself. It is merely in the nature of our understanding that we think of attributes apart from their substance, the latter being imagined to be in possession and control of the former. There is, however, in fact no substance *per se*, independent of its attributes, and no attributes detached from that which unites them. And this is one of the fundamental conceptions of Buddhism, that there is no soul-in-itself considered apart from its various manifestations such as imagination, sensation, intellectuation, etc. The innumerable ripples and waves and billows of mentation that are stirred in the depths of the Tathâgata-Garbha, are not things foreign or external to it, but they are all particular expressions of the same essence, they are working out its immanent destiny. So continues the *Lankâvatâra Sûtra*:

[1] This is translated from the Chinese of Çikṣananda; the Sanskrit reads as follows:

"Tarangâ hi udadher yadvat pavanapratyaya îritâ,
Nṛtyamânâh pravartante vyucchedaç ca na vidhyate:
Âlayodhyas tathâ nityam viṣayapavana îritaḥ,
Cittâis tarangavijñânâir nṛtyamânâḥ pravartate."

"The saline crystal and its red-bluishness,
The milky sap and its sweetness,
Various flowers and their fruits,
The sun and the moon and their luminosity:
These are neither separable nor inseparable.
As waves are stirred in the water,
Even so the seven modes of mentation
Are awakened in the Mind and united with it.
When the waters are troubled in the ocean,
We have waves that roll each in its own way:
So with the Mind All-Conserving.
When stirred, therein diverse mentations arise:
Citta, Manas, and Manovijñâna.
These we distinguish as attributes,
In substance they differ not from each other;
For they are neither attributing nor attributed.
The sea-water and the waves,
One varies not from the other:
It is even so with the Mind and its activities;
Between them difference nowhere obtains.
Citta is karma-accumulating,
Manas reflects an objective world,
Manovijñâna is the faculty of judgment,
The five Vijñânas are the differentiating senses." [1]

[1] From the Chinese. The Sanskrit reads as follows:
"Nîle rakte ⁝tha lavaṇe çankhe kṣîre ca çârkare,
Kaṣayâiḥ phalapuṣpâdyâih kiraṇâ yatha bhâskare:
No ' nyena ca nânanyena tarangâ hi udadher matâ;
Vijñânâni tathâ sapta, cittena saha samyuktâ.
Udadheḥ pariṇâmo ' sâu tarangânâm vicitratâ,
Âlayam hi tathâ cittam vijñânâkhyam pravartate;
Cittam manaç ca vijñânam lakṣaṇârtham prakalpyate;
Âbhinna lakṣanâ hi aṣṭâu na lakṣyâ na ca lakṣaṇâ.
Udadheç ca tarangânâm yathâ nâsti viçeṣanâ.
Vijñânânam tathâ citte pariṇâmo na labhyate.
Cittena cîyate karmaḥ, manasâ ca vicîyate,
Vijñânena vijânâti, dṛçyam kalpeti pañcabhiḥ."

The Manas.

The Âlayavijñâna which is sometimes, as in the preceding quotations, simply called *citta* (mind), is, as such, no more than a state of Suchness, allowing itself to be influenced by the principle of birth-and-death, i. e., by Ignorance; and there has in it taken place as yet no "awakening" or "stirring up" (*vṛtti*), from which results a consciousness. When the Manas is evolved, however, we have a sign of mentality thereby set in motion, for the Manas, according to the Mahâyânists, marks the dawn of consciousness in the universe.

The Manas, deriving its reason of consciousness from the Citta or Âlaya, reflects on it as well as on an external world, and becomes conscious of the distinction between me and not-me. But since this not-I or external world is nothing but an unfoldment of the Âlaya itself, the Manas must be said really to be self-reflecting, when it discriminates between subject and object. If the Âlaya is not yet conscious of itself, the Manas is, as the latter comes to realise the state of self-awareness. The Âlaya is perhaps to be compared in a sense to the Kantian "ego of transcendental apperception"; while the Manas is the actual center of self-consciousness. But the Manas and the Âlaya (or Citta) are not two different things in the sense that one emanates from the other or that one is created by the other. It is better to understand the Manas as a state or condition of the Citta in its evolution.

Now, the Manas is not only contemplative, but capable of volition. It awakens the desire to cling to the state of individuation, it harbors egoism, passion, and prejudice; it wills and creates: for Ignorance, the principle of birth-and-death, is there in its full force, and the absolute identity of Suchness is here forever departed. Therefore, the Manas really marks the beginning of concrete, particularising consciousness-waves in the eternal ocean of the All-Conserving Mind. The mind which was hitherto indifferent and neutral here acquires a full consciousness; discriminates between ego and non-ego; feels pain and pleasure; clings to that which is agreeable and shrinks from that which is disagreeable; urges activities according to judgments, false or truthful; memorises what has been experienced, and stores it all: — in short, all the modes of mentation come into play with the awakening of the Manas.

According to Açvaghoṣa, with the evolution of the Manas there arise five important psychical activities which characterise the human mind. They are: (1) motility, that is the capability of creating karma; (2) the power to perceive; (3) the power to respond; (4) the power to discriminate; and (5) individuality. Through the exercise of these five functions, the Manas is able to create according to its will, to be a perceiving subject, to respond to the stimuli of an external world, to deliver judgments over what it likes and what it dislikes, and finally to retain all its own "karma-seeds" in the past and to mature them for the future, according to circumstances.

With the advent of the Manas, the evolution of the Citta is complete. Practically, it is the consummation of mentality, for self-consciousness is ripe now. The will can affirm its ego-centric, dualistic activities, and the intellect can exercise its discriminating, reasoning, and image-retaining faculties. The Manas now becomes the center of psychic coördination. It receives messages from the six senses and pronounces over the impressions whatever judgments, intellectual or volitional, which are needed at the time for its own conservation. It also reflects on its own sanctum, and, perceiving there the presence of the Âlaya, wrongfully jumps to the conclusion that herein lies the real, ultimate ego-soul, from which it derives the notions of authority, unity, and permanency.

As is evident, the Manas is a double-edged sword. It may destroy itself by clinging to the error of ego-conception, or it may, by a judicious exercise of its reasoning faculty, destroy all the misconceptions that arise from a wrong interpretation of the principle of Ignorance. The Manas destroys itself by being overwhelmed by the dualism of *ego* and *alter*, by taking them for final, irreducible realities, and by thus fostering absolute ego-centric thoughts and desires, and by making itself a willing prey of an indomitable egoism, religiously and morally. On the other hand, when it sees an error in the conception of the absolute reality of individuals, when it perceives a play of Ignorance in the dualism of me and not-me, when it recognises the *raison d'être* of existence in the essence of Tathâgatahood, i. e., in Suchness, when it realises that the Âlaya which is mistaken for the ego is no more than an innocent and irreproachable reflection of the cosmic Garbha, it at once transcends the sphere of particularity and becomes the very harbinger of eternal enlightenment.

Buddhists, therefore, do not see any error or evil in the evolution of the Mind (*âlaya*). There is nothing faulty in the awakening of consciousness, in the dualism of subject and object, in the individualising operation of birth-and-death (*samsâra*), only so long as our Manas keeps aloof from the contamination of false egoism. The gravest error, however, permeates every fiber of our mind with all its wickedness and irrationality, as soon as the nature of the evolution of the Âlaya is wrongfully interpreted by the abuse of the functions of the Manas. [1]

[1] A little digression here. It has frequently been affirmed of the ethics of Mahâyânism that as it has a nihilistic tendency its morality turns towards asceticism ignoring the significance of the sentiment and instinct It is true that Mahâyânism perfectly agrees with Vedantism when the latter declares: "If the killer thinks that he kills, if the killed thinks that he is killed, they do not understand; for this one does not kill, nor is that one killed." (*The Katopanishad*, II. 19.) This belief in non-action (Laotzean *Wu Wei*) apparently denies the existence of a world of relativity, but he will be a superficial critic who will stop short at this absolute aspect of Mahâyâna

Though Mahâyânism most emphatically denies the existence of a personal ego which is imagined to be lodging within the body and to be the spiritual master of it, it does not necessarily follow that it denies the unity of consciousness or personality or individuality. In fact, the assumption of Manovijñâna by Buddhists most conclusively proves that they have an ego in a sense, the denial of whose empirical existence is tantamount to the denial of the most concrete facts of our daily experiences. What is most persistently negated by them is not the existence of ego, but its final, ultimate reality. But to discuss this subject more fully we have a special chapter below devoted to "Âtman."

The Sâmkhya Philosophy and Mahâyânism

If we draw a comparison between the Sâmkhya philosophy and Mahâyânism, the Âlayavijñâna may

philosophy and refuses to consider its practical side. As we have seen above, Buddhists do not conceive the evolution of the Manovijñâna as a fault on the part of the cosmic mind, nor do they think the assertion of Ignorance altogether wrong and morally evil. Therefore, Mahâyânism does not deny the claim of reality to the world of the senses, though of course relatively, and not absolutely.

Again, "Tat tvam asi" (thou art it) or "I am the Buddha" — this assertion, though arrogant it may seem to some, is perfectly justifiable in the realm of absolute identity, where the serene light of Suchness alone pervades. But when we descend on earth and commingle in the hurly-burly of our practical, dualistic life, we cannot help suffering from its mundane limitations. We hunger, we thirst, we grieve at the loss of the dearest, we feel remorse over errors committed.

be considered an unification of Soul (*puruṣa*) and Nature (*prakṛtî*), and the Manovijñâna a combination of Buddhi (intellect) or Mahat (great element) with Ahankâra (ego). According to the *Sâmkhyakârika* (11), the essential nature of Prakṛtî is the power of creation, or, to use Buddhist phraseology, it is blind activity; while that of Puruṣa is witnessing (*sakṣitvâ*) and perceiving (*drastṛtvâ*). (*The Kârika*, 19.) A modern philosopher would say, Puruṣa is intelligence and Prakṛtî the will; and when they are combined and blended in one, they make Hartmann's *Unbewusste Geist* (unconscious spirit). The All-Conserving Mind (*Âlaya*) in a certain sense resembles the Unconscious, as it is the manifestation of Suchness, the principle of enlightenment, in its evolutionary aspect as conditioned by Ignorance; and Ignorance apparently

Mahâyânism does not teach the annihilation of those human passions and feelings.

There was once a recluse-philosopher, who was considered by the villagers to have completely vanquished all natural desires and human ambitions They almost worshipped him and thought him to be superhuman. One day early in Winter, a devotee approached him and reverentially inquired after his health. The sage at once responded in verse:

"A hermit truly I am, world-renounced;
Yet when the ground is white with snow,
A chill goes through me and I shiver."

A false conception of religious saintliness as cherished by so many pious-hearted, but withal ignorant, minds, has led them into some of the grossest superstitions, whose curse is still lingering even among us. Our earthly life has so many limitations and tribulations. The ills that the flesh is heir to must be relieved by some material, scientific methods.

corresponds to the will as the principle of blind activity. The Sâmkhya philosophy is an avowed dualism and permits the existence of two principles independent of each other. Mahâyânism is fundamentally monistic and makes Ignorance merely a condition necessary to the unfolding of Suchness [1] Therefore, what the Sâmkhya splits into two, Mahâyânism puts together in one.

So is the parallelism between the Manovijñâna, and Buddi and Ahankâra. Buddhi, intellect, is defined as *adhyavasâya* (*Kârika*, 23), while Ahankâra is interpreted as *abhimanas* (*Kârika*, 24), which is evidently self-consciousness. As to the exact meaning of *adhyavasâya*, there is a divergence of opinion: "ascertainment," "judgment," "determination," "apprehension" are some of the English equivalents chosen for it. But the inner signification of Buddhi is clear enough; it indicates the awakening of knowledge, the dawn of rationality, the first shedding of light on the dark recesses of unconsciousness; so the commentators give as the synonyms *mati* (understanding), *khyâti* (cognition), *jñânam*, *prajñâ*, etc, the last two of these, which mean knowledge or intelligence, being also technical terms of Mahâyânism. And, as we have seen above, these senses are what the Buddhists give to their Manovijñâna, save that the

[1] That the Buddhist Ignorance corresponds to the Sâmkhya Prakṛti can be seen also from the fact that some Samkhya commentators give to Prakṛti as its synonyms such terms as *çâkti* (energy) which reminds of karma or sankâra, *tamas* (darkness), *mâyâ*, and even the very word *avidyâ* (ignorance)

latter in addition has the faculty of discriminating between *teum* and *meum*, while in the Sâmkhya this is reserved for Ahankâra. Thus, here, too, in place of the Sâmkhya dualism, we have the Buddhist unity.

Another point we have to take notice here in comparing the two great Hindu religio-philosophical systems, is that the Sâmkhya philosophy pluralises the Soul (*puruṣa*, *Kârika*, 18), while Buddhism postulates one universal Citta or Âlaya. According to the followers of Kapila, therefore, there must be as many souls as there are individuals, and at every departure or advent of an individual there must be assumed a corresponding soul passing away or coming into existence, though we do not know its whence and whither. Buddhism, on the other hand, denies the existence of any individual mind apart from the All-Conserving Mind (*Âlaya*) which is universal. Individuality first appears at the awakening of the Manovijñâna. The quintessence of the Mind is Suchness and is not subject to the limitations of time and space as well as the law of causation. But as soon as it asserts itself in the world of particularisation, it negates itself thereby, and, becoming specialised, gives rise to individual souls. [1]

[1] This view of the oneness of the Âlaya or Citta (mind) may not be acceptable to some Mahâyânists, particularly to those who advocate the Yogâcâra philosophy; but the present author is here trying to expound a more orthodox and more typical and therefore more widely-recognised doctrine of Mahâyânism, i. e.. that of Açvaghoṣa.

CHAPTER VII.

THE THEORY OF NON-ATMAN OR NON-EGO.

IF I am requested to formulate the ground-principles of the philosophy of Mahâyâna Buddhism, and, indeed, of all the schools of Buddhism, I would suggest the following:

(1) All is momentary (*sarvam kṣanikam*),

(2) All is empty (*sarvam çûnyam*).

(3) All is without self (*sarvam anâtmam*).

(4) All is such as it is (*sarvam tathâtvam*).

These four tenets, as it were, are so closely interrelated that, stand or fall, they all inevitably share one and the same fate together. Whatever different views the various schools of Buddhism may hold on points of minor importance, they all concur at least on these four principal propositions.

Of these four propositions, the first, the second, and the fourth have been elucidated above, more or less explicitly. If the existence of a relative world is the work of ignorance and as such has no final reality, it must be considered illusory and empty; though it does not necessarily follow that on this account our life is not worth living. We must not confuse the moral value of existence with the ontological problem of its phenomenality. It all depends on our subjective attitude whether or not our world and life become full of significance. When the illusiveness or phenomenality of individual existences is granted and we use the world accordingly, that is, "as not abusing it," we escape the error and curse of egoism and take things as they are presented to us, as reflecting the Dharma of Suchness. We no more cling to forms of particularity as something ultimate and absolutely real and as that in which lies the essence of our life. We take them for such as they are, and recognise their reality only in so far as they are considered a partial realisation of Suchness, and do not go any further. Suchness, indeed, lies not hidden *behind* them, but exists immanently *in* them. Things are empty and illusory so long as they are particular things and are not thought of in reference to the All that is Suchness and Reality.

From this, it logically follows that in this world of relativity all is momentary, that nothing is permanent, so far as isolated, particular existences are concerned. Even independently of the statement made above, the doctrine of universal impermanency is an almost self-evident truth experienced everywhere, and does not require any special demonstration to prove its validity. The desire for immortality which is so conspicuous and persistent in all the stages of development of the religious consciousness that the very desire has been thought to be the essence of all religious systems, is the most conclusive proof that things on this earth are in a constant flux of becoming, and that there is nothing permanent or stationary in our individual existences; if otherwise, people would never have sought for immortality.

If this be granted as a fact of our everyday experience, we naturally ask: "Why are things so changeable? Why is life so fleeting? What is it that makes things so mutable and transitory?" To this, the Buddhist's answer is: Because the universe is a resultant product of many efficient forces that are acting according to different karmas; — the destiny of those forces being that no one force or no one set of forces can constantly be predominant over all the others, but that when one has exhausted its potential karma, it is replaced by another that has been steadily coming forward in the meantime. Hence the universal cadence of birth and death, of the spring and the fall, of the tide and the ebb, of integration and disintegration. Where there is attraction, there is repulsion; where there is the centripetal force, there is the centrifugal force. Because it is the law of karma that at the very moment of birth the arms of death are around the neck of life. The universe is nothing but a grand rhythmic manifestation of certain forces working in conformity to their predetermined laws; or, to use Buddhist terminology, this *lokadhâtu* (material world) consists in a concatenation of *hetus* (causes) and *pratyayas* (conditions) regulated by their karma.

If this were not so, there would be either a certain fixed state of things in which perfect equillibrium would be maintained, or an inexpressible confusion of things of which no knowledge or experience would be possible. In the former case, we should have universal stagnation and eternal death; in the latter case, there would be no universe, no life, nothing but absolute chaos. Therefore, so long as we have the world before us, in which all the possible varieties of particularisation are manifested it cannot be otherwise than in a state of constant vicissitudes and therefore of universal transitoriness.

Now, the Buddhist argument for the theory of non-ego is this: If individual existences are due to relations obtaining between diverse forces, which act sometimes in unison with and sometimes in opposition to one another as predetermined by their karma, they cannot be said to have any transcendental agency behind them, which is a permanent unity and absolute dictator. In other words, there is no âtman or ego-soul behind our mental activities, and no thing-in-itself (*svabhâva*), so to speak, behind each particular form of existence. This is called the Buddhist theory of non-âtman or non-ego.

Âtman

Buddhists use the term "âtman" in two senses: first, in the sense of personal ego, [1] and secondly, in

[1] *Pudgala* or *pudgalasamjña* is sometimes used by Mahâyânists as a synonym of âtman. The Buddhist âtman in the

that of thing-in-itself, perhaps, with a slight modification of its commonly accepted meaning. Let us use the term "âtman" here in its first sense as equivalent to ***bhûtâtman***, for we are going first to treat of the doctrine of non-ego, and later of that of no-thing-in-itself.

Âtman is usually translated "life," "ego," or "soul," [1] and is a technical term used both by Vedanta philosophers and Buddhists. But we have to note at the beginning that they do not use the term in the same sense. When the Vedanta philosophy, especially the later one, speaks of âtman as our inmost self which is identical with the universal Brahma, it is used in its most abstract metaphysical sense and does not mean the soul whatever, as the latter is

sense of ego-substratum may be considered to correspond to the Vedantist Jîvâtman, which is used in contradistinction to Paramâtman, the supreme being or Brahma.

[1] Mahâyâna Buddhists generally understand the essential characteristic of âtman to consist in freedom, and by freedom they mean eternality, absolute unity, and supreme authority. A being that is transitory is not free, as it is conditioned by other beings, and therefore it has no âtman. A being that is an aggregate of elemental matter or forms of energy is not absolute, for it is a state of mutual relationship, and therefore it has no âtman. Again, a being that has no authoritative command over itself and other beings, is not free, for it will be subjected to a power other than itself, and therefore it has no âtman. Now, take anything that we come across in this world of particulars; and does it not possess one or all of these three qualities: transitoriness, compositeness, and helplessness or dependence? Therefore, all concrete individual existences not excepting human beings have no âtman, have no ego, that is eternal, absolute, and supreme.

commonly understood by vulgar minds. On the other hand, Buddhists understand by âtman this vulgar, materialistic conception of the soul (*bhûtâtman*) and positively denies its existence as such. If we, for convenience' sake, distinguish between phenomenal and noumenal in our notion of ego or soul, the âtman of Buddhism is the phenomenal ego, namely, a concrete agent that is supposed to do the acting, thinking, and feeling; while the âtman of Vedantists is the noumenal ego as the *raison d' être* of our psychical life. The one is in fact material, however ethereal it might be conceived. The other is a highly metaphysical conception transcending the reach of human discursive knowledge. The latter may be identified with Paramâtman and the former with Jîvâtman. Paramâtman is a universal soul from which, according to Vedantism, emanates this world of phenomena, and in a certain sense it may be said to correspond to the Tathâgata-garbha of Buddhism. Jîvâtman is the ego-soul as it is conceived by ignorant people as an independent entity directing all the mental activities. It is this latter âtman that was found to be void by Buddha when he arose from his long meditation, declaring:

"Many a life to transmigrate,
Long quest, no rest, hath been my fate,
Tent-designer [1] inquisitive for:
Painful birth from state to state.

[1] Tent-designer is a figurative term for the ego-soul. Following the prevalent error, the Buddha at first made an

"Tent-designer! I know thee now;
Never again to build art thou:
Quite out are all thy joyful fires,
Rafter broken and roof-tree gone,
Gain eternity—dead desires."[1]

Buddha's First Line of Inquiry.

Buddhism finds the source of all evils and sufferings in the vulgar material conception of the ego-soul, and concentrates its entire ethical force upon the destruction of the ego-centric notions and desires. The Buddha seems, since the beginning of his wandering life, to have conceived the idea that the way of salvation must lie somehow in the removal of this egoistic prejudice, for so long as we are not liberated from its curse we are liable to become the prey of the three venomous passions: covetousness, infatuation, and anger, and to suffer the misery of birth and death and disease and old age. Thus, when he received his first instructions from the Sâmkhya philosopher, Arada, he was not satisfied, because he did not teach how to abandon this ego-soul itself. The Buddha argued: "I consider that the embodied ego-soul, though freed from the evolvent-evolutes,[2]

earnest search after the ego that was supposed to be snugly sitting behind our mental experiences, and the result was this utterance.

[1] *The Dharmapada*, vs. 153—154. Tr. by A. J. Edmunds.

[2] *Prakṛtivikṛtayas*. This is a technical term of Sâmkhya philosophy and means the modes of Prakrti, as evolved from it and as further evolving on. See Satis Chandra Banarji, *Samkhya-Philosophy*, p. XXXIII et seq.

is still subject to the condition of birth and has the condition of a seed. The seed may remain dormant so long as it is deprived of the opportunity of coming into contact with the requisite conditions of quickening and being quickened, but since its germinating power has not been destroyed, it will surely develop all its potentialities as soon as it is brought into that necessary contact. Even though the ego-soul free from entanglement [i. e. from the bondage of Prakṛti] is declared to be liberated, yet, so long as the ego-soul remains, there can be no absolute abandonment of it, there can be no real abandonment of egoism."[1]

The Buddha then proceeds to indicate the path through which he reached his final conclusion and declares: "There is no real separation of the qualities and their subject; for fire cannot be conceived apart from its heat and form." When this argument is logically carried out, it leads nowhere but to the Buddhist doctrine of non-âtman, that says: The existence of an ego-soul cannot be conceived apart from sensation, perception, imagination, intelligence, volition, etc., and, therefore, it is absurd to think that there is an independent individual soul-agent which makes our consciousness its workshop.

To imagine that an object can be abstracted from its qualities, not only logically but in reality, that there is some unknown quantity that is in

[1] The passages quoted here as well as one in the next paragraph are taken from Açvaghoṣa's *Buddhacarita*.

possession of such and such characteristic marks (*lakṣana*) whereby it makes itself perceivable by our senses, says Buddhism, is wrong and unwarranted by reason. Fire cannot be conceived apart from its form and heat; waves cannot be conceived apart from the water and its commotion; the wheel cannot exist outside of its rim, spokes, axle, etc. All things, thus, are made of ***hetus*** and ***pratyayas***, of causes and conditions, of qualities and attributes; and it is impossible for our pudgala or âtman or ego or soul to be any exception to this universal condition of things.

Let me in this connection state an interesting incident in the history of Chinese Buddhism. Hui-K'e, the second patriarch of the Dhyâna sect in China, was troubled with this ego-problem before his conversion. He was at first a faithful Confucian, but Confucianism did not satisfy all his spiritual wants. His soul was wavering between agnosticism and scepticism, and consequently he felt an unspeakable anguish in his inmost heart. When he learned of the arrival of Bodhidharma in his country, he hastened to his monastery and implored him to give him some spiritual advice. But Bodhidharma did not utter a word, being seemingly absorbed in his deep meditation. Hui-K'e, however, was determined to obtain from him some religious instructions at all hazards. So it is reported that he was standing at the same spot seven days and nights, when he at last cut off his left arm with the sword he was carrying (being a military officer) and placed it before Dharma, saying: "This arm is a token of my sincere desire to be instructed in the Holy Doctrine. My soul is troubled and annoyed; pray let your grace show me the way to pacify it." Dharma quietly arose from his meditation and said: "Where is your soul? Bring it here and I will have it pacified." Hui-K'e replied: "I have been searching for it all these years, but I have never succeeded in laying a hand on it." Dharma then exclaimed: "There, I have your soul pacified!" At this, it is said, a flash of spiritual enlightenment went across the mind of Hui-K'e, and his "soul"[1] was pacified once for all.

The Skandhas.

When the five skandhas are combined according to their previous karma and present a temporal existence in the form of a sentient being, vulgar minds imagine that they have here an individual entity sustained by an immortal ego-substratum. In fact, the material body (*rûpakâya*) alone is not what makes the ego-soul, nor the sensation (*vedanâ*), nor the deeds (*sanskâra*), nor the consciousness (*vijñâna*), nor the conception (*samjñâ*); but only when they are all combined in a certain form they make a sentient being. Yet this combination is not the work of a certain independent entity, which, according to its own will, combines the five skandhas in one form and then hides itself in it. The combination of the constituent elements, Buddhism declares, is achieved by themselves after their karma. When a certain number of atoms of hydrogen and of oxygen are brought together, they attract each other on their own accord or owing to their own karma, and the result is water. The ego of water, so to speak, did not will to bring the two elements and make itself out of them. Even so is it with the existence of a sentient being, and there is no need of hypostasising a fabulous ego-monster behind the combination of the five skandhas.

Skandha (*khanda* in Pâli) literally means "aggregate" or "aglomeration", and, according to the Chinese exegetists, it is called so, because our personal existence is an aggregate of the five constituent elements of being, because it comes to take a definite individual form when the skandhas are brought together according to their previous karma. The first of the five aggregates is matter (*rûpa*), whose essential quality is thought to consist in resistance. The material part of our existence in the five sense-organs called *indryas*: eyes, ears, nose, tongue, and the body. The second skandha is called sensation or sense-impression (*vedanâ*), which results from the contact of the six vijñânas (senses) with the viṣaya (external world). The third is called *samjñâ* which corresponds to our conception. It is the psychic power by which we are enabled to form the abstract images of particular objects. The fourth is *sanskâra* which may be rendered action or deed. Our intelligent consciousness, responding to impressions received which are either agreeable or disagreeable or indifferent, acts accordingly; and these acts bear fruit in the coming generations.

Sanskâra, the fourth constituent of being, comprises two categories, mental (*caitta*) and non-mental (*cittaviprayukta*). And the mental is subdivided into six: fundamental (*mahâbhûmi*), good (*kuçala*), tormenting (*kleça*), evil (*akuçala*), tormenting minor (*upakleça*), and indefinite (*aniyata*). It may be interesting to enumerate what all these sankâras are, as they shed light on the practical ethics of Buddhism.

There are ten fundamental sanskâras belonging to the category of mental or psychic activities: 1. cetanâ (mentation), 2. sparça (contact), 3. chanda (desire), 4. mati (understanding), 5. smṛti (recollection), 6. manaskara (concentration), 7. adhimokṣa (unfettered intelligence), 8. samâdhi (meditation). The ten good sanskâras are: 1. çraddhâ (faith), 2. vîrya (energy), 3. upekṣa (complacency), 4. hrî (modesty), 5. apatrapâ (shame), 6 alobha (non-covetousness), 7. adveṣa (freedom from hatred), 8. ahimsa (gentleness of heart), 9. praçradbhi (mental repose), 10. apramâda (attentiveness).

The six tormenting sanskâras are as follows: 1. moha (folly), 2. pramâda (wantonness), 3. kâusidya (indolence), 4. açrâddhya (scepticism), 5. styāna (slothfulness), 6. âuddhatpa (unsteadiness).

The two minor evil sanskâras are: 1. ahrîkatâ, state of not being modest, or arrogance, or self-assertiveness, and 2. anapatrapa, being lost to shame, or to be without conscience.

The ten minor tormenting sanskâras are: 1. krodha (anger), 2. mrakṣa (secretiveness), 3. mâtsarya (niggardliness), 4. îrṣya (envy). 5. pradâça (uneasiness), 6. vihimsâ (noxiousness), 7. upanâha (malignity), 8. mâyâ (trickiness), 9. çâthya (dishonesty), 10. mada (arrogance).

The eight indefinite sanskâras are: 1. kâukṛtya (repentance), 2. middha (sleep), 3. vitarka (inquiry), 4. vicâra (investigation), 5. râga (excitement), 6. pratigha (wrath), 7. mâna (self-reliance), 8. vicikitsâ (doubting).

The second grand category of sanskâra which is not included under "mental" or "psychic," comprises fourteen items as follows: 1. prâpti (attainment), 2. aprâpti (non-attainment), 3. sabhâgatâ (grouping), 4 asanjñika (unconsciousness), 5. asanjñisamâpatti (unconscious absorption in religious meditation), 6. nirodhasamâpatti (annihilation-trance of a heretic), 7. jîvita (vitality), 8. jâti (birth), 9. sthiti (existing), 10. jarâ (decadence), 11. anityatâ (transitoriness), 12. nâmakâya (name), 13. padakâya (phrase), 14. vyañjanakâya (sentence).

Now, to return to the main problem. The fifth skandha is called *vijñâna*, commonly rendered consciousness, which, however, is not quite correct. The vijñâna is intelligence or mentality, it is the psychic power of discrimination, and in many cases it can be translated by sense. There are, according to Hînayânists, six vijñânas or senses: visual, auditory, olfactory, gustatory, tactual, and cogitative; according to Mahâyânism there are eight vijñânas: the manovijñâna and the âlayavijñâna, being added to the above six. This psychological phase of Mahâyâna philosophy is principally worked out by the Yogâcâra school, whose leading thinkers are Asanga and Vasubandhu.

King Milinda and Nâgasena

Buddhist literature, Northern as well as Southern, abounds with expositions of the doctrine of non-ego, as it is one of the most important foundation-stones on which the magnificent temple of Buddhism is built. The dialogue[1] between King Milinda and Nâgasena, among many others, is very interesting for various reasons and full of suggestive thoughts, and we have the following discussion of theirs concerning the problem of ego abstracted from the Dialogue.

At their first meeting the King asks Nâgasena, "How is your Reverence known, and what is your name?"

To this the monk-philosopher replies: "I am known as Nâgasena, and it is by that name that my brethren in the faith address me. But although parents give such a name as Nâgasena, or Sûrasena, Vîrasena, or Sîhasena, yet this Nâgasena and so on—is only a generally understood term, a designation in common use. For there is no permanent self involved in the matter."

Being greatly surprised by this answer, the King

[1] *The Questions of King Milinda, Sacred Books of the East,* Vol. XXXV.

volleys upon Nâgasena a series of questions as follows:

"If there be no permanent self involved in the matter, who is it, pray, who gives to you members of the Order your robes and food and lodging and necessaries for the sick? Who is it who enjoys such things when given? Who is it who lives a life of righteousness? Who is it who devotes himself to meditation? Who is it who attains to the goal of the Excellent Way, to the Nirvâna of Arhatship? And who is it who destroys living creatures? who is it who takes what is not his own? who is it who lives an evil life of worldly lusts, who speaks lies, who drinks strong drink, who in a word commits any one of the five sins which work out their bitter fruit even in this life? If that be so, there is neither merit nor demerit; there is neither doer nor cause of good or evil deeds; there is neither fruit nor result of good or evil karma. If we are to think that were a man to kill you there would be no murder, [1] then it follows that there are no real masters or teachers in your Order, that your ordinations are void. You tell me that your brethren in the Order are in the habit of addressing you as Nâgasena. Now, what is that Nâgasena? Do you mean to say that the hair is Nâgasena?"

This last query being denied by the Buddhist sage, the King asks: "Or is it the nails, the skin, the flesh, the nerves, the bones, the marrow, the kidneys,

[1] This reminds us of the passage quoted elsewhere from the *Katha-Upanishad;* cf. the footnote to it.

the heart, the liver, the abdomen, the spleen, the lungs, the larger intestines, the smaller intestines, the faeces, the bile, the phlegm, the pus, the blood, the sweat, the fat, the tears, the serum, the saliva, the mucus, the oil that lubricates the joints, the urine, or the brain or any or all of these, that is Nâgasena?

"Is it the material form that is Nâgasena, or the sensations, or the ideas, or the confections (deeds), or the consciousness, that is Nâgasena?"

To all these questions, the King, having received a uniform denial, exclaims in excitement: "Then, thus, ask as I may, I can discover no Nâgasena. Nâgasena is a mere empty sound. Who then is the Nâgasena that we see before us?[1] It is a falsehood that your Reverence has spoken, an untruth?"

Nâgasena does not give any direct answer, but quietly proposes some counter-questions to the King. Ascertaining that he came in a carriage to the Buddhist philosopher, he asks: "Is it the wheel, or the framework, or the ropes, or the spokes of the wheels, or the goad, that are the chariot?"

To this, the king says, "No," and continues: "It is on account of its having all these things that it

[1] As cited elsewhere, Bodhi-Dharma of the Dhyâna sect, when questioned in a similar way, replied, "I do not know." Walt Whitman echoes the same sentiment in the following lines:

"A child said, what is the grass? fetching it to me with full hands;
How could I answer the child? I do not know what it is, any more than he."

comes under the generally understood term, the designation in common use, of 'chariot.'"

"Very good," says Nâgasena, "Your Majesty has rightly grasped the meaning of 'chariot.' And just even so it is on account of all these things you questioned me about the thirty-two kinds of organic matter in a human body, and the five skandhas (constituent elements of being) that I come under the generally-understood term, the designation in common use, of 'Nâgasena.'"

Then, the sage quotes in way of confirmation a passage from the *Samyutta Nikâya*: "Just as it is by the condition precedent of the co-existence of its various parts that the word 'chariot' is used, just so it is that when the skandhas are there we talk of a 'being.'"

* * *

To further illustrate the theory of non-âtman from earlier Buddhist literature, let me quote the following from the *Jâtaka Tales* (No. 244):

The Bodhisattva said to a pilgrim. "Will you have a drink of Ganges-water fragrant with the scent of the forest?"

The pilgrim tried to catch him in his words: "What is the Ganges? Is the sand the Ganges? Is the water the Ganges? Is the hither bank the Ganges? Is the further bank the Ganges?"

But the Bodhisattva retorted, "If you except the

water, the sand, the hither bank, and the further bank, where can you find any Ganges?"

Following this argument we might say, "Where is the ego-soul, except imagination, volition, intellection, desire, aspiration, etc.?"

Ananda's Attempts to Locate the Soul.

In the *Surangama Sutra* [1], Buddha exposes the absurdity of the hypothesis of an individual concrete soul-substance by subverting Ândanda's seven successive attempts to determine its whereabouts. Most people who firmly believe in personal immortality, will see how vague and chimerical and logically untenable is their notion of the soul, when it is critically examined as in the following case. Ânanda's conception of the soul is somewhat puerile, but I doubt whether even in our enlightened age the belief

[1] There seem to be two Chinese translations of this Sûtra, one by Kumârajîva and the other by Paramârtha, but apparently they are different texts bearing the same title. Besides these two, there is another text entirely in Chinese transliteration. Owing to insufficiency of material at my disposal here, I cannot say anything definite about the identity or diversity of these documents. The following discussion that is reported to have taken place between the Buddha and Ananda is an abstract prepared from the first and the second fasciculi of Paramârtha's (?) translation. Beal gives in his *Catena of Buddhist Scriptures from the Chinese* (pp. 286 – 369) an English translation of the first four fasc. of the *Surangama*. Though this translation is not quite satisfactory in many points the reader may find there a detailed account of the discussion which is here only partially and roughly recapitulated.

entertained by the multitude is any better than his.

When questioned by the Buddha as to the locality of the soul, Ânanda asserts that it resides within the body. Thereupon, the Buddha says: "If your intelligent soul resides within your corporeal body, how is it that it does not see your inside first? To illustrate, what we see first in this lecture hall is the interior and it is only when the windows are thrown open that we are able to see the outside garden and woods. It is impossible for us who are sitting in the hall to see the outside only and not to see the inside. Reasoning in a similar way, why does not the soul that is considered to be within the body see the internal organs first such as the stomach, heart, veins etc.? If however it does not see the inside, surely it cannot be said to reside within the body."

Ânanda now proposes to solve the problem by locating the soul outside the body. He says that the soul is like a candle-light placed without this hall. Where the light shines everything is visible, but within the room there are no candles burning, and therefore here prevails nothing but darkness. This explains the incapacity of the soul to see the inside of the body. But the Buddha argues that "it is impossible for the soul to be outside. If so, what the soul feels may not be felt by the body, and what the body feels may not be felt by the soul, as there is no relationship between the two. The fact, however, is that when you, Ânanda, see my hand thus stretched, you are conscious that you have the perception of it. As far as there is a correspondence between the soul and the body, the soul cannot be said to be residing outside the body."

The third hypothesis assumed by Ânanda is that the soul hides itself just behind the sense-organs. Suppose a man put a pair of lenses over his eyes. Cannot he see the outside world through them? The reason why it cannot see the inside is that it resides within the sense-organs.

But says the Buddha: "When we have a lens over an eye, we perceive this lens as well as the outside world. If the soul is hidden behind the sense-organ, why does it not see the sense-organ itself? As it does not in fact, it cannot be residing in the place you mention."

Ânanda proposes another theory. "Within, we have the stomach, liver, heart, etc.: without, we have so many orifices. Where the internal organs are, there is darkness; but where we have openings, there is light. Close the eyes and the soul sees the darkness inside. Open the eyes and it sees the brightness outside. What do you say to this theory?"

The Buddha says: "If you take the darkness you see when the eyes are closed for your inside, do you consider this darkness as something confronting your soul, or not? In the first case, wherever there prevails a darkness, that must be thought to be your interior organs. In the latter case, seeing is impossible, for seeing presupposes the existence of subject and object. Besides this, there is another difficulty. Granting your supposition that the eye could turn itself inward or outward and see the darkness of the interior or the brightness of the external world, it could also see your own face when the eye is opened. If it could not do so, it must be said to be incapable of turning the sight inward."

The fifth assumption as made by Ânanda is that the soul is the essence of understanding or intelligence, which is not within, nor without, nor in the middle, but which comes into actual existence as soon as it confronts the objective world, for it is taught by the Buddha that the world exists on account of the mind and the mind on account of the world.

To this the Buddha replies: "According to your argument, the soul must be said to exist before it comes in contact with the world; otherwise, the contact cannot have any sense. The soul, then, exists as an individual presence, not after nor at the time of a contact with the external world, but assuredly before the contact. Granting this, we come back again to the old difficulties: Does the soul come out of your inside, or does it come in from the outside? In case of the first alternative, the soul must be able to see its own face."

Ânanda interrupts: "Seeing is done by the eyes, and the soul has nothing to do with it."

The Buddha objects: "If so, a dead man has eyes just as perfect as a living man.[1] He must be able

[1] Cf the following which is extracted from the *Questions of King Milinda* (Sacred Books of the East, vol. XXXV,

to see things, but if he sees at all, he cannot be dead. Well, if your intelligent soul has a concrete existence, should it be thought simple or compound? Should it be thought of as filling the body or being present only in a particular spot? If it is a simple unit, when one of your limbs is touched, all the four will at once be conscious of the touch, which really means no touch. If the soul is a compound body, how can it distinguish itself from another soul? If it is filling the body all over, there will be no localisation of sensation, as must be the case according to the first supposition of a simple soul-unit. Finally, if it occupies only a particular part of the body, you may experience certain feelings on that spot only, and all the other parts will remain perfectly anesthetic. All these hypotheses are against the actual facts of our experience and cannot be logically maintained."

For the sixth time, Ânanda ventures to untie the Gordian knot of the soul-problem. "As the soul cannot be located neither within nor without, it must be somewhere in the middle." But the Buddha again refutes this, saying: "This 'middle' is extremely indefinite. Should it be located as a point in space or somewhere on the body? If it is on the surface of the body,

133): "If there be a soul [distinct from the body] which does all this, then if the door of the eye were thrown down [if the eye were plucked out] could it stretch out its head, as it were, through the larger aperture and [with greater range] see forms much more clearly than before? Could one hear sounds better if the ears were cut off, or taste better if the tongue were pulled out, or feel touch better if the body were destroyed?"

it is not the middle; if it is in the body, it is then within. If it is said to occupy a point in space, how should that point be indicated? Without an indication, a point is no point; and if an indication is needed, it can be fixed anywhere arbitrarily, and then there will be no end of confusion."

Ânanda interposes and says that he does not mean this kind of "middle." The eye and the color conditioning each other, there comes to exist visual perception. The eye has the faculty to discriminate, and the color-world has no sensibility; but the perception takes place in their "middle," that is, in their interaction; and then it is said that there exists a soul.

Says the Buddha: "If the soul, as you say, exists in the relation between the sense-organs (*indṛya*) and their respective sense-objects (*viṣaya*), should we consider the soul as uniting and partaking the natures of these two incongruous things, viṣaya and indṛya? If the soul partakes something of each, it has no characteristics of its own. If it unites the two natures, the distinction between subject and object exists no more. 'In the middle' is an empty word; that is to say, to conceive the soul as the relation between the indṛyas and the viṣayas is to make it an airy nothing."

The seventh and final hypothesis offered by Ânanda is that the soul is the state of non-attachment, and that, therefore, it has no particular locality in which it abides. But this is also mercilessly attacked by the Buddha who declares: "Attachment presupposes the existence of beings to which a mind may be attached.

Now, should we consider these things (*dharmas*) such as the world, space, land, water, birds, beasts, etc. as existing or not existing? If the external world does not exist, we cannot speak about non-attachment, as there is nothing to attach from the first. If the external world really is, how can we manage not to come in contact with it? When we say that things are devoid of all characteristic marks, it amounts to the declaration that they are non-existent. But they are not non-existent, they must have certain characteristics that distinguish themselves. Now, the external world has certainly some marks (*lakṣana*) and it must by all means be considered as existing. There then is no room for your theory of non-attachment."

At this, Ânanda surrenders and the Buddha discloses his theory of Dharmakâya, which we shall expound at some length in the chapter specially devoted to it.

* * *

By way of a summary of the above, let me remark that the Buddhists do not deny the existence of the so-called empirical ego in contradistinction to the noumenal ego, which latter can be considered to correspond to the Buddhist âtman. Vasubandhu in his treatise on the Yogâcâra's idealistic philosophy declares that the existence of âtman and dharma is only hypothetical, provisional, apparent, and not in any sense real and ultimate. To express this in modern terms, the soul and the world, or subject and object, have only relative existence, and no absolute reality can be ascribed to them. Psychologically speaking, every one of us has an ego or soul which means the unity of consciousness; and physically, this world of phenomena is real either as a manifestation of one energy or as a composite of atoms or electrons, as is considered by physicists.

To confine ourselves to the psychological question, what Buddhism most emphatically insists on is the non-existence of a concrete, individual, irreducible soul-substance, whose immortality is so much coveted by most unenlightened people. Individuation is only relative and not absolute. Buddhism knows how far the principle could safely and consistently be carried out, and its followers will not forget where to stop and destroy the wall, almost adamantine to some religionists, of individualism. Absolute individualism, as the Buddhists understand it, incapacitates us to follow the natural flow of sympathy; to bathe in the eternal sunshine of divinity which not only surrounds but penetrates us; to escape the curse of individual immortality which is strangely so much sought after by some people; to trace this mundane life to its fountainhead of which it drinks so freely, yet quite unknowingly; to rise rejuvenated from the consuming fire of Kâla (Chronos). To think that there is a mysterious something behind the empirical ego and that this something comes out triumphantly after the fashion of the immortal phœnix from the funeral pyre of corporeality, is not Buddhistic.

What I would remark here in connection with this

problem of the soul, is its relation to that of Âlaya-vijñâna, of which it is said that the Buddha was very reluctant to talk, on account of its being easily confounded with the notion of the ego. The Âlaya, as was explained, is a sort of universal soul from which our individual empirical souls are considered to have evolved. The Manas which is the first offspring of the Âlaya is endowed with the faculty of discrimination, and from the wrongful use of this faculty there arises in the Manas the conception of the Âlaya as the ego, — the real concrete soul-substratum.

The Âlaya, however, is not a particular phenomenon, for it is a state of Suchness in its evolutionary disposition and has nothing in it yet to suggest its concrete individuality. When the Manas finds out its error and lifts the veil of Ignorance from the body of the Âlaya, it soon becomes convinced of the ultimate nature of the soul, so called. For the soul is not individual, but supra-individual.

Âtman and the "Old Man."

When the Buddhists exclaim: "Put away your egoism, for the ego is an empty notion, a mere word without reality," some of our Christian readers may think that if there is no ego, what will become of our personality or individuality? Though this point will become clearer as we proceed, let us remark here that what Buddhism understands by ego or âtman may be considered to correspond in many respects to the Christian notion of "flesh" or the "old man," which is the source of all our sinful acts. Says Paul: "I am crucified with Christ; nevertheless I live; yet not I, but Christ liveth in me: and the life which I live now in the flesh I live by the faith of the Son of God, who loved me and gave himself for me." (Gal. ii, 20.) When this passage is interpreted by the Buddhists, the "I" that was annihilated through crucifixion, is our false notion of an ego-soul (*âtman*); and the "I" that is living through the grace of God is the Bodhi, a reflex in us of the Dharmakâya.

When Christians put the spirit and the flesh in contrast and advise us to "walk in the spirit" and not to "fulfil the lust of the flesh," it must be said that they understand by the flesh our concrete, material existence whose characteristic is predominantly individual, and by the spirit, that which transcends particularity and egoism; for "love, joy, peace, long-suffering, faith, meekness, temperance," and suchlike virtues are possible only when our egocentric, âtman-made desires are utterly abnegated. Buddhism is more intellectual than Christianity or Judaism and prefers philosophical terms which are better understood than popular language which leads often to confusion. Compared with the Buddhists' conception of âtman, the "flesh" lacks in perspicuity and exactitude, not to speak of its dualistic tendency which is extremely offensive to the Buddhists.

The Vedantic Conception.

Though the doctrine of non-âtman is pre-eminently Buddhistic, other Hindu philosophers did not neglect to acknowledge its importance in our religious life. Having grown in the same soil under similar circumstances, the following passage which is taken from the *Yogavâsistha* (which is supposed to be a Vedantic work, Upaçama P., ch. LII, 31, 44) sounds almost like Buddhistic:

"I am absolute, I am the light of intelligence, I am free from the defilement of egoism. O thou that art unreal! I am not bound by thee, the seed of egoism." [1]

The author then argues: Where shall we consider the ego-soul, so called, to be residing in this body of flesh and bones? and what does it look like? We move our limbs, but the movement is due to the vital airs (*vâta*). We think, but consciousness is a manifestation of the great mind (*mahâcitta*). We cease to exist, but extinction belongs to the body (*kâya*). Now, take apart what we imagine to constitute our personal existence. The flesh is one thing, the blood is another, and so on with mentation (*bodha*) and vitality (*spanda*). The ear hears, the tongue tastes, the eye sees, the mind

[1] Nirvikalpo 'smi ciddipo nirahankaravasanaḥ
Tvaya ahankarabijena na saṁbaddho 'smi asanmaya (31)

thinks, but what and where is that which we call "ego"?

Then comes the conclusion: "In reality, there is no such thing as the ego-soul, nor is there any mine and thine, nor imagination. All this is nothing but the manifestation of the universal soul which is the light of pure intelligence." [1]

Nâgârjuna on the Soul.

In conclusion, let me quote some passage bearing on the subject from Nâgârjuna's *Discourse on the Middle Path* (chapter 9): [2] "Some say that there are seeing, hearing, feeling, etc., because there is something which exists even prior to those [manifestations]. For how could seeing, etc. come from that which does not exist? Therefore, it must be admitted that that being [i. e. soul] existed prior to those [manifestations].

"But [this hypothesis of the prior (*pûrva*) or independent existence of the soul is wrong, because] how could that being be known if it existed prior to seeing, feeling, etc.? If that being could exist without seeing, etc., the latter too could surely exist without that being. But how could a thing which could not be known by any sign exist before it is known? How could *this* exist without *that*, and how could

[1] Yathâ bhûtatayâ na ahammano na tvam na vâsanâ
Atmâ çuddhacidabhasaḥ kevalo yam vijṛbhate. (44)

[2] The following is a somewhat free translation of the original Chinese of Kumârajîva, which pretty closely agrees with the Sanskrit text published by the Buddhist Text Society of India.

that exist without *this?* [Are not all things relative and conditioning one another?]

"If that being called soul could not exist prior to all manifestations such as seeing, etc., how could it exist prior to each of them taken individually?

"If it is the same soul that sees, hears, feels, etc., it must be assumed that the soul exists prior to each of these manifestations. This, however, is not warranted by facts. [Because in that case one must be able to hear with the eyes, see with the ears, as one soul is considered to direct all these diverse faculties at its will.]

"If, on the other hand, the hearer is one, and the seer is another, the feeler must be still another. Then, there will be hearing, seeing, etc. simultaneously,— which leads to the assumption of a plurality of souls.[1] [This too is against experience.]

"Further, the soul does not exist in the element (*bhûta*) on which seeing, hearing, feeling, etc. depend. [To use modern expression, the soul does not exist in the nerves which respond to the external stimuli.]

"If seeing, hearing, feeling, etc. have no soul that exists prior to them, they too have no existence as such. For how could *that* exist without *this*, and *this* without *that?* Subject and object are mutually conditioned. The soul as it is has no independent, individual reality whatever. Therefore, the hypothesis that contends for the existence of an ego-soul prior

[1] The Sanskrit text does not give this passage.

to simultaneous with, or posterior to, seeing, etc., is to be abandoned as fruitless, for the ego-soul existeth not."

Non-âtman-ness of Things.

The word "âtman" is used by the Buddhists not only psychologically in the sense of soul, self, or ego, but also ontologically in the sense of substance or thing-in-itself or thinginess; and its existence in this capacity is also strongly denied by them. For the same reason that the existence of an individual ego-soul is untenable, they reject the hypothesis of the permament existence of an individual object as such. As there is no transcendent agent in our soul-life, so there is no real, eternal existence of individuals as individuals, but a system of different attributes, which, when the force of karma is exhausted, ceases to subsist. Individual existences cannot be real by their inherent nature, but they are illusory, and will never remain permanent as such; for they are constantly becoming, and have no selfhood though they may so appear to our particularising senses on account of our subjective ignorance. They are in reality çûnya and anâtman, they are empty and void of âtman.

Svabhâva.

The term "sabhâva" (self-essence or noumenon) is sometimes used by the Mahâyânists in place of âtman, and they would say that all dharmas have no self-essence, *sarvam dharmam niḥsvabhâvam*, which is to say, that all things in their phenomenal aspect are devoid of individual selves, that it is only due to our ignorance that we believe in the thinginess of things, whereas there is no such thing as svabhâva or âtman or noumenon which resides in them. Svabhâva and âtman are thus habitually used by Buddhists as quite synonymous.

What do they exactly understand by "svabhâva" whose existence is denied in a particular object as perceived by our senses? This has never been explicitly defined by the Mahâyânists, but they seem to understand by svabhâva something concrete, individual, yet independent, unconditional, and not subject to the law of causation (*pratyayasamutpâda*). It, therefore, stands in opposition to çûnyatâ, emptiness, as well as to conditionality. Inasmuch as all beings are transient and empty in their inherent being, they cannot logically be said to be in possession of self-essence which defies the law of causation. All things are mutually conditioning and limiting, and apart from their relativity they are non-existent and cannot be known by us. Therefore, says Nâgârjuna, "If substance be different from attribute, it is then beyond comprehension." [1] For "a jag is not to be known independent of matter et cetera, and matter in turn is not to be known independent of ether et cetera." [2]

[1] Lakṣyâl lakṣaṇam anyac cet syât tal lakṣyam alakṣanam.

[2] Rûpâdi vyatirekena yathâ kumbho na vidyate,
Vâhyâdi vyatireṇa tathâ rûpam na vidyate.

As there is no subject without object, so there is no substance without attribute; for one is the condition for the other. Does self-essence then exist in causation? No, " whatever is subject to conditionality, is by its very nature tranquil and empty." (*Pratîtya yad yad bhavati, tat tac çântam svabhâvataḥ.*) Whatever owes its existence to a combination of causes and conditions is without self-essence, and therefore it is tranquil (*çânta*), it is empty, it is unreal (*asat*), and the ultimate nature of this universal emptiness is not within the sphere of intellectual demonstrability, for the human understanding is not capable of transcending its inherent limitations.

Says Pingalaka, a commentator of Nâgârjuna: "The cloth exists on account of the thread; the matting is possible on account of the rattan. If the thread had its own fixed, unchangeable self-essence, it could not be made out of the flax. If the cloth had its own fixed, unchangeable self-essence, it could not be made from the thread. But as in point of fact the cloth comes from the thread and the thread from the flax, it must be said that the thread as well as the cloth had no fixed, unchangeable self-essence. It is just like the relation that obtains between the burning and the burned. They are brought together under certain conditions, and thus there takes place a phenomenon called burning. The burning and the burned, each has no reality of its own. For when one is absent the other is put out of existence. It is so with all things in this world, they are all empty, without self, without absolute existence, they are like the will-'o-the-wisp."[1]

The Real Significance of Emptiness.

From these statements it will be apparent that the emptiness of things (*çûnyatâ*) does not mean nothingness, as is sometimes interpreted by some critics, but it simply means conditionality or transitoriness of all phenomenal existences, it is a synonym for aniyata or pratîtya. Therefore, emptiness, according to the Buddhists, signifies, negatively, the absence of particularity, the non-existence of individuals as such, and positively, the ever-changing state of the phenomenal world, a constant flux of becoming, an eternal series of causes and effects. It must never be understood in the sense of annihilation or absolute nothingness, for nihilism is as much condemned by Buddhism as naïve realism. "The Buddha proclaimed emptiness as a remedy for all doctrinal controversies, but those who in turn cling to emptiness are beyond treatment." A medicine is indispensable as long as there is a disease to heal, but it turns poisonous when applied after the restoration of perfect health. To make this point completely clear, let me quote the following from Nâgârjuna's *Mâdhyamika Çâstra* (Chap. XXIV). "[Some one may object to the Buddhist doctrine of emptiness, declaring:] If all is void (*çûnya*) and

[1] Abstracted from Pingalaka's *Commentary on the Mâdhyamika Çâstra*, Chapter VII. The Chinese translation is by Kumârajîva.

there is neither creation nor destruction, then it must be concluded that even the Fourfold Noble Truth does not exist. If the Fourfold Noble Truth dœs not exist, the recognition of Suffering, the stoppage of Accumulation, the attainment of Cessation, and the advancement of Discipline, — all must be said to be unrealisable. If they are altogether unrealisable, there cannot be any of the four states of saintliness; and without these states there cannot be anybody who will aspire for them. If there are no wise men, the Sangha is then impossible. Further, as there is no Fourfold Noble Truth, there is no Good Law (*saddharma*); and as there is neither Good Law nor Sangha, the existence of Buddha himself must be an impossibility. Those who talk of emptiness, therefore, must be said to negate the Triple Treasure (*triratna*) altogether. Emptiness not only destroys the law of causation and the general principle of retribution (*phalasadbhâvam*), but utterly annihilates the possibility of a phenomenal world."

"[To this it is to be remarked that]

" Only he is annoyed over such scepticism who understands not the true significance and interpretation of emptiness (*çûnyatâ*).

"The Buddha 's teaching rests on the discrimination of two kinds of truth (*satya*): absolute and relative. Those who do not have any adequate knowledge of them are unable to grasp the deep and subtle meaning of Buddhism. [The essence of being, dharmata, is beyond verbal definition or intellectual comprehension, for there is neither birth nor death in it, and it is even like unto Nirvâna. The nature of Suchness, tattva, is fundamentally free from conditionality, it is tranquil, it distances all phenomenal frivolities, it discriminates not, nor is it particularised].[1]

"But if not for relative truth, absolute truth is unattainable, and when absolute truth is not attained, Nirvâna is not to be gained.

"The dull-headed who do not perceive the truth rightfully go to self-destruction, for they are like an awkward magician whose trick entangles himself, or like an unskilled snake-catcher who gets himself hurt. The World-honored One knew well the abstruseness of the Doctrine which is beyond the mental capacity of the multitudes and was inclined not to disclose it before them.

"The objection that Buddhism onesidedly adheres to emptiness and thereby exposes itself to grave errors, entirely misses the mark; for there are no errors in emptiness. Why? Because it is on account of emptiness that all things are at all possible, and without emptiness all things will come to naught. Those who deny emptiness and find fault with it, are like a horseman who forgets that he is on horseback.

"If they think that things exist because of their self-essence (*svabhâva*), [and not because of their emptiness,] they thereby make things come out of causelessness (*ahetupratyaya*), they destroy those

[1] The passage in parentheses is taken from Chandrakîrti's *Commentary on Nâgârjuna*, pp. 180—181.

relations that exist between the acting and the act and the acted; and they also destroy the conditions that make up the law of birth and death.

"All is declared empty because there is nothing that is not a product of universal causation (*pratyaya-samutpâda*). This law of causation, however, is merely provisional, though herein lies the middle path.

"As thus there is not an object (*dharma*) which is not conditioned (*pratîtya*), so there is nothing that is not empty.

"If all is not empty, then there is no death nor birth, and withal disappears the Fourfold Noble Truth.

"How could there be Suffering, if not for the law of causation? Impermanence is suffering. But with self-essence there will be no impermanence. [So long as impermanence is the condition of life, self-essence which is a causeless existence, is out of question.] Suppose Suffering is self-existent, then it could not come from Accumulation, which in turn becomes impossible when emptiness is not admitted. Again, when Suffering is self-existent, then there could be no Cessation, for with the hypothesis of self-essence Cessation becomes a meaningless term. Again, when Suffering is self-existent, then there will be no Path. But as we can actually walk on the Path, the hypothesis of self-essence is to be abandoned.

"If there is neither Suffering nor Cessation, it must be said that the Path leading to the Cessation of Suffering is also non-existent.

"If there is really self-essence, Suffering could not

be recognised now, as it had not been recognised, for self-essence as such must remain forever the same. [That is to say, enlightened minds, through the teaching of Buddha, now recognise the existence of Suffering, though they did not recognise it when they were still uninitiated. If things were all in a fixed, self-determining state on account of their self-essence, it would be impossible for those enlightened men to discover what they had never observed before. The recognition of the Fourfold Noble Truth is only possible when this phenomenal world is in a state of constant becoming, that is, when it is empty as it really is.]

"As it is with the recognition of Suffering, so it is with the stoppage of Accumulation, the attainment of Cessation, the realisation of Path as well as with the four states of saintliness.

"If, on account of self-essence, the four states of saintliness were unattainable before, how could they be realised now, still upholding the hypothesis of self-essence? [But we can attain to saintliness as a matter of fact, for there are many holy men who through their spiritual discipline have emerged from their former life of ignorance and darkness. If everything had its own self-essence which makes it impossible to transform from one state to another, how could a person desire to ascend, if he ever so desire, higher and higher on the scale of existence?]

"If there were no four states of saintliness (*catvâri phalâni*), then there would be no aspirants for it.

And if there were no eight wise men (*puruṣapuñgala*), there could exist no Sangha.

"Again, when there could not be the Fourfold Noble Truth, the Law would be impossible, and without the Sangha and the Law how could the Buddha exist? You might say: 'A Buddha does not exist on account of wisdom (*Bodhi*), nor does wisdom exist on account of the Buddha.' But if a man did not have Buddha-essence [that is, Bodhi] he could not hope to attain to Buddhahood, however strenuously he might exert himself in the ways of Bodhisattva.

"Further, if all is not empty but has self-essence, [i. e. if all is in a fixed, unchangeable state of sameness], how could there be any doing? How could there be good and evil? If you maintain that there is an effect (*phala*) which does not come from a cause good or evil, [which is the practical conclusion of the hypothesis of self-essence], then it means that retribution is independent of our deed, good or evil. [But is this justified by our experience?]

"If it must then be admitted that our deed good or evil becomes the cause of retribution, retribution must be said to come from our deed, good or evil; then how could we say there is no emptiness?

"When you negate the doctrine of emptiness, the law of universal causation, you negate the possibility of this phenomenal world. When the doctrine of emptiness is negated, there remains nothing that ought to be done; and a thing is called done which is not yet accomplished; and he is said to be a doer who has not done anything whatever. If there were such a thing as self-essence, the multitudinousness of things must be regarded as uncreated and imperishable and eternally existing which is tantamount to eternal nothingness.

"If there were no emptiness there would be no attainment of what has not yet been attained, nor would there be the annihilation of pain, nor the extinction of all the passions (*sarvakleça*).

"Therefore, it is taught by the Buddha that those who recognise the law of universal causation, recognise the Buddha as well as Suffering, Accumulation, Cessation, and the Path."

* * *

The Mahâyânistic doctrines thus formulated and transmitted down to the present days are: There is no such thing as the ego; mentation is produced by the co-ordination of various vijñânas or senses.

Individual existences have no selfhood or self-essence or reality, for they are but an aggregate of certain qualities sustained by efficient karma. The world of particulars is the work of Ignorance as declared by Buddha in his Formula of Dependence (Twelve Nidânas). When this veil of Mâya is uplifted, the universal light of Dharmakâya shines in all its magnificence. Individual existences then as such lose their significance and become sublimated and ennobled in the oneness of Dharmakâya. Egoistic prejudices are forever vanquished, and the aim of our lives is no more the gratification of selfish cravings, but the glorification of Dharma as it works its own way through the multitudinousness of things. The self does not stand any more in a state of isolation (which is an illusion), it is absorbed in the universal body of Dharma, it recognises itself in other selves animate as well as inanimate, and all things are in Nirvâna. When we reach this state of ideal enlightenment, we are said to have realised the Buddhist life.

CHAPTER VIII.

KARMA.

Definition.

KARMA, or Sanskâra which is sometimes used as its synonym,—though the latter gives a slightly different shade of meaning,—comes from the Sanskrit root *kṛ*, "to do," "to make," "to perform," "to effect," "to produce," etc. Both terms mean activity in its concrete as well as in its abstract sense, and form an antithesis to intelligence, contemplation, or ideation in general. When karma is used in its most abstract sense, it becomes an equivalent to "beginningless ignorance," which is universally inherent in nature, and corresponds to the Will or blind activity of Schopenhauer; for ignorance as we have seen above is a negative manifestation of Suchness (*Bhûta-tathâtâ*) and marks the beginning or unfolding of a phenomenal world, whose existence is characterised by incessant activities actuated by the principle of karma. When Goethe says in Faust, "In Anfang war die That," he uses the term "That" in the sense of karma as it is here understood.

When karma is used in its concrete sense, it is the

principle of activity in the world of particulars or nâmarûpas: it becomes in the physical world the principle of conservation of energy, in the biological realm that of evolution and heredity etc., and in the moral world that of immortality of deeds. Sanskara, when used as an equivalent of karma, corresponds to this concrete signification of it, as it is the case in the Twelve Chains of Dependence (*Nidânas*, or *Pratyâyasamutpâda*).[1] Here it follows ignorance (*avidyâ*) and precedes consciousness (*vijñâna*). Ignorance in this case means simply privation of enlightenment, and does not imply any sense of activity which is expressed in Sanskâra. It is only when it is coupled with the latter that it becomes the principle of activity, and creates as its first offspring consciousness or mentality. In fact, ignorance and blind activity are one, their logical difference being this: the former emphasises the epistemological phase and the latter the ethical; or, we might say, one is statical and the other dynamical. If we are to draw a comparison between the first four of the Twelve Nidânas and the several processes of evolution that takes place in the Tathâgata-garbha as described above, we can take Ignorance and the principle of blind activity, san-

[1] The Twelve Nidânas are: (1) Ignorance (*avidyâ*), (2) action (*sanskâra*), (3) Consciousness (*vijñâna*), (4) Name-and-form (*nâmarûpa*), (5) Six Sense-organs (*âyatana*), (6) Contact (*sparça*), (7) Sensation (*vedanâ*), (8) Desire (*trṣnâ*), (9) Attachment (*upâdâna*), (10) Procreation (*bhâva*), (11) birth (*jati*), (12) Old Age, Death, etc. (*jarâ*, *marana*, *çoka*, etc.)

skâra, in the Twelve Chains as corresponding to the All-conserving Soul (*âlayavijñâna*), and the Vijñâna, consciousness of the Twelve Chains, to the Manovijñâna, and the Nâmârûpa to this visible world, ***viṣaya***, in which the principle of karma works in its concrete form.

As we have a special chapter devoted to "Ignorance" as an equivalent of karma in its abstract sense, let us here treat of the Buddhist conception of karma in the realm of names and forms, i. e. of karma in its concrete sense. But we shall restrict ourselves to the activity of karmaic causation in the moral world, as we are not concerned with physics or biology.

The Working of Karma.

The Buddhist conception of karma briefly stated is this: Any act, good or evil, once committed and conceived, never vanishes like a bubble in water, but lives, potentially or actively as the case may be, in the world of minds and deeds. This mysterious moral energy, so to speak, is embodied in and emanates from every act and thought, for it does not matter whether it is actually performed, or merely conceived in the mind. When the time comes, it is sure to germinate and grow with all its vitality. Says Buddha:

> "Karma even after the lapse of a hundred kalpas,
> Will not be lost nor destroyed;
> As soon as all the necessary conditions are ready,
> Its fruit is sure to ripe." [1]

[1] From a Chinese Mahâyâna sutra.

Again,

> "Whatever a man does, the same he in himself will find,
> The good man, good: and evil he that evil has designed;
> And so our deeds are all like seeds, and bring forth fruit
> in kind." [1]

A grain of wheat, it is said, which was accidentally preserved in good condition in a tomb more than a thousand years old, did not lose its germinating energy, and, when planted with proper care, it actually started to sprout. So with karma, it is endowed with an enormous vitality, nay, it is even immortal. However remote the time of their commission might have been, the karma of our deeds never dies; it must work out its own destiny at whatever cost, if not overcome by some counteracting force. The law of karma is irrefragable.

The irrefragability of karma means that the law of causation is supreme in our moral sphere just as much as in the physical, that life consists in a concatenation of causes and effects regulated by the principle of karma, that nothing in the life of an individual or a nation or a race happens without due cause and sufficient reason, that is, without previous karma. The Buddhists, therefore, do not believe in any special act of grace or revelation in our religious realm and moral life. The idea of deus ex machina is banned in Buddhism. Whatever is suffered or enjoyed morally in our present life is due to the karma, accumulated

[1] The Pâli Jâtaka, no. 222. Translation by W. H. Rouse.

since the beginning of life on earth. Nothing sown nothing reaped.

Whatever has been done leaves an ineffable mark in the individual's life and even in that of the universe; and this mark will never be erased save by sheer exhaustion of the karma or by the interruption of an overwhelming counter-karma. In case the karma of an act is not actualised during one's own life-time, it will in that of one's successors, who may be physical or spiritual. Not only "the evil that men do lives after them," but also the good, for it will not be "interred with their bones," as vulgar minds imagine. We read in the *Samyukta Nikâya*, III, 1 — 4:

"Assailed by death, in life's last throes,
At quitting of this human state,
What is it one can call his own?
What with him take as he goes hence?
What is it follows after him,
And like a shadow ne'er departs?

"His good deeds and his wickedness,
Whate'er a mortal does while here;
'Tis this that he can call his own,
This with him take as he goes hence.
This is what follows after him,
And like a shadow ne'er departs.

"Let all, then, noble deeds perform,
A treasure-store for future weal;
For merit gained this life within,
Will yield a blessing in the next." [1]

[1] Warren's *Buddhism in Translations*, p. 214.

In accordance with this karmaic preservation, Buddhists do not expect to have their sins expatiated by other innocent people so long as their own hearts remain unsoftened as ever. But when the all-embracing love of Buddhas for all sentient beings kindles even the smallest spark of repentance and enlightenment in the heart of a sinner, and when this ever-vacillating light grows to its full magnitude under propitious conditions, the sinner gets fully awakened from the evil karma of eons, and enters, free from all curses, into the eternity of Nirvâna.

Karma and Social Injustice.

The doctrine of karma is very frequently utilised by some Buddhists to explain a state of things which must be considered cases of social injustice.

There are some people who are born rich and noble and destined to enjoy all forms of earthly happiness and all the advantages of social life, though they have done nothing that justifies them in luxuriating in such a fashion any more than their poor neighbors. These people, however, are declared by some pseudo-Buddhists to be merely harvesting the crops of good karma they had prepared in their former lives. On the other hand, the poor, needy, and low that are struggling to eke out a mere existence in spite of their moral rectitude and honest industry, are considered to be suffering the evil karma which had been accumulated during their previous lives. The law of moral retribution is never suspended, as they reason, on account of the changes which may take place in a mortal being. An act, good or evil, once performed, will not be lost in the eternal succession and interaction of incidents, but will certainly find the sufferer of its due consequence, and it does not matter whether the actor has gone through the vicissitudes of birth and death. For the Buddhist conception of individual identity is not that of personal continuity, but of karmaic conservation. Whatever deeds we may commit, they invariably bear their legitimate fruit and follow us even after death. Therefore, if the rich and noble neglect to do their duties or abandon themselves to the enjoyment of sensual pleasures, then they are sure in their future births, if not in their present life, to gather the crops they have thus unwittingly prepared for themselves. The poor, however hard their lot in this life, can claim their rightful rewards, if they do not get despaired of their present sufferings and give themselves up to temptations, but dutifully continue to do things good and meritorious. Because as their present fate is the result of their former deeds, so will be their future fortune the fruit of their present deeds.

This view as held by some pseudo-Buddhists gives us a wrong impression about the practical working of the principle of karma in this world of nâmarûpas, for it tries to explain by karmaic theory the phenomena which lie outside of the sphere of its applicability. As I understand, what the theory of karma proposes to explain is not cases of social injustice and economic inequality, but facts of moral causation.

The overbearing attitude of the rich and the noble, the unnecessary sufferings of the poor, the over-production of criminals, and suchlike social phenomena arise from the imperfection of our present social organisation, which is based upon the doctrine of absolute private ownership. People are allowed to amass wealth unlimitedly for their own use and to bequeath it to the successors who do not deserve it in any way. And they do not pay regard to the injuries this system may incur upon the general welfare of the community to which they belong, and upon other members individually. The rich might have slaughtered economically and consequently politically and morally millions of their brethren before they could reach places of social eminence they now occupy and enjoy to its full extent. They might have sacrificed hundreds of thousands of victims on the altar of Mammon in order to carry out their vast scheme of self-aggrandisement. And, what is worse, the wealth thus accumulated by an individual is allowed by the law to be handed down to his descendants, who are in a sense the parasitic members of the community. They are privileged to live upon the sweat and blood of others, who know not where to lay their heads, and who are daily succumbing to the heavy burden, not of their free choice, but forced upon them by society.

Let us here closely see into the facts. There is one portion of society that does almost nothing toward the promotion of the general welfare, and there is another portion that, besides carrying the burden not of its own, is heroically struggling for bare existence. These sad phenomena which, owing to the imperfection of social organisation, we daily witness about us,—should we attribute them to diversity of individual karma and make individuals responsible for what is really due to the faulty organisation of the community to which they belong? No, the doctrine of karma certainly must not be understood to explain the cause of our social and economical imperfection.

The region where the law of karma is made to work supreme is our moral world, and cannot be made to extend also over our economic field. Poverty is not necessarily the consequence of evil deeds, nor is plenitude that of good acts. Whether a person is affluent or needy is mostly determined by the principle of economy as far as our present social system is concerned. Morality and economy are two different realms of human activity. Honesty and moral rectitude do not necessarily guarantee well-being. Dishonesty and the violation of the moral law, on the contrary, are very frequently utilised as handmaids of material prosperity. Do we not thus see many good, conscientious people around us who are wretchedly poverty-stricken? Shall we take them as suffering the curse of evil karma in their previous lives, when we can understand the fact perfectly well as a case of social injustice? It is not necessary by any means, nay, it is even productive of evil, to establish a relation between the two things that in the nature of their being have no causal dependence. Karma ought not to be made accountable for economic inequality.

A virtuous man is contented with his cleanliness of conscience and purity of heart. Obscure as is his present social position, and miserable as are his present pecuniary conditions, he has no mind to look backward and find the cause of his social insignificance there, nor is he anxious about his future earthly fortune which might be awaiting him when his karmaic energy appears in a new garment. His heart is altogether free from such vanities and anxieties. He is sufficent unto himself as he is here and now. And, as to his altruistic aspect of his moral deeds, he is well conscious that their karma would spiritually benefit everybody that gets inspired by it, and also that it would largely contribute to the realisation of goodness on this earth. Why, then, must we contrive such a poor theory of karma as is maintained by some, in order that they might give him a spiritual solace for his material misfortune?

Vulgar people are too eager to see everything and every act they perform working for the accumulation of earthly wealth and the promotion of material welfare. They would want to turn even moral deeds which have no relation to the economic condition of life into the opportunities to attain things mundane They would desire to have the law of karmaic causation applied to a realm, where prevails an entirely different set of laws. In point of fact, what proceeds from meritorious deeds is spiritual bliss only, — contentment, tranquillity of mind, meekness of heart, and immovability of faith, — all the heavenly treasures which could not be corrupted by moth or rust. And what more can the karma of good deeds bring to us? And what more would a man of pious heart desire to gain from his being good? "Take no thought for your life, what ye shall eat, or what ye shall drink, nor yet for your body, what ye shall put on. Is not the life more than meat and the body more than raiment?" Let us then do away with the worldly interpretation of karma, which is so contrary to the spirit of Buddhism.

As long as we live under the present state of things, it is impossible to escape the curse of social injustice and economic inequality. Some people must be born rich and noble and enjoying a superabundance of material wealth, while others must be groaning under the unbearable burden imposed upon them by cruel society. Unless we make a radical change in our present social organisation, we cannot expect every one of us to enjoy equal opportunity and fair chance. Unless we have a certain form of socialism installed which is liberal and rational and systematic, there must be some who are economically more favored than others. But this state of affairs is a phenomenon of worldly institution and is doomed to die away sooner or later. The law of karma, on the contrary, is an eternal ordinance of the will of the Dharmakâya as manifested in this world of particulars. We must not confuse a transient accident of human society with an absolute decree issued from the world-authority.

An Individualistic View of Karma.

There is another popular misconception concerning the doctrine of karma, which seriously mars the true interpretation of Buddhism. I mean by this an individualistic view of the doctrine. This view asserts that deeds, good or evil, committed by a person determine only his own fate, no other's being affected thereby in any possible way, and that the reason why we should refrain from doing wrong is: for we, and not others, have to suffer its evil consequences. This conception of karma which I call individualistic, presupposes the absolute reality of an individual soul and its continuance as such in a new corporeal existence which is made possible by its previous karma. Because an individual soul is here understood as an independent unit, which stands in no relation to others, and which therefore neither does influence nor is influenced by them in any wise. All that is done by oneself is suffered by oneself only and no other people have anything to do with it, nor do they suffer a whit thereby.

Buddhism, however, does not advocate this individualistic interpretation of karmaic law, for it is not in accord with the theory of non-âtman, nor with that of Dharmakâya.

According to the orthodox theory, karma simply means the conservation or immortality of the inner force of deeds regardless of their author's physical identity. Deeds once committed, good or evil, leave permanent effects on the general system of sentient beings, of which the actor is merely a component part; and it is not the actor himself only, but everybody constituting a grand psychic community called "Dharmadhâtu" (spiritual universe), that suffers or enjoys the outcome of a moral deed.

Because the universe is not a theatre for one particular soul only; on the contrary, it belongs to all sentient beings, each forming a psychic unit; and these units are so intimately knitted together in blood and soul that the effects of even apparently trifling deeds committed by an individual are felt by others just as much and just as surely as the doer himself. Throw an insignificant piece of stone into a vast expanse of water, and it will certainly create an almost endless series of ripples, however imperceptible, that never stop till they reach the furthest shore. The tremulation thus caused is felt by the sinking stone as much as the water disturbed. The universe that may seem to crude observers merely as a system of crass physical forces is in reality a great spiritual community, and every one of sentient beings forms its component part. This most complicated, most subtle, most sensitive, and best organised mass of spiritual atoms transmits its current of moral electricity from one particle to another with utmost rapidity and surety. Because this community is at bottom an expression of one Dharmakâya. However diversified and dissimilar it may appear in its material individual aspect, it is after all no more than an evolution of one pervading essence, in which the multitudinousness of things finds its unity and identity. Therefore, it is for the interests of the community at large, and not for their own welfare only, that sincere Buddhists refrain from transgressing moral laws and are encouraged to promote goodness. Those whose spiritual insight thus penetrates deep into the inner unity and interaction of all human souls are called Bodhisattvas.

It is with this spirit, let me repeat, that pious Buddhists do not wish to keep for themselves any merits created by their acts of love and benevolence, but wish to turn them over (*parivarta*) to the deliverance of all sentient creatures from the darkness of ignorance. The most typical way of concluding any religious treatise by Buddhists, therefore, runs generally in the following manner:

"The deep significance of the three karmas as taught by Buddha,
I have thus completed elucidating in accord with the Dharma and logic:
By dint of this merit I pray to deliver all sentient beings
And to make them soon attain to perfect enlightenment."[1]

Or,

"All the merits arising from this my exposition
May abide and be universally distributed among all beings;
And may they ascend in the scale of existence and increase in bliss and wisdom,

[1] *On the Completion of Karma*, by Vasubandhu. Nanjo, No. 1222.

And soon attain to an enlightenment supreme, perfect, great, and far-reaching." [1]

The reason why a moral deed performed by one person would contribute to the attainment by others of supreme enlightenment, is that souls which are ordinarily supposed to be individual and independent of others are not so in fact, but are very closely intermingled with one another, so that a stir produced in one is sooner or later transmitted to another influencing it rightfully or wrongfully. The karmaic effect of my own deed determines not only my own future, but to a not little extent that of others; hence those invocations just quoted by pious Buddhists who desire to dedicate all the merits they can attain to the general welfare of the masses.

The ever-increasing tendency of humanity to widen and facilitate communication in every possible way is a phenomenon illustrative of the intrinsic oneness of human souls. Isolation kills, for it is another name for death. Every soul that lives and grows desires to embrace others, to be in communion with them; to be supplemented by them, and to expand infinitely so that all individual souls are brought together and united in the one soul. Under this condition only a man's karma is enabled to influence other people, and his merits can be utilised for the promotion of general enlightenment

[1] *The Distinguishing of the Mean*, by Vasubandhu. Nanjo, 1248.

Karma and Determinism.

If the irrefragability of karma means the predetermination of our moral life, some would reason, the doctrine is fatalism pure and simple. It is quite true that our present life is the result of the karma accumulated in our previous existences, and that as long as the karma preserves its vitality there is no chance whatever to escape its consequences, good or evil. It is also true that as the meanest sparrow shall not fall on the ground without the knowledge of God, and as the very hairs of our heads are all numbered by him, so even a single blade of grass does not quiver before the evening breeze without the force of karma. It is also true that if our intellect were not near-sighted as it is, we could reduce a possible complexity of the conditions under which our life exists into its simplest terms, and thus predict with mathematical precision the course of a life through which it is destined to pass. If we could record all our previous karma from time immemorial and all its consequences both on ourselves and on those who come in contact with us, there would be no difficulty in determining our future life with utmost certainty. The human intellect, however, as it happens, is incapable of undertaking a work of such an enormous magnitude, we cannot perceive the full significance of determinism; but, from the divine point of view, determinism seems to be perfectly justified, for there cannot be any short-sightedness on the part of a world-soul as to the destiny of the universe, which is nothing but its own expression. It is only from the human point of view that we feel uncertain about our final disposition and endeavor to explain existence now from a mechanical, now from a teleological standpoint, and yet, strange enough, at the bottom of our soul we feel that there is something mysterious here which makes us cry, either in despair or in trustful resignation, "Let thy will be done." While this very confidence in "thy will" proves that we have in our inmost consciousness and outside the pale of intellectual analysis a belief in the supreme order, which is absolutely preordained and which at least is not controllable by our finite, limited, fragmentary mind, yet the doctrine of karma must not be understood in the strictest sense of fatalism.

As far as a general theory of determinism is concerned, Buddhism has no objection to it. Grant that there is a law of causation, that every deed, actualised or thought of, leaves something behind, and that this something becomes a determining factor for our future life; then how could we escape the conclusion that "each of us is inevitable" as Whitman sings? Religious confidence in a divine will that is supposed to give us always the best of things, is in fact no more than a determinism. But if, in applying the doctrine to our practical life, we forget to endeavor to unfold all the possibilities that might lie in us, but could be awakened only after strenuous efforts, there will be no moral characters, no personal responsibility, no noble aspirations; the mind will be nothing but a reflex nervous system and life a sheer machinery.

In fact karma is not a machine which is not incapable of regeneration and self-multiplication. Karma is a wonderful organic power; it grows, it expands, and even gives birth to a new karma. It is like unto a grain of mustard, the least of all seeds, but, being full of vitality, it grows as soon as it comes in contact with the nourishing soil and becometh a tree so that the birds of the air come and lodge in the branches thereof. Its mystery is like that of sympathetic waves that pass through all the hearts which feel the great deeds of a hero or listen to the story of a self-sacrificing mother. Karma, good or evil, is contagious and sympathetic in its work. Even a most insignificant act of goodness reaps an unexpectedly rich crop. Even to the vilest rogue comes a chance for repentance by dint of a single good karma ever effected in his life, which has extended through many a kalpa. And the most wonderful thing in our spiritual world is that the karma thus bringing repentance and Nirvâna to the heart of the meanest awakens and rekindles a similar karma potentially slumbering in other hearts and leads them to the final abode of enlightenment.

Inasmuch as we confine ourselves to general, superficial view of the theory of karma, it leads to a form of determinism, but in our practical life which is a product of extremely complicated factors, the doctrine of karma allows in us all kinds of possibilities and all chances of development. We thus escape the mechanical conception of life, we are saved from the despair of predetermination, though this is true to a great extent;

and we are assured of the actualisation of hopes, however remote it may be. Though the curse of evil karma may sometimes hang upon us very heavily, there is no reason to bury our aspirations altogether in the grave; on the contrary, let us bear it bravely and perform all the acts of goodness to destroy the last remnant of evil and to mature the stock of good karma.

The Maturing of Good Stock (kuçalamûla) and the Accumulation of merits (puṇyaskandha).

One of the most significant facts, which we cannot well afford to ignore while treating of the doctrine of karma, is the Buddhist belief that Çâkyamuni reached his supreme Buddhahood only after a long practise of the six virtues of perfection (*pâramitâs*) through many a rebirth. This belief constitutes the very foundation of the ethics of Buddhism and has all-important bearings on the doctrine of karma.

The doctrine of karma ethically considered is this: Sentient beings can attain to perfection not by an intervention from on high, but through long, steady, unflinching personal efforts towards the actualisation of ideals, or, in other words, towards the maturing of good stock (*kuçalamûla*) and the accumulation of of merits (*punyaskandha*). This can be accomplished only through the karma of good deeds untiringly practised throughout many a generation. Each single act of goodness we perform to-day is recorded with strict accuracy in the annals of human evolution and is so much the gain for the cause of righteousness. On the contrary, every deed of ill-will, every thought of self-aggrandisement, every word of impurity, every assertion of egoism, is a drawback to the perfection of humanity. To speak concretely, the Buddha represents the crystalisation in the historical person of Çâkyamuni of all the good karma that was accumulated in innumerable kalpas previous to his birth. And if Devadatta, as legend has him, was really the enemy of the Buddha, he symbolises in him the evil karma that was being stored up with the good deeds of all Buddhas. Later Buddhism has thus elaborated to represent in these two historical figures the concrete results of good and evil karma, and tries to show in what direction its followers should exercise their spiritual energy.

The doctrine of karma is, therefore, really the theory of evolution and heredity as working in our moral field. As Walt Whitman fitly sings, in every one of us, "converging objects of the universe" are perpetually flowing, through every one of us is "afflatus surging and surging — the current and index." And these converging objects and this afflatus are no more than our karma which is interwoven in our being and which is being matured from the very beginning of consciousness upon the earth. Each generation either retards or furthers the maturing of karma and transmits to the succeeding one its stock either impaired or augmented. Those who are blind enough not to see the significance of life, those who take their ego for the sole reality, and those who ignore the spiritual inheritance accumulated from time immemorial, — are the most worthless, most ungrateful, and most irresponsible people of the world. Buddhism calls them the children of Mâra engaged in the work of destruction.

Dr. G. R. Wilson of Scotland states a very pretty story about a royal robe in his article on "The Sense of Danger" (*The Monist*, 1903, April), which graphically illustrates how potential karma stored from time out of mind is saturated in every fibre of our subliminal consciousness or in the Âlayavijñâna, as Buddhists might say. The story runs as follows:

"An Oriental robe it was, whose beginning was in a prehistoric dynasty of which the hieroglyphics are undecipherable. With that pertinacity and durability so characteristic of the East, this royal garment has been handed down, not through hundreds of years, but through hundreds of generations,—generations, some of them, unconsciously long and stale and dreary; others short and quick and merry. A garment of kings, this, and of queens, a garment to which, as tradition prescribed, each monarch added something of quality,—a jewel of price, a patch of gold, a hem of rich embroidery,—and with each contribution a legend, worked into the imperishable fibre, told the story of the giver. Did something of the personality of these kings and queens linger in the work of their hands? If so, the robe was no dead thing, no mere covering to be lightly assumed or lightly laid aside, but a living power, royal influence, and the wearer, all unwitting, must have taken on something of the character of the dead. It is a princess of the royal blood, perhaps, sensitive and mystical, trembling on the apprehensive verge of monarchy, who dons the robe, and as she dons it, tingles to its message. These great rubies that blaze upon its front are the souvenirs of bloody conquerors. As she fingers them idly, she is thrilled with an emotion she does not understand, for in her blood something answers to the fighting spirit they embody. Pearls are for peace. That rope has been strung by kings and queens who favored art and learning; and as the girl's fingers stray towards them the inspiration changes and her mind reverts to the purposes of the civilised scholar. Here is a gaudy hem, the legacy of an unfaithful queen, steeped in intrigue all her life until her murder ended it; and as the maiden lifts it to examine it more closely, she learns with shame and blushes, yet not knowing what has wrought this change in her, that, deep down in her character, are mischievous possibilities, possibilities of wickedness and disgrace that will dog the footsteps of her reign. Suchlike are the suggestions which the hidden parts of the mind bring forth, and in such subtle manner are they born."

The doctrine of karma thus declares that an act of love and good-will you are performing here is not for your selfish interests, but it simply means the appreciation of the works of your worthy ancestors and the discharge of your duties towards all humanity and your contribution to the world-treasury of moral ideals. Mature good stock, accumulate merits, purify evil karma, remove the ego-hindrance, and cultivate love for all beings; and the heavenly gate of Nirvâna will be opened not only to you, but to the entire world.

We can sing with Walt Whitman the immortality of karma and the eternal progress of humanity, thus:

> "Did you guess anything lived only its moment?
> The world does not so exist—no part palpable or impalpable so exist;
> No consummation exists without being from some long previous consummation—and that from some other,
> Without the farthest conceivable one coming a bit nearer the beginning than any." [1]

Immortality

We read in the *Milinda-pañha*:

"Your Majesty, it is as if a man were to ascend to the story of a house with a light, and eat there; and the light in burning were to set fire to the thatch; and the thatch in burning were to set fire to the house; and the house in burning were to set fire to the village; and the people of the village were to seize him, and say, 'Why, O man, did you set fire to the village?' and he were to say, 'I did not set fire to the village. The fire of the lamp by whose light I ate was a different one from the one which set fire to the village';

[1] "Manhattan's Streets I Saunter'd, Pondering." I might have quoted the whole poem, if not for limitation of space.

and they, quarreling, were to come to you. Whose cause, Your Majesty, would you sustain?"

"That of the people of the village, Reverend Sir," etc.

"And why?"

"Because, in spite of what the man might say, the latter fire sprang from the former."

"In exactly the same way, Your Majesty, although the name and form which is born into the next existence is different from the name and form which is to end at death, nevertheless, it is sprung from it. Therefore is one not freed from one's evil deeds."

The above is the Buddhist notion of individual identity and its conservation, which denies the immortality of the ego-soul and upholds that of karma.

Another good way, perhaps, of illustrating this doctrine is to follow the growth and perpetuation of the seed. The seed is in fact a concrete expression of karma. When a plant reaches a certain stage of development, it blooms and bears fruit. This fruit contains in it a latent energy which under favorable conditions grows to a mature plant of its own kind. The new plant now repeats the processes which its predecessors went through, and an eternal perpetuation of the plant is attained. The life of an individual plant cannot be permanent according to its inherent nature, it is destined to be cut short some time in its course. But this is not the case with the current of an ever-lasting vitality that has been running in the plant ever since the beginning of the world. Because this current is not individual in its nature and stands above the vicissitudes which take place in the life of particular plants. It may not be manifested in its kinetic form all the time, but potentially it is ever present in the being of the seed. Changes are simply a matter of form, and do not interfere with the current of life in the plant, which is preserved in the universe as the energy of vegetation.

This energy of vegetation is that which is manifested in a mature plant, that which makes it blossom in the springtime, that which goes to seed, that which lies apparently dormant in the seeds, and that which resuscitates them to sprout among favorable surroundings. This energy of vegetation, this mysterious force, when stated in Buddhist phraseology, is nothing else than the vegetative expression of karma, which in the biological world constitutes the law of heredity, or the transmission of acquired character, or some other laws which might be discovered by the biologist. And it is when this force manifests itself in the moral realm of human affairs that karma obtains its proper significance as the law of moral causation.

Now, there are several forms of transmission, by means of which the karma of a person or a people or a nation or a race is able to perpetuate itself to eternity. A few of them are described below.

One may be called genealogical, or, perhaps, biological. Suppose here are descendants of an illustrious family, some of whose ancestors distinguished themselves by bravery, or benevolence, or intelligence, or by some other praiseworthy deeds or faculties. These people are as a rule respected by their neighbors as if their ancestral spirits were transmitted through generations and still lingering among their consanguineous successors. Some of them in the line might have even been below the normal level in their intellect and morals, but this fact does not altogether nullify the possibility and belief that others of their family might some day develop the faculties possessed by the forefathers, dormant as they appear now, through the inspiration they could get from the noble examples of the past. The respect they are enjoying and the possibility of inspiration they may have are all the work of the karma generated by the ancestors. The author or authors of the noble karma are all gone now, their bones have long returned to their elements, their ego-souls are no more, their concrete individual personalities are things of the past; but their karma is still here and as fresh as it was on the day of its generation and will so remain till the end of time. If some of them, on the other hand, left a black record behind them, the evil karma will tenaciously cling to the history of the family, and the descendants will have to suffer the curse as long as its vitality is kept up, no matter how innocent they themselves are.

Here one important thing I wish to note is the mysterious way in which evil karma works. Evil does not always generate evils only; it very frequently turns out to be a condition, if not a cause, which will induce a moral being to overcome it with his utmost spiritual efforts. His being conscious of the very fact that his family history is somehow besmirched with dark spots, would rekindle in his heart a flickering light of goodness. His stock of good karma finally being brought into maturity, his virtues would then eclipse the evils of the past and turn a new page before him, which is full of bliss and glory. Everything in this world, thus, seems to turn to be merely a means for the final realisation of Good. Buddhists ascribe this spiritual phenomenon to the virtues of the upâya (expediency) of the Dharmakâya or Amitâbha Buddha. [1]

To return to the subject. It does not need any further illustration to show that all these things which have been said about the family are also true of the race, the tribe, clan, nation, or any other form of community. History of mankind in all its manifold aspects of existence is nothing but a grand drama visualising the Buddhist doctrine of karmaic immortality. It is like an immense ocean whose boundaries nobody knows and the waves of events now swelling and surging, now ebbing, now whirling, now refluxing, in all times, day and night, illustrate how the laws

[1] If we understand the following words of Tolstoi in the light which we gain from the Buddhist doctrine of karmaic immortality, we shall perhaps find more meaning in them than the author himself wished to impart: "My brother who is dead acts upon me now more strongly than he did in life; he even penetrates my being and lifts me up towards him."

of karma are at work in this actual life. One act provokes another and that a third and so on to eternity without ever losing the chain of karmaic causation.

Next, we come to a form of karma which might be called historical. By this I mean that a man's karma can be immortalised by some historical objects, such as buildings, literary works, productions of art, implements, or instruments. In fact, almost any object, human or natural, which, however insignificant in itself, is associated with the memory of a great man, bears his karma, and transmits it to posterity.

Everybody is familiar with the facts that all literary work embodies in itself the author's soul and spirit, and that posterity can feel his living presence in the thoughts and sentiments expressed there, and that whenever the reader draws his inspiration from the work and actualises it in action, the author and the reader, though corporeally separate and living in different times, must be said spiritually feeling the pulsation of one and the same heart. And the same thing is true of productions of art. When we enter a gallery decorated with the noble works of Græcean or Roman artists, we feel as if we were breathing right in the midst of these art-loving people and seem to reawaken in us the same impressions that were received by them. We forget, as they did, the reality of our particular existence, we are unconsciously raised above it, and our imagination is filled with things not earthly. What a mysterious power it is!—the power by which those inanimate objects carry us away to a world of ideals! What a mysterious power it is that reawakens the spirits of by-gone artists on a sheet of canvas or in a piece of marble! It was not indeed entirely without truth that primitive or ignorant people intuitively believed in the spiritual power of idols. What they failed to grasp was the distinction between the subjective presence of a spirit and its objective reality. As far as their religious feeling, and not their critical intellect, was concerned, they were perfectly justified in believing in idolatry. Taking all in all, these facts unmistakably testify the Buddhist doctrine of the immortality of karma. A chord of karma touched by mortals of bygone ages still vibrates in their works, and the vibration with its full force is transmitted to the sympathetic souls down to the present day.

Architectural creations bear out the doctrine of karma with no less force than works of art and literature. As the uppermost bricks on an Egyptian pyramid would fall on the ground with the same amount of energy that required to raise them up in the times of Pharaohs; as a burning piece of coal in the furnace that was dug out from the heart of the earth emits the same quantity of heat that it absorbed from the sun some hundred thousand years ago; even so every insignificant bit of rock or brick or cement we may find among the ruins of Babylonian palaces, Indian topes, Persian kiosks, Egyptian obelisks, or Roman pantheons, is fraught with the same spirit and soul that actuated the ancient peoples to construct those gigantic architectural wonders. The spirit is here, not in its individual form, but in its karmaic presence. When we pick these insignificant, unseemly pieces, our souls become singularly responsive to inspirations coming from those of the past, and our mental eyes vividly perceive the splendor of the gods, glory of the kings, peace of the nation, prosperity of the peoples, etc., etc. Because our souls and theirs are linked with the chain of karmaic causation through the medium of those visible remains of ancient days. Because the karma of those old peoples is still breathing its immortality in those architectural productions and sending its sympathetic waves out to the beholders. When thus we come to be convinced of the truth of the immortality of karma, we can truly exclaim with Christians, "O death, where is thy sting? O grave, where is thy victory?"

It is hardly necessary to give any further illustration to establish the doctrine of karma concerning its historical significance. All scientific apparatus and instruments are an undying eye-witness of the genius of the inventors. All industrial machines and agricultural implements most concretely testify the immortality of karma created by the constructors, in exact proportion as they are beneficial to the general welfare and progress of humanity. The instruments or machines or implements may be superseded by later and better ones, and possibly altogether forgotten by succeeding generations, but this does not annul the fact that the improved ones were only possible through the knowledge and experience which came from the use of the older ones, in other words, that the ideas and thoughts of the former inventors are still surviving through those of their successors, just as much as in the case of genealogical karma-transmission. Whatever garb the karma of a person may wear in its way down to posterity, it is ever there where its inspiration is felt. Even in an article of most trivial significance, even in a piece of rag, or in a slip of time-worn paper, only let there be an association with the memory of the deceased; and an unutterable feeling imperceptibly creeps into the heart of the beholder; and if the deceased were known for his saintliness or righteousness, this would be an opportunity for our inspiration and moral elevation according to how our own karma at that moment is made up.

We now come to see more closely the spiritual purport of karmaic activity. Any intelligent reader could infer from what has been said above what important bearing the Buddhist doctrine of karma has on our moral and spiritual life. The following remarks, however, will greatly help him to understand the full extent of the doctrine and to pass an impartial judgment on its merits.

Here, if not anywhere else, looms up most conspicuously the characteristic difference between Buddhism and Christianity as to their conception of soul-activity. Christianity, if I understand it rightly, conceives our soul-phenomena as the work of an individual ego-entity, which keeps itself mysteriously hidden somewhere within the body. To Christians, the soul is a metaphysical being, and its incarnation in the flesh is imprisonment. It groans after emancipation, it craves for the celestial abode, where, after bodily death, it can enjoy all the blessings due to its naked existence. It finds the nectar of immortality up in Heaven and in the presence of God the father and Christ the son, and not in the perpetuation of karma in this universe. The soul of the wicked, on the other hand, is eternally damned, if it is conceded that they have any soul. As soon as it is liberated from the bodily incarceration, it is hurled into the infernal fire, and is there consumed suffering unspeakable agony. Christianity, therefore, does not believe in the transmigration or reincarnation of a soul. A soul once departed from the flesh never returns to it; it is either living an eternal life in Heaven or suffering an instant annihilation in Hell. This is the necessary conclusion from their premises of an individual concrete ego-soul.

Buddhism, however, does not teach the metaphysical existence of the soul. All our mental and spiritual experiences, it declares, are due to the operations of karma which inherits its efficiency from its previous "seeds of activity" (*karmabîja*), and which has brought the five skandhas into the present state of co-ordination. The present karma, while in its force, generates in turn the "seeds of activity" which under favorable conditions grow to maturity again. Therefore, as long as the force of karma is thus successively generated, there are the five skandhas constantly coming into existence and working co-ordinately as a person. Karma-reproduction, so to speak, effected in this manner, is the Buddhist conception of the transmigration of a soul.

A Japanese national hero, General Kusunoki Masashige, who was an orthodox Buddhist, is said to have uttered the following words when he fell in the battle-field: "I will be reborn seven times yet and complete discharging my duties for the Imperial House." And he did not utter these words to no purpose. Because even to-day, after the lapse of more than seven hundred years, his spirit is still alive among his countrymen, and indeed his bronze statue on horseback is solemnly guarding the Japanese Imperial palace. He was reborn more than seven times and will be reborn as long as the Japanese as a nation exist on earth. This constant rebirth or reincarnation means no more nor less than the immortality of karma. Says Buddha: "Ye disciples, take after my death those moral precepts and doctrines which were taught to you for my own person, for I live in them." To live in karma, and not as an ego-entity, is the Buddhist conception of immortality. Therefore, the Buddhists will perfectly agree with the sentiment expressed by a noted modern poet in these lines:

"We live in deeds, not years; in thoughts, not in breaths:
In feelings, not in figures on a dial,
We should count time by heart-throbs. He most lives
Who thinks most, feels the noblest, acts the best."

Some may like to call this kind of immortality unsatisfactory, and impetuously demand that the ego-soul, instead of mysterious force of karma, should be made immortal, as it is more tangible and better appreciated by the masses. The Buddhist response to such a demand would be; "If their intellectual and moral insight is not developed enough to see truth in the theory of karma, why, we shall let them adhere as long as they please to their crude, primitive faith and rest contented with it." Even the Buddha could not make children find pleasure in abstract metaphysical problems, whatever truth and genuine spiritual consolation there might be in them. What their hearts are after are toys and fairy-tales and parables. Therefore, a motto of Buddhism is: "Minister to the patients according to their wants and conditions." We cannot make a plant grow even an inch higher by artificially pulling its roots; we have but to wait till it is ready for development. Unless a child becomes a man, we must not expect of him to put away childish things.

The conclusion that could be drawn from the above is obvious If we desire immortality, let there be the maturing of good karma and the cleansing of the heart from the contamination of evils. In good karma we are made to live eternally, but in evil one we are doomed, not only ourselves but every one that follows our steps on the path of evils. Karma is always generative; therefore, good karma is infinite bliss, and evil one is eternal curse. It was for this reason that at the appearance of the Buddha in the Jambudvîpa heaven and earth resounded with the joyous acclamation of gods and men. It was a signal triumph for the cause of goodness. The ideal of moral perfection found a concrete example in the person of Çâkyamuni. It showed how the stock of good karma accumulated and matured from the beginning of consciousness on earth could be crystalised in one person and brought to an actuality even in this world of woes. The Buddha, therefore, was the culmination of all the good karma previously stored up by his spiritual ancestors. And he was at the same time the starting point for the fermentation of new karma, because his moral "seeds of activity" which were generated during his lifetime have been scattered liberally wherever his virtues and teachings could be promulgated. That is, his karma-seeds have been sown in the souls of all sentient beings. Every one of these seeds which are infinte in number will become a new centre of moral activity. In proportion how strong it grows and begins to bear fruit, it destroys the seeds of evil doers. Good karma is a combined shield and sword, while it protects itself it destroys all that is against it. Therefore, good karma is not only statically immortal, but it is dynamically so; that is to say, its immortality is not a mere absence of birth and death, but a constant positive increase in its moral efficiency.

Pious Buddhists believe that every time Buddha's name is invoked with a heart free from evil thoughts, he enters right into the soul and becomes integral part of his being. This does not mean, however, that

Buddha's ego-substratum which might have been enjoying its immortal spiritual bliss in the presence of an anthropomorphic God descends on earth at the invocation of his name and renders in that capacity whatever help the supplicant needs. It means, on the other hand, that the Buddhist awakens in his personal karma that which constituted Buddhahood in the Buddha and nourishes it to maturity. That which constitutes Buddhahood is not the personal ego of the Buddha, but his karma. Every chemical element, whenever occasioned to befree itself from a combination, never fails to generate heat which it absorbed at the time of combination with other elements; and this takes place no matter how remote the time of combination was. It is even so with the karma-seed of Buddha. It might have been in the barren soil of a sinful heart, and, being deeply buried there for many a year, might have been forgotten altogether by the owner. But, sooner or later, it will never fail to grow under favorable conditions and generate what it gained from the Buddha in the beginning of the world. And this regeneration will not be merely chemical, but predominantly biological; for it is the law which conditions the immortality of karma.

PRACTICAL BUDDHISM.

CHAPTER IX.

THE DHARMAKÂYA.

WE have considered the doctrine of Suchness (*Bhûtatathâtâ*) under "Speculative Buddhism," where it appeared altogether too abstract to be of any practical use to our earthly life. The theory as such did not seem to have any immediate bearings on our religious consciousness. The fact is, it must pass through some practical modification before it fully satisfies our spiritual needs. As there is no concrete figure in this world that is a perfect type of mathematical exactitude,—since everything here must be perceived through our more or less distorted physical organs; even so with pure reason: however perfect in itself, it must appear to us more or less modified while passing through our affective-intellectual objectives. This modification of pure reason, however, is necessary from the human point of view; because mere abstraction is contentless, lifeless, and has no value for our practical life, and again, because our religious cravings will not be satisfied with empty concepts lacking vitality.

We may sometimes ignore the claims of reason

and rest satisfied, though usually unconsciously, with assertions which are conflicting when critically examined, but we cannot disregard by any means those of the religious sentiment, which finds satisfaction only in the very fact of things. If it ever harbored some flagrant contradictions in the name of faith, it was because its ever-pressing demands had to be met with even at the expense of reason. The truth is: the religious consciousness first of all demands fact, and when it attains that, it is not of much consequence to it whether or not its intellectual interpretation is logically tenable. If on the other hand logic be all-important and demand the first consideration and the sentiment had to follow its trail without a murmuring, our life would surely lose its savory aspect, turn tasteless, our existence would become void, the world would be a mere succession of meaningless events, and what remains would be nothing else than devastation, barreness, and universal misery. The truth is, in this life the will predominates and the intellect subserves; which explains the fact that while all existing religions on the one hand display some logical inaccuracy and on the other hand a mechanical explanation of the world is gaining ground more and more, religion is still playing an important part everywhere in our practical life. Abstraction is good for the exercises of the intellect, but when it is the question of life and death we must have something more substantial and of more vitality than theorisation. It may not be a mathematically exact and certain proposition, but it must be a working, living, real theory, that is, it must be a faith born of the inmost consciousness of our being.

What practical transformations then has the doctrine of Suchness, in order to meet the religious demands, to suffer?

God.

Buddhism does not use the word God. The word is rather offensive to most of its followers, especially when it is intimately associated in vulgar minds with the idea of a creator who produced the world out of nothing, caused the downfall of mankind, and, touched by the pang of remorse, sent down his only son to save the depraved. But, on account of this, Buddhism must not be judged as an atheism which endorses an agnostic, materialistic interpretation of the universe. Far from it. Buddhism outspokenly acknowledges the presence in the world of a reality which transcends the limitations of phenomenality, but which is nevertheless immanent everywhere and manifests itself in its full glory, and in which we live and move and have our being.

God or the religious object of Buddhism is generally called Dharmakâya-Buddha and occasionally Vairocana-Buddha or Vairocana-Dharmakâya-Buddha; still another name for it is Amitâbha-Buddha or Amitâyur-Buddha, — the latter two being mostly used by the followers of the Sukhâvatî sect of Japan and China.

Again, very frequently we find Çâkyamuni, the Buddha, and the Tathâgata stripped of his historical personality and identified with the highest truth and reality. These, however, by no means exhaust a legion of names invented by the fertile imagination of Buddhists for their object of reverence as called forth by their various spiritual needs.

Dharmakâya.

Western scholars usually translate Dharmakâya by "Body of the Law" meaning by the Law the doctrine set forth by Çâkyamuni the Buddha. It is said that when Buddha was preparing himself to enter into eternal Nirvâna, he commanded his disciples to revere the Dharma or religion taught by him as his own person, because a man continues to live in the work, deeds, and words left behind himself. So, Dharmakâya came to be understood by Western scholars as meaning the person of Buddha incarnated in his religion. This interpretation of the term is not very accurate, however, and is productive of some very serious misinterpretations concerning the fundamental doctrines of Mahâyânism. Historically, the Body of the Law as the Buddha incarnate might have been the sense of Dharmakâya, as we can infer from the occasional use of the term in some Hînayâna texts. But as it is used by Eastern Buddhists, it has acquired an entirely new significance, having nothing to do with the body of religious teachings established by the Buddha.

This transformation in the conception of Dharmakâya has been effected by the different interpretation the term Dharma came to receive from the hand of the Mahâyânists. Dharma is a very pregnant word and covers a wide range of meaning. It comes from the root *dhṛ*, which means "to hold," "to carry", "to bear," and the primitive sense of dharma was "that which carries or bears or supports," and then it came to signify "that which forms the norm, or regulates the course of things," that is, "law," "institution," "rule," "doctrine," then, "duty," "justice," "virtue," "moral merit," "character," "attribute," "essential quality," "substance," "that which exists," "reality," "being," etc., etc. The English equivalent most frequently used for dharma by Oriental scholars is law or doctrine. This may be all right as far as the Pâli texts go; but when we wish to apply this interpretation to the Mahâyâna terms, such as Dharmadhâtu, Dharmakâya, Dharmalakṣa, Dharmaloka, etc., we are placed in an awkward position and are at a loss how to get at the meaning of those terms. There are passages in Mahâyâna literature in which the whole significance of the text depends upon how we understand the word dharma. And it may even be said that one of the many reasons why Christian students of Buddhism so frequently fail to recognise the importance of Mahâyânism is due to their misinterpretation of dharma. Max Mueller, therefore, rightly remarks in his introduction to an English translation of the *Vajracchedika Sûtra*, when he says: "If we were always to translate dharma by law, it seems to me that the whole drift of our treatise would become unintelligible." Not only that particular text of Mahâyânism, but its entire literature would become utterly incomprehensible.

In Mahâyânism Dharma means in many cases "thing," "substance," or "being," or "reality," both in its particular and in its general sense, though it is also frequently used in the sense of law or doctrine. Kâya may be rendered "body," not in the sense of personality, but in that of system, unity, and organised form. Dharmakâya, the combination of dharma and kâya, thus means the organised totality of things or the principle of cosmic unity, though not as a purely philosophical concept, but as an object of the religious consciousness. Throughout this work, however, the original Sanskrit form will be retained in preference to any English equivalents that have been used heretofore; for Dharmakâya conveys to the minds of Eastern Buddhists a peculiar religious flavor, which, when translated by either God or the All or some abstract philosophical terms, suffers considerably.

Dharmakâya as Religious Object.

As aforesaid, the Dharmakâya is not a product of philosophical reflection and is not exactly equivalent to Suchness; it has a religious signification as the object of the religious consciousness. The Dharmakâya is a soul, a willing and knowing being, one that is will and intelligence, thought and action. It is, as understood by the Mahâyânists, not an abstract metaphysical principle like Suchness, but it is living spirit, that manifests itself in nature as well as in thought. The universe as an expression of this spirit is not a meaningless display of blind forces, nor is it an arena for the struggle of diverse mechanical powers. Further, Buddhists ascribe to the Dharmakâya innumerable merits and virtues and an absolute perfect intelligence, and makes it an inexhaustible fountain-head of love and compassion; and it is in this that the Dharmakâya finally assumes a totally different aspect from a mere metaphysical principle, cold and lifeless.

The *Avatamsaka Sûtra* gives some comprehensive statements concerning the nature of the Dharmakâya as follows:

"The Dharmakâya, though manifesting itself in the triple world, is free from impurities and desires. It unfolds itself here, there, and everywhere responding to the call of karma. It is not an individual reality, it is not a false existence, but is universal and pure. It comes from nowhere, it goes to nowhere; it does not assert itself, nor is it subject to annihilation. It is forever serene and eternal. It is the One, devoid of all determinations. This Body of Dharma has no boundary, no quarters, but is embodied in all bodies. Its freedom or spontaneity is incomprehensible, its spiritual presence in things corporeal is incomprehensible. All forms of corporeality are involved therein, it is able to create all things. Assuming any concrete material body as required by the nature and condition of karma, it illuminates all creations. Though it is the treasure of intelligence, it is void of particularity. There is no place in the universe where this Body does not prevail. The universe becomes, but this Body forever remains. It is free from all opposites and contraries, yet it is working in all things to lead them to Nirvâna."

More Detailed Characterisation.

The above gives us a general, concise view as to what the Dharmakâya is, but let me quote the following more detailed description of it, in order that we may more clearly and definitely see into the characteristically Buddhistic conception of the highest being. [1]

"O ye, sons of Buddha! The Tathâgata [2] is not a particular dharma, nor a particular form of activity, nor has it a particular body, nor does it abide in a particular place, nor is its work of salvation confined to one particular people. On the contrary, it involves in itself infinite dharmas, infinite activities, infinite bodies, infinite spaces, and universally works for the salvation of all things.

"O ye, sons of Buddha! It is like unto space. Space [3] contains in itself all material existences and all the vacuums that obtain between them. Again, it establish-

[1] The *Avatamsaka Sûtra,* Chinese translation by Buddhabhadra, fas. XXXIV.

[2] That is the Dharmakâya personified.

[3] In Hindu philosophy space is always conceived as an objective entity in which all things exist.

es itself in all possible quarters, and yet we cannot say of it that it is or it is not in this particular spot, for space has no palpable form. Even so with the Dharkâya of the Tathâgata. It presents itself in all places, in all directions, in all dharmas, and in all beings; yet the Dharmakâya itself has not been thereby particularised. Because the Body of the Tathâgata has no particular body but manifests itself everywhere and anywhere in response to the nature and condition of things.

"O ye, sons of Buddha! It is like unto space. Space is boundless, comprehends in itself all existence, and yet shows no trace of passion [partiality]. It is even so with the Dharmakâya of the Tathâgata. It illuminates all good works worldly as well as religious, but it betrays no passion or prejudice. Why? Because the Dharmakâya is perfectly free from all passions and prejudices.[1]

"O ye, sons of Buddha! It is like unto the Sun. The benefits conferred by the light of the sun upon all living beings on earth are incalculable: e. g. by dispelling darkness it gives nourishment to all trees, herbs, grains, plants, and grass; it vanquishes humidity; it illuminates ether whereby benefitting all the

[1] This should be understood in the sense that "God maketh his sun to rise on the evil and on the good, and sendeth rain on the just and on the unjust." The Dharmakâya is universal in its love, as space is in its comprehensiveness Because it is absolutely free from human desires and passions that are the product of egoism and therefore tend always to be discriminative and exclusive.

living beings in air; its rays penetrate into the waters whereby bringing forth the beautiful lotus-flowers into full blossom; it impartially shines on all figures and forms and brings into completion all the works on earth. Why? Because from the sun emanate infinite rays of life-giving light.

"O ye, sons of Buddha! It is even so with the Sun-Body of the Tathâgata which in innumerable ways bestows benefits upon all beings That is, it benefits us by destroying evils, all good things thus being quickened to growth; it benefits us with its universal illumination which vanquishes the darkness of ignorance harbored in all beings; it benefits us through its great compassionate heart which saves and protects all beings; it benefits us through its great loving heart which delivers all beings from the misery of birth and death; it benefits us by the establishment of a good religion whereby we are all strengthened in our moral activities; it benefits us by giving us a firm belief in the truth which cleanses all our spiritual impurities; it benefits by helping us to understand the doctrine by virtue of which we are not led to disavow the law of causation; it benefits us with a divine vision which enables us to observe the metempsychosis of all beings; it benefits us by avoiding injurious deeds which may destroy the stock of merits accumulated by all beings; it benefits us with an intellectual light which unfolds the mind-flowers of all beings; it benefits us with an aspiration whereby we are enlivened to practice all that constitutes Buddhahood. Why? Because the Sun-

Body of the Tathâgata universally emits the rays of the Light of Intelligence.

"O ye, sons of Buddha! When the day breaks, the rising sun shines first on the peaks of all the higher mountains, then on those of high mountains, and finally all over the plains and fields; but the sunlight itself does not make this thought: I will shine first on all the highest mountains and then gradually ascending higher and higher shine on the plains and fields. The reason why one gets the sunlight earlier than another is simply because there is a gradation of height on the surface of the earth.

"O ye, sons of Buddha! It is even so with the Tathâgata who is in possession of innumerable and immeasurable suns of universal intelligence. The innumerable rays of the Light of Intelligence, emanating everlastingly from the spiritual Body of the Tathâgata, will first fall on the Bodhisattvas and Mahâsattvas who are the highest peaks among mankind, then on the Nidânabuddhas, then on the Çrâvakas, then on those beings who are endowed with definitely good character, as they will each according to his own capacity unhesitatingly embrace the doctrine of deliverance, and finally on all common mortals whose character may be either indefinite or definitely bad, providing them with those conditions which will prove beneficial in their future births But the Light of Intelligence emanating from the Tathâgata does not make this thought: 'I will first shine on the Bodhisattvas and then gradually pass over to all common mortals, etc.' The Light is universal and illuminates everything without any prejudice, yet on account of the diversity that obtains among sentient beings as to their character, aspirations, etc., the Light of Intelligence is diversely perceived by them.

"O ye, sons of Buddha! When the sun rises above the horizon, those people born blind, on account their defective sight, cannot see the light at all, but they are nevertheless benefited by the sunlight, for it gives them just as much as to any other beings all that is necessary for the maintenance of life: it dispels dampness and coldness and makes them feel agreeable, it destroys all the injurious germs that are produced on account of the absence of sunshine, and thus keeps the blind as well as the not-blind comfortable and healthy.

"O ye, sons of Buddha! It is even so with the Sun of Intelligence of the Tathâgata. All those beings whose spiritual vision is blinded by false doctrine, or by the violation of Buddha's precepts, or by ignorance, or by evil influences, never perceive the Light of Intelligence; because they are devoid of faith. But they are nevertheless benefited by the Light; for it disperses indiscriminately for all beings the sufferings arising from the four elements, and gives them physical comforts; for it destroys the root of all passions, prejudices, and pains for unbelievers as well as for believers... By virtue of this omnipresent Light of Intelligence, the Bodhisattvas will attain perfect purity and the knowledge of all things, the Nidânabuddhas and Çravakas will destroy all passions and desires; mortals poorly endowed and those born blind will rid of impurities, control the senses, and believe in the four views;[1] and those creatures living in the evil paths of existence such as hell, world of ghosts, and the animal realm, will be freed from their evils and torture and will, after death, be born in the human or celestial world....

"O ye, sons of Buddha! The Light of Dharmakâya is like unto the full moon which has four wondrous attributes: (1) It outdoes in its brilliance all stars and satellites; (2) It shows in its size increase and decrease as observable in the Jambudvîpa; (3) Its reflection is seen in every drop or body of clear water; (4) Whoever is endowed with perfect sight, perceives it vis-a-vis.

"O ye, sons of Buddha! Even so with the Dharmakâya of the Tathâgata, that has four wondrous attributes: (1) It eclipses the stars of the Nidânabuddhas, Çrâvakas, etc.; (2) It shows in its earthly life a certain variation which is due to the different natures of the beings to whom it manifests itself,[2] while the Dharmakâya

[1] The four views are: That the physical body is productive of impurities; that sensuality causes pain; that the individual soul is not permanent; and that all things are devoid of the Atman.

[2] That is to say: The Dharmakâya, that assumes all forms of existence according to what class of being it is manifesting itself, is sometimes conceived by the believers to be a short-lived god, sometimes an immortal spirit, sometimes a celestial being of one hundred kalpas, and sometimes an existence of only a moment. As there are so many different dispositions,

itself is eternal and shows no increase or decrease in any way; (3) Its reflection is seen in the Bodhi (intelligence) of every pure-hearted sentient being; (4) All who understand the Dharma and obtain deliverance, each according to his own mental calibre, think that they have really recognised in their own way the Tathâgata face to face, while the Dharmakâya itself is not a particular object of understanding, but universally brings all Buddha-works into completion.

"O ye, sons of Buddha! The Dharmakâya is like unto the Great Brahmarâja who governs three thousand chiliocosms. The Râja by a mysterious trick makes himself seen universally by all living beings in his realm and causes them to think that each of them has seen him face to face; but the Râja himself has never divided his own person nor is he in possession of diverse features.

"O ye, sons of Buddha! Even so with the Tathâgata; he has never divided himself into many, nor has he ever assumed diverse features. But all beings, each according to his understanding and strength of faith, recognise the Body of the Tathâgata, while he has never made this thought that he will show himself to such and such particular people and not to others. . .

"O ye, sons of Buddha! The Dharmakâya is like unto the maniratna in the waters, whose wondrous

characters, karmas, intellectual attainments, moral environments, etc., so there are as many Dharmakâyas as subjectively represented in the minds of sentient beings, though the Dharmakâya, objectively considered, is absolutely one.

light transforms everything that comes in contact with it to its own color. The eyes that perceive it become purified. Wherever its illumination reaches, there is a marvelous display of gems of every description, which gives pleasure to all beings to see.

"O ye, sons of Buddha! It is even so with the Dharmakâya of the Tathâgata, which may rightly be called the treasure of treasures, the thesaurus of all merits, and the mine of intelligence. Whoever comes in touch with this light, is all transformed into the same color as that of the Buddha. Whoever sees this light, all obtains the purest eye of Dharma. Whoever comes in touch with this light, rids of poverty and suffering, attains wealth and eminence, enjoys the bliss of the incomparable Bodhi"......

Dharmakâya and Individual Beings.

From these statements it is evident that the Dharmakâya or the Body of the Tathâgata, or the Body of Intelligence, whatever it may be designated, is not a mere philosophical abstraction, standing aloof from this world of birth and death, of joy and sorrow, calmly contemplates on the folly of mankind; but that it is a spiritual existence which is "absolutely one, is real and true, and forms the raison d'être of all beings, transcends all modes of upâya, is free from desires and struggles [or compulsion], and stands outside the pale of our finite understanding."[1] It is

[1] Asanga's *General Treatise on Mahâyânism. (Mahâyâna samparigraha).*

also evident that the Dharmakâya, though itself free from ignorance (*avidyâ*) and passion (*kleça*) and desire (*tṛṣnâ*), is revealed in the finite and fragmental consciousness of human being, so that we can say in a sense that "this body of mine is the Dharmakâya"—though not absolutely; and also in a generalised form that "the body of all beings is the Dharmakâya, and the Dharmakâya is the body of all beings,"—though in the latter only imperfectly and fractionally realised. As we thus partake something in ourselves of the Dharmakâya, we all are ultimately destined to attain Buddhahood when the human intelligence, Bodhi, is perfectly identified with, or absorbed in, that of the Dharmakâya, and when our earthly life becomes the realisation of the will of the Dharmakâya.

The Dharmakâya as Love.

Here an important consideration forces itself upon us which is, that the Dharmakâya is not only an intelligent mind but a loving heart, that it is not only a god of rigorism who does not allow a hair's breadth deviation from the law of karma, but also an incarnation of mercy that is constantly belaboring to develop the most insignificant merit into a field yielding rich harvests. The Dharmakâya relentlessly punishes the wrong and does not permit the exhaustion of their karma without sufficient reason; and yet its hands are always directing our life toward the actualisation of supreme goodness. "Pangs of nature, sins of will, defects of doubt, and stains of blood,"—discouraging and gloomy indeed is the karma of evil-doers! But the Dharmakâya, infinite in love and goodness, is incessantly managing to bring this world-transaction to a happy terminus. Every good we do is absorbed in the universal stock of merits which is no more nor less than the Dharmakâya. Every act of lovingkindness we practice is conceived in the womb of Tathâgata, and therein nourished and matured, is again brought out to this world of karma to bear its fruit. Therefore, no life walks on earth with aimless feet; no chaff is thrown into the fire unquenchable. Every existence, great or insignificant, is a reflection of the glory of the Dharmakâya and as such worthy of its all-embracing love.

For further corroboration of this view let us cite at random from a Mahâyâna sutra: [1]

"With one great loving heart
The thirsty desires of all beings he quencheth with coolness refreshing;
With compassion, of all doth he think,
Which like space knows no bounds;
Over the world's all creation
With no thought of particularity he revieweth.

"With a great heart compassionate and loving,
All sentient beings by him are embraced;
With means (*upâya*) which are pure, free from stain, and all excellent,
He doth save and deliver all creatures innumerable.

[1] The *Avatamsaka Sûtra*, chap. 13, "On Merit."

"With unfathomable love and with compassion
All creations caressed by him universally;
Yet free from attachment his heart is.

"As his compassion is great and is infinite,
Bliss unearthly on every being he confereth,
And himself showeth all over the universe;
He'll not rest till all Buddhahood truly attains."

Later Mahâyânists' view of the Dharmakâya.

The above has been quoted almost exclusively from the so-called sûtra literature of Mahâyâna Buddhism, which is distinguished from the other religio-philosophical treatises of the school, because the sûtras are considered to be the accounts of Buddha himself as recorded by his immediate disciples.[1] Let us now see by way of further elucidation what views were held concerning the Dharmakâya by such writers as Asanga, Vasubandhu, etc.

We read in the *General Treatise on Mahâyânism* by Asanga and Vasubandhu the following statement:

"When the Bodhisattvas think of the Dharmakâya, how have they to picture it to themselves?

"Briefly stated, they will think of the Dharmakâya by picturing to themselves its seven characteristics, which constitute the faultless virtues and essential

[1] This is by no means the case, for some of the Mahâyâna sûtras are undoubtedly productions of much later writers than the immediate followers of the Buddha, though of course it is very likely that some of the most important Mahâyâna canonical books were compiled within a few hundred years after the Nirvana of the Master.

functions of the Kâya. (1) Think of the free, unrivaled, unimpeded activity of the Dharmakâya, which is manifested in all beings; (2) Think of the eternality of all perfect virtues in the Dharmakâya; (3) Think of its absolute freedom from all prejudice, intellectual and affective; (4) Think of those spontaneous activities that uninterruptedly emanate from the will of the Dharmakâya; (5) Think of the inexhaustible wealth, spiritual and physical, stored in the Body of the Dharma; (6) Think of its intellectual purity which has no stain of onesidedness; (7) Think of the earthly works achieved for the salvation of all beings by the Tathâgatas who are reflexes of the Dharmakâya."

As regards the activity of the Dharmakâya, which is shown in every Buddha's work of salvation, Asanga enumerates five forms of operation: (1) It is shown in his power of removing evils which may befall us in the course of life, though the Buddha is unable to cure any physical defects which we may have, such as blindness, deafness, mental abberration, etc. (2) It is shown in his irresistible spiritual domination over all evil-doers, who, base as they are, cannot help doing some good if they ever come in the presence of the Buddha. (3) It is shown in his power of destroying various unnatural and irrational methods of salvation which are practiced by followers of asceticism, hedonism, or Ishvaraism. (4) It is shown in his power of curing those diseased minds that believe in the reality, permanency, and indivisibility of the ego-soul, that is, in the pudgalavâda. (5) It is shown in his inspiring influence over those Bodhisattvas who have not yet attained to the stage of immovability as well as over those Çrâvakas whose faith and character are still in a state of vacillation.

The Freedom of the Dharmakâya.

Those spiritual influences over all beings of the Dharmakâya through the enlightened mind of a Buddha, which we have seen above as stated by Asanga, are fraught with religious significance. According to the Buddhist view, those spiritual powers everlastingly emanating from the Body of Dharma have no trace of human elaboration or constrained effort, but they are a spontaneous overflow from its immanent necessity, or, as I take it, from its free will. The Dharmakâya does not make any conscious, struggling efforts to shower upon all sentient creatures its innumerable merits, benefits, and blessings. If there were in it any trace of elaboration, that would mean a struggle within itself of divers tendencies, one trying to gain ascendency over another. And it is apparent that any struggle and its necessary ally, compulsion, are incompatible with our conception of the highest religious reality. Absolute spontaneity and perfect freedom is one of those necessary attributes which our religious consciousness cannot help ascribing to its object of reverence. Buddhists therefore repeatedly affirm that the activity of the Dharmakâya is perfectly free from all effort and coercion, external and internal. Its every act of creation or salvation or love emanates from its own free will, unhampered by any struggling exertion which characterises the doings of mankind. This free will which is divine, standing in such a striking contrast with our own "free will" which is human and at best very much limited, is called by the Buddhists the Dharmakâya's "Purvapranidhânabala."[1]

As the Dharmakâya works of its own accord it does not seek any recompense for its deed; and it is evident that every act of the Dharmakâya is always for the best welfare of its creatures, for they are its manifestations and it must know what they need. We do not have to ask for our "daily bread,"

[1] "Purvapranidhânabala" is frequently translated "the power of original (or primitive) prayer." Literally, pûrva means "former" or "original" or "primitive"; and pranidhâna, "desire" or "vow or "prayer"; and bala, "power." So far as literary rendering is concerned, "power of original prayer" seems to be the sense of the original Sanskrit. But when we speak of primitive prayers of the Dharmakâya or Tathâgata, how shall we understand it? Has prayer any sense in this connection? The Dharmakâya can by its own free will manifest in any form of existence and finish its work in whatever way it deems best. There is no need for it to utter any prayer in the agony of struggle to accomplish. There is in the universe no force whatever which is working against it so powerfully as to make it cry for help; and there cannot be any struggle or agony in the activity of the Dharmakâya. The term prayer therefore is altogether misleading and inaccurate and implicates us in a grave error which tends to contradict the general Buddhist conception of Dharmakâya. We must dispense with the term entirely in order to be in perfect harmony with the fundamental doctrine of Buddhism. This point will receive further consideration later.

nor have we to praise or eulogise its virtues to court its special grace, nor is there any necessity for us to offer prayer or supplication to the Dharmakâya. Consider the lilies of the field which neither toil nor spin,—and I might add,—which ask not for any favoritism from above; yet are they not arrayed even better than Solomon in all his glory? The Dharmakâya shines in its august magnificence everywhere there is life, nay, even where there is death. We are all living in the midst of it and yet, strange to say, as "the fish knows not the presence of water about itself," and also as "the mountaineers recognise not the mountains among which they hunt," even so we know not whence that power comes whose work is made manifest in us and whither it finally leadeth us. In spite of this profound ignorance, we really feel that we are here, and thereby we rest supremely contented. For we believe that all this is wrought through the mysterious and miraculous will of the Dharmakâya, who does all excellent works and seeks no recompense whatever.

The Will of the Dharmakâya.

Summarily speaking, the Dharmakâya assumes three essential aspects as reflected in our religious consciousness: first, it is intelligence (*prajñâ*); secondly, it is love (*karunâ*); and thirdly, it is the will (*pranidhânabala*). We know that it is intelligence from the declaration that the Dharmakâya directs the course of the universe, not blindly but rationally; we know again that it is love because it embraces all beings with fatherly tenderness;[1] and finally we must assume that it is a will, because the Dharmakâya has firmly set down its aim of activity in that good shall be the final goal of all evil in the universe. Without the will, love and intelligence will not be realised; without love, the will and intelligence will lose their impulse; without intelligence, love and the will will be irrational. In fact, the three are coordinates and constitute the oneness of the Dharmakâya; and by oneness I mean the absolute, and not the numerical, unity of all these three things in the being of the Dharmakâya, for intelligence and love and the will are differentiated as such only in our human, finite consciousness.

Some Buddhists may not agree entirely with the view here expounded. They may declare: "We conform to your view when you say the Dharmakâya is intelligence and love, as this is expressly stated in the sûtras and çâstras; but we do not see how it could be made a will. Indeed, the Scriptures say that the Dharmakâya is in possession of the Pranidhânabala, but this bala or power is not necessarily the will, it is the power of prayers or intense vows. The Dharmakâya actually made solemn vows, and their spiritual energy abiding in the world of particulars works out its original plan and makes possible the universal salvation of all creatures."

It is quite true that the word pranidhânabala means

[1] "I am the father of all beings, and they are my children." (The *Avatamsaka*, the *Pundarîka*, etc.)

literally "the power of original prayers." But this literary rendering totally ignores its inner significance without which the nature of the Dharmakâya would become unintelligible. We admit that the Dharmakâya knows no higher existence by which it is conditioned, nor has it any fragmentary, limited consciousness like that of human being, nor has it any intrinsic want by which it is necessitated to appeal to something other than itself. It is, therefore, utterly nonsensical to speak of its prayer, "original" or borrowed, as some Buddhists are inclined to think. On the other hand, we are perfectly justified in saying that whatever is done by the Dharmakâya is done by its own free will independent of all the determinations that might affect it from outside.

But I can presume the reason why they speak of the prayers of the Dharmakâya instead of its will. Here we have an instance of emotional outburst. The fervency of the intense religious sentiment not infrequently carries us beyond the limits of the intellect, landing us in a region full of mysteries and contradictions. It anthroposises everything beyond the proper measure of intellection and ascribes all earthly human feelings and passions to an object which the mind well-balanced demands to be above all the forms of human helplessness. The Buddhists, especially those of the Sukhâvatî sect,[1] recognise the exist-

[1] To get more fully acquainted with the significance of the Sukhâvatî doctrine, the reader is advised to look up the Sukhâvatî sûtras in the *Sacred Books of the East*, Vol. XLIX.

ence of an all-powerful will, all-embracing love, and all-knowing intelligence in the Dharmakâya, but they want to represent it more concretely and in a more humanly fashion before the mental vision of the less intellectual followers. The result thus is that the Dharmakâya in spite of its absoluteness made prayers to himself to emancipate all sentient beings from the sufferings of birth and death. But are not these self-addressed prayers of the Dharmakâya which sprang out of its inmost nature exactly what constitutes its will?

CHAPTER X.

THE DOCTRINE OF TRIKÂYA.

(Buddhist Theory of Trinity.)

The Human and the Super-human Buddha.

ONE of the most remarkable differences between the Pâli and the Sanskrit, that is, between the Hînayâna and the Mahâyâna Buddhist literature, is in the manner of introducing the characters or persons who take principal parts in the narratives. In the former, sermons are delivered by the Buddha as a rule in such a natural and plain language as to make the reader feel the presence of the teacher, fatherly-hearted and philosophically serene; while in the latter generally we have a mysterious, transcendent figure, more celestial than human, surrounded and worshipped by beings of all kinds, human, celestial, and even demoniac, and this mystical central character performing some supernatural feats which might well be narrated by an intensely poetical mind.

In the Pâli scriptures, the texts as a rule open with the formula, "Thus it was heard by me" (*Evam me sutam*), then relate the events, if any, which induced the Buddha to deliver them, and finally lead the reader to the main subjects which are generally written in lucid style. Their opening or introductory matter is very simple, and we do not notice anything extraordinary in its further development. But with the Mahâyâna texts it is quite different. Here we have, as soon as the curtain rises with the stereotyped formula, "Evam mayâ çrutam," a majestic prologue dramatically or rather grotesquely represented, which prepares the mind of the audience to the succeeding scenes, in which some of the boldest religio-philosophical proclamations are brought forth. The perusal of this introductory part alone will stupefy the reader by its rather monstrous grandeur, and he may without much ado declare that what follows must be extraordinary and may be even nonsensical.

The following is an illustration showing the typical manner of introducing the characters in the Mahâyâna texts. [1]

"Thus it was heard by me. Buddha was once staying at Râjagriha, on the Gridhrakuta mountain. He was in the Hall of Ratnachandra in the Double Tower of Chandana. Ten years passed since his attainment of Buddhahood. He was surrounded by a hundred thousand Bhikṣus and Bodhisattvas and Mahâsattvas numbering sixty times as many as the sands of the Ganges. All of them were in possession of the greatest spiritual energy; they had paid homage to thousands of hundred mil-

[1] What follows is selected from a short sûtra called *The Mahâvaipulya-Tathâgatagarbha Sûtra*, translated into Chinese by Buddhabhadra of the Eastern Tsin dynasty (A.D, 371-420). Nanjo, No 384.

lions of niyutas[1] of Buddhas; they were able to set rolling the never-sliding-back Wheel of Dharma; and whoever heard their names could establish themselves firmly in the Highest Perfect Knowledge. Their names were. . . . [Here about fifty Bodhisattvas are mentioned.]

"All these Bodhisattvas numbering sixty times as many as the sands of the Ganges coming from innumerable Buddha-countries were accompanied by numberless Devas, Nâgas, Yakṣas, Gandharvas, Açuras, Garudas, Kinnaras, and Mahoragas. [2] This great assembly all joined in revering, honoring, paying homage to the Bhagavat, the World-honored One.

"At this time the Bhagavat in the Double Tower of Chandana seated himself in the assigned seat, entered upon a samâdhi, and displayed a marvelous phenomenon. There appeared innumerable lotus-flowers with thousand-fold petals and each flower as large as a carriage-wheel. They had perfectly beautiful color and fragrant odour, but their petals containing celestial beings in them were not yet unfolded. They all were raised now by themselves high up in the heavens and hung over the earth like a canopy of pearls. Each one of these lotus-flowers emitted innumerable rays of light and simultaneously grew in size with wonderful vitality. But through the divine power of Buddha they all of

[1] *Niyuta* is an exceedingly large number, but generally considered to be equal to one billion.

[2] All these are unhuman forms of existence, including demons, dragon-kings, winged beasts, etc.

a sudden changed color and withered. All the celestial Buddhas sitting cross-legged within the flowers now came into full view, shone with innumerable hundred thousand-fold rays of light. At this moment the transcendent glory of the spot was beyond description." . . .

As is here thus clearly shown, the Buddha in the Mahâyâna scriptures is not an ordinary human being walking in a sensuous world; he is altogether dissimilar to that son of Suddhodana, who resigned the royal life, wandered in the wilderness, and after six years' profound meditation and penance discovered the Fourfold Noble Truth and the Twelve Chains of Dependence; and we cannot but think that the Mahâyâna Buddha is the fictitious creation of an intensely poetic mind. Let it be so. But the question which engages us now is, "How did the Buddhists come to relegate the human Buddha to oblivion, as it were, and assign a mysterious being in his place invested with all possible or sometimes impossible majesty and supernaturality?" This question, which marks the rise of Mahâyâna Buddhism, brings us to the doctrine of Trikâya,—which in a sense corresponds to the Christian theory of trinity.

According to this doctrine, the Buddhists presume a triple existence of the Tathâgata, that is, the Tathâgata is conceived by them as manifesting himself in three different forms of existence: the Body of Transformation, the Body of Bliss, and the Body of Dharma. Though they are conceived as three, they are in fact all the manifestations of one Dharmakâya,—the Dharmakâya that revealed itself in the historical Çâkyamuni

Buddha as a Body of Transformation, and in the Mahâyâna Buddha as a Body of Bliss. However differently they may appear from the human point of view, they are nothing but the expression of one eternal truth, in which all things have their *raison d'être*.

An Historical View.

At present we are not in possession of any historical documents that will throw light on the question as to how early this doctrine of Trikâya or Buddhist trinity conception came to be firmly established among Northern Buddhists and found its way in an already-finished form as such into the Mahâyâna scriptures. As far as we know, it was Açvaghoṣa, the first Mahâyâna philosopher, who incorporated this conception in his *Discourse on the Awakening of Faith in the Mahâyâna* as early as the first century before Christ. This work, as the author declares, is a sort of synopsis of the Mahâyâna teachings, elucidating their principal features as taught by the Buddha in his various sûtras. It is not an original work which expounds the individual views of Açvaghoṣa concerning Buddhism. He wrote the book in a concise and comprehensive form, in order that the later generations who remote from the Buddha could not have the privilege of being inspired by his august presence, might peruse it with concentration of mind and synthetically grasp the whole significance of many lengthy and voluminous sûtras. Therefore, in the *Awakening of Faith*, we are supposed not to find any Mahâyâna doctrines that were not already taught by the Buddha and incorporated in the sûtras. Everything Açvaghoṣa treats in his work must be considered merely a recapitulation of the doctrines which were not only formulated but firmly established as the Mahâyâna faith long before him. His is simply the work of a recorder. He carefully scanned all the Mahâyâna scriptures that had existed prior to his time and faithfully collected all the principal teachings of Mahâyânism here and there scatteringly told in them. His merit lies in compilation and systematisation.

This being the case, we must assume that all the doctrines that are found in Açvaghoṣa and distinct from those usually held to be Hînayânistic are the teachings elaborated by Buddhists from the time of Buddha's death down to the time of Açvaghoṣa. But as the latter apparently believes all these doctrines as Buddha's own and raises no doubt concerning their later origin, even if they were so, we must assume again that these doctrines were in a state of completion long before Açvaghoṣa's time. If our calculation is correct that he lived in the first century before Christ, the Mahâyâna faith must be said to have been formulated at least two hundred years prior to his age,—taking this presumably as the time that is required for the formulation and dogmatical establishment of a doctrine. This calculation places the development of the Mahâyâna faith during the first century after the Buddha, and, we know, it was during this time that so many schools and divisions,—

among which we must also find the so-called "primitive" Buddhism of Ceylon, arose among the Buddhists,—each claiming to be the only authentic transmission of the Buddha's teaching. Did Mahâyânism come out of this turmoil of contention? Did it boldly raise itself from this chaos and claim to have solved all the questions and doubts that agitated the minds of Buddhists after the Nirvâna? For certain we do not know anything concerning the chronology of the development of Buddhist philosophy and dogmas in India, at least before Açvaghoṣa; but, as far as our Chinese Buddhist literature records, we must conclude that this was most probably the case.

To give our readers a glimpse of the state of things that were taking place in those early days of Buddhism in India, I will quote some passages from Vasumitra's *Discourse on the Points of Controversy by the Different Schools of Buddhism*,—the work once refered to in the beginning of this book. The two principal schools that arose soon after the Nirvâna of the Buddha were, as is well known, the Elders and the Great Council, and though they were further divided into a number of smaller sections and their views became so complex and intermixed that some of the Elders shared similar views with the Great Council School and vice versa, yet we can fairly distinguish one from the other and describe the the essential peculiarities of each school. These points of difference, generally speaking, are as follows, confining ourselves to their conceptions about the Buddha:

(1) According to the School of the Great Council, the Buddha's personality is transcendental (*lokottara*), and all the Tathâgatas are free from the defilements that might come from the material existence (*bhâva-âçrava*).[1] For in the Buddha all evil passions hereditary and acquired were eternally uprooted, and his presence on earth was absolutely spotless. (*The Vibhaṣa*, CLXXIII.) Contending this view, the Elders held that the Buddha's personality was not free from Bhâvâçrava, though his mind was fully enlightened. His corporeal existence was the product of blind love veiled with ignorance and tangled with attachment. If this were not so, the Buddha's feature would not have awakened an impure affection in the heart of a maiden, an ill-will in the heart of a highwayman, stupidity in the mind of an ascetic, and arrogance in that of a haughty Brahman. These incidents which

[1] Âçrava literally means "oozing," or "flowing out," and the Chinese translators rendered it by *lou*, dripping, or leaking. Roughly speaking, it is a general name for evils, principally material and sensuous. According to an Indian Buddhist scholar, Âçrava has threefold sense: (1) "keeping," for it retains all sentient beings in the whirlpool of birth and death; (2) "flowing," for it makes all sentient beings run in the stream of birth and death; (3) "leaking," or "oozing," for it lets such evils as avarice, anger, lust, etc., ooze out from the six sense-organs after the fashion of an ulcer, which lets out blood and filthy substance. The cause of Âçrava is a blind will, and its result is birth and death. Specifically, Bhâvâçrava is one of the three Âçravas, which are (1) kâmâçrava, (2) vidyâçrava, and (3) bhâvâçrava. The first is egotistic desires, the second is ignorance, and the third is the material existence which we have to suffer on account of our previous karma.

happened during the life of the Buddha evince that his corporeal presence was apt to agitate others' hearts, and to that extent it was contaminated by Bhâvâçrava.

(2) The Great Council School insists that every word uttered by a Tathâgata has a religious, spiritual meaning and purports to the edification of his fellow-beings; that his one utterance is variously interpreted by his audience each according to his own disposition, but all to his spiritual welfare; that every instruction given out by the Buddha is rational and perfect. Against these views the Elders think that the Buddha occasionally uttered things which had nothing to do with the enlightenment of others; that even with the Buddha something was out of his attainment, for instance, he could not make every one of his hearers perfectly understand his preachings; that though the Buddha never taught anything irrational and heretical, yet all his speeches were not perfect, he said some things which had no concern with rationality or orthodoxy.

(3) The corporeal body (*rûpakâya*) of the Buddha has no limits (*koṭi*); his majestic power has no limits; every Buddha's life is unlimited; a Buddha knows no fatigue, knows not when to rest, always occupying himself with the enlightenment of all sentient beings and with the awakening in their hearts of pure faith. Against these tendencies of the Great Council School to deify the historical Buddha, the Elders generally insist on the humanity of Buddhahood. Though the

Elders agree with the Great Council in that the body assumed by the Buddha as the result of his untiring accumulation of good karma through eons of his successive existences possesses a wonderful power, spiritual and material, they do not conceive it to be beyond all limitations.

(4) The Great Council School says that with the Buddha sleep is not necessary and he has no dreams. The Elders admit that the Buddha never dreams, but denies that he does not need any sleep.

(5) As the Buddha is always in the state of a deep, exalted spiritual meditation, it is not necessary for him to think what to say when requested to answer certain questions. Though he might appear to the inquirers as if he thoroughly cogitates over the problems presented to him for solution, the Buddha's response is in fact immediate and without any efforts. The Elders, on the other hand, presume the Buddha's mental calculation as to how to express his ideas as best suited to the understanding of the audience. Indeed, he does not cogitate over the problem itself, for with him everything is transparent, but he thinks over the best method of presenting his ideas before his pupils.

Our thoughtful readers must have noticed here that the conceptions of the Buddha as entertained by the Mahâsaṇgika School (Great Council) closely resemble those of the Mahâyâna Buddhism. Though we are still unable to trace step by step the development of Mahâyânism in India, the hypothesis assumed by most of Japanese Buddhist scholars is that the Mahâsangika was Mahâyânistic in tendency.

Now to return to the doctrine of Dharmakâya and Trikâya. When we consider these controversies as above stated, it is apparent that among many other questions which arose soon after the demise of the Buddha Çâkyamuni, there was one, which in all probability most agitated the minds of his disciples. I mean the question of the personality of Buddha. Was he merely a human being like ourselves? Then, how could he reach such a height of moral perfection? Or was he a divine being? But Buddha himself did not communicate anything to his disciples concerning his divinity, nor did he tell them to accept the Dharma on account of his divine personality, but solely for the sake of truth. But for all that how could the disciples ever eradicate from their hearts the feeling of sacred reverence for their teacher, which was so indelibly engraved there? Whenever they recalled the sermons, anecdotes, or gâthâs of their master, the truth and spirit embodied in them and the author must have become so closely associated that they could not but ask themselves: "What in the Buddha caused him to perceive and declare these solemn profound truths? What was it that formed in him such a noble majestic character? What was there in the mind of Buddha that raised him to such a perfection of intellectual and religious life? How was it possible that, possessed of such exalted moral and spiritual virtues, Buddha too had to succumb to the law of birth and death that is the lot of common mortals? Some such questions must have been repeatedly asked before they could answer them by the doctrines of Dharmakâya and Trikâya.

Who was the Buddha?

The evidence that these questions were constantly disturbing the minds of the disciples ever since the Master's entrance into Parinirvâna, is scatteringly revealed throughout the Buddhist texts both Southern and Northern. The regret of the immediate followers that they did not ask the Buddha to prolong his earthly life, while the Buddha told them that he could do so if he wished, and their lamentation over the remains of the Blessed One, "How soon the Light of the World has passed away!" [1] — these utterances may be considered the first drops foreboding the showers of doubt and speculation as to his personality.

According to the *Suvarna Prabhâ Sûtra*,[2] a Bodhisattva, by the name of Ruciraketu, was greatly annoyed by the doubt why Çâkyamuni Tathâgata had such a short life terminating only at eighty. He

[1] The *Mahâparinibbâna sutta*.

[2] There are three Chinese translations of this sûtra: the first, by Dharmarakṣa during the first two decades of the fifth century A. D.; the second, by Paramârtha of the Liang dynasty, who came to China A. D. 546 and died A. D. 569; and the third, by I-tsing of the Tang dynasty who came back from his Indian pilgrimage in the year 695 and translated this sûtra A. D. 703. The last is the only complete Chinese translation of the *Suvarnâ Prabhâ*. A part of the orginal Sanskrit text recovered in Nepal was published by the Buddhist Text Society of India in 1898. Nanjo, Nos. 126, 127, 130.

taught the disciples that those who did not injure any living beings, and those who generously practised charity, in their former lives, could enjoy a considerably long life on earth; why then was the life of the Blessed One himself cut so short, who practised those virtues from time immemorial? The sûtra now records that this doubt was dispelled by the declaration of four Tathâgatas who mysteriously appeared to the sceptic and told him that "Every drop of water in the vast ocean can be counted, but the age of Çâkyamuni none can measure. Crush the mount Sumeru into particles as fine as mustard seeds and we can count them, but the age of Çâkyamuni none can measure..... the Buddha never entered into Parinirvana; the Good Dharma will never perish. He showed an earthly death merely for the benefits of sentient beings."....

Here we have the conception of a spiritual Dharmakâya germinating out of the corporeal death of Çâkyamuni.[1] Here we have the bridge that spans

[1] The notion that great men never die seems to be universal. Spiritually they would never perish, because the ideas that moved them and made them prominent in the history of humanity are born of truth. And in this sense every person who is possessed of worthy thoughts is immortal, while souls that are made of trumpery are certainly doomed to annihilation. But the masses are not satisfied with this kind of immortality. They must have something more tangible, more sensual, and more individual. The notion of bodily resurrection of Christ is a fine illustration of this truth. When the followers of Christ opened the master's grave, they did not find his body, so says legend, and they at once conceived the idea

the wide gap between the human Çâkyamuni Buddha and the spiritual existence of the Dharmakâya. The Buddha did not die after he partook of the food offered by Chunda. His age was not eighty. His life did not pass to an airy nothingness when his cinerary urns were divided among kings and Brahmans. His virtues and merits which were accumulated throughout innumerable kalpas, could not come to naught so abruptly. What constituted the essence of his life—and that of ours too—could not perish with the vicissitudes of the corporeal existence. The Buddha as a particular individual being was certainly subject to transformation—so is every mortal, but his truth must abide forever His Dharmakâya is above birth and death and even above Nirvâna; but his Body of Transformation comes out of the womb of Tathâgata as destined by karma and vanishes into it when the karma exhausts its force. The Buddha who is still seated at the summit of the Gridhrakuta, delivering to all beings the message of joy and bliss, and who among other precious teachings bequeathed to us

of resurrection, for they reasoned that such a great man as Jesus could not suffer the same fate that befalls common mortals only. The story of his corporeal resurrection now took wing and went wild; some heard him speak to them, some saw him break bread, and others even touched his wounds. What a grossly materialistic conception early Christians (and alas, even some of the twentieth century) cherished about resurrection and immortality! It is no wonder, therefore, that primitive Buddhists raised a serious question about the personality of Buddha which culminated in the conception of the Sambhogakâya, Body of Bliss, by Mahâyânists.

such sûtras as the *Avatamsaka*, the *Pundarîka*, etc., is no more nor less than an expression of the eternal spirit. Thus came the doctrine of Dharmakâya to be formulated by the Mahâyânists, and from this the transition to that of Trikâya was but a natural sequence. Because one without the other could not give an adequate solution of the problems above cited.

The Trikâya as Explained in the Suvarna Prabhâ.

What then is the Trikâya or triple body of the Tathâgata? It is (1) Nirmâna Kâya, the Body of Transformation; (2) Sambhoga Kâya, the Body of Bliss; and (3) Dharma Kâya, the Body of Dharma. If we draw a parallelism between the Buddhist and the Christian trinity, the Body of Transformation may be considered to correspond to Christ in the flesh, the Body of Bliss either to Christ in glory or to Holy Ghost, and Dharmakâya to Godhead.

Let us again quote from the *Suvarna Prabhâ*, in which (I-tsing's translation, chap. III.) we find the following statements concerning the doctrine of Trikâya.

"The Tathâgata, when he was yet at the stage of discipline, practised divers deeds of morality for the sake of sentient beings. The practise finally attained perfection, reached maturity, and by virtue of its merits he acquired a wonderful spiritual power. The power enabled him to respond to the thoughts, deeds, and livings of sentient beings. He thoroughly understood them and never missed the right opportunity [to respond to their needs]. He revealed himself in the right place and in the right moment; he acted rightly, assuming various bodily forms [in response to the needs of mortal souls]. These bodily forms are called the Nirmânakâya of the Tathâgata.

"But when the Tathâgatas, in order to make the Bodhisattvas thoroughly conversant with the Dharma, to instruct them in the highest reality, to let them understand that birth-and-death (*samsâra*) and Nirvâna are of one taste, to destroy the thoughts of the ego, individuality, and the fear [of transmigration], and to promote happiness, to lay foundation for innumerable Buddha-dharmas, to be truly in accord with Suchness, the knowledge of Suchness, and the Spontaneous Will, manifest themselves to the Bodhisattvas in a form which is perfect with the thirty-two major and eighty minor features of excellence and shining with the halo around the head and the back, the Tathâgatas are said to have assumed the Body of Bliss or Sambhogakâya. [1]

"When all possible obstacles arising from sins [material, intellectual, and emotional] are perfectly removed, and when all possible good dharmas are preserved, there would remain nothing but Suchness and the knowledge of Suchness,—this is the Dharmakâya.

"The first two forms of the Tathâgata are provisional [and temporal] existences; but the last one is a reality, wherein the former two find the reason of

[1] Compare this to the transfigured Christ.

their existence. Why? Because when deprived of the Dharma of Suchness and of knowledge of non-particularity, no Buddha-dharma can ever exist; because it is Suchness and Knowledge of Suchness that absorbs within itself all possible forms of Buddha-wisdom and renders possible a complete extinction of all passions and sins [arising from particularity]."

According to the above, the Dharmakâya which is tantamount to Suchness or Knowledge of Suchness is absolute; but like the moon whose image is reflected in a drop of water as well as in the boundless expanse of the waves, the Dharmakâya assumes on itself all possible aspects from the grossest material form to the subtlest spiritual existence. When it responds to the needs of the Bodhisattvas whose spiritual life is on a much higher plane than that of ordinary mortals, it takes on itself the Body of Bliss or Sambhogakâya. This Body is a supernatural existence, and almost all the Buddhas in the Mahâyâna scriptures belong to this class of being. Açvaghoṣa (p. 101) says: "The Body has infinite forms. The form has infinite attributes. The attribute has infinite excellences. And the accompanying fruition, that is, the region where they are destined to be born [by their previous karma], also has infinite merits and ornamentations. Manifesting itself everywhere, the Body of Bliss is infinite, boundless, limitless, unintermittent [in its activity] which comes directly from the Mind [Dharmakâya]."

But the Buddhas revealed to the eyes of common

mortals are not of this kind They are common mortals themselves, and the earthly Çâkyamuni who came out of the womb of Mâyâdevî and passed away under the sâla trees at the age of eighty years was one of them. He was essentially a manifestation of the Dharmakâya, and as such we ordinary people also partake something of him. But the masses, unless favored by good karma accumulated in the past, are generally under the spell of ignorance. They do not see the glory of Dharmakâya in its perfect purity shining in the lilies of the field and sung by the fowls of the air. They are blindly groping in the dark wilderness, they are vainly seeking, they are wildly knocking. To the needs of these people the Dharmakâya responds by assuming an earthly form as a human Buddha.

Revelation in All Stages of Culture.

En passant, let us remark that it is in this sense that Christ is conceived by Buddhists also as a manifestation of the Dharmakâya in a human form. He is a Buddha and as such not essentially different from Çâkyamuni The Dharmakâya revealed itself as Çâkyamuni to the Indian mind, because that was in harmony with its needs. The Dharmakâya appeared in the person of Christ on the Semitic stage, because it suited their taste best in this way. The doctrine of Trikâya, however, goes even further and declares that demons, animal gods, ancestor-worship, nature-worship, and what not, are all due to the activity and revelation of the Dharmakâya responding to the spiritual needs of barbarous and half-cultured people. The Buddhists think that the Dharmakâya never does things that are against the spiritual welfare of its creatures, and that whatever is done by it is for their best interests at that moment of revelation, no matter how they comprehend the nature of the Dharmakâya. The Great Lord of Dharma never throws a pearl before the swine, for he knows the animal's needs are for things more substantial. He does not reveal himself in an exalted spiritual form to the people whose hearts are not yet capable of grasping anything beyond the grossly material. As they understand animal gods better than a metaphysical or highly abstracted being, let them have them and derive all possible blessings and benefits through their worshiping. But as soon as they become dissatisfied with the animal or human-fashioned gods, there must not be a moment's hesitation to let them have exactly what their enlightened understanding can comprehend.[1]

[1] Cf. I Cor. XIII, II. "When I was a child, I spake as a child, I understood as a child, I thought as a child, but when I became a man, I put away childish things." This point of our ever-ascending spiritual progress is well illustrated in the *Saddharma-pundarîka Sûtra*. See Chapters II, III, IV, V, and XI. The following passage quoted from chap. II, p. 49 (Kern's translation) will give a tolerably adequate view concerning diversity of means and unity of purpose as here expounded: "Those highest of men have, all of them, revealed most holy laws by means of illustrations, reasons and arguments, with many hundred proofs of skillfulness (*upâyakauçalya*). And all of them have manifested but one vehicle and introduced but one on earth; by one vehicle have they led to full ripeness inconceivably many thousands of kotis of beings." As was

They are thus all the while being led, though unconsciously on their part, to the higher and higher region of mystery, till they come fully to grasp the true and real meaning of the Dharmakâya in its absolute purity, or, to use Christian terminology, till "we all, with open face beholding as in a glass the glory of the Lord, are changed into the same image from glory, even as by the Spirit of the Lord." (2 Cor III. 18.)

The Mahâyânists now argue that the reason why Çâkyamuni entered into Parinirvana when his worldly career was thought by him to be over is that by this his resignation to the law of birth and death, he wished to exemplify in him the impermanency of worldly life and the folly of clinging to it as final reality. As for his Dharmakâya, it has an eternal life, it was never born, and it would never perish; and when called by the spiritual needs of the Bodhisattvas, it will cast off the garb of absoluteness and preach in the form of a Sambhogakâya "never-ceasing sermons which run like a stream for ever and aye." It will be evident from this that Buddhists are ready to consider all religious or moral leaders of mankind, whatever their nationality, as the Body of Transformation of the Dharmakâya. Translated into Christian thoughts, God reveals himself in every being that is worthy of him. He reveals himself not only at a certain

elsewhere noted, this doctrine is sometimes known as the theory of Upâya. Upâya is very difficult term to translate into English; it literally means "way," "method," or "strategy." For fuller interpretation see p. 298, footnote.

period in history, but everywhere and all the time. His glory is perceived throughout all the stages of human culture. This manifestation, from the very nature of God, cannot be intermittent and sporadic as is imagined by some "orthodox Christians." The following from St. Paul's first Epistle to the Corinthians Chap. XII), when read in this connection, sounds almost like a Buddhist philosopher's utterance: "Now there are diversities of gifts, but the same Spirit. And there are diversities of administrations, but the same Lord. And there are diversities of operations, but it is the same God which worketh all in all. But the manifestation of the Spirit is given to every man to profit withal For to one is given by the Spirit the word of wisdom; to another the word of knowledge by the same Spirit; to another faith by the same Spirit; to another the gifts of healing by the same Spirit; to another the working of miracles; to another prophecy; to another divers kinds of tongues; to another the interpretation of tongues; but all these worketh that one and the selfsame Spirit, dividing to every man severally as he will. For as the body is one and hath many members, and all the members of that one body, being many, are one body: so also is Christ. For by one Spirit are we all baptised into one body, whether we be Jews or Gentiles, whether we be bond or free; and have been all made to drink into one Spirit."

The Sambhogakâya.

One peculiar point in the doctrine of Trikâya, which modern minds find rather difficult to comprehend, is the conception of the Sambhogakâya, or the Body of Bliss. We can understand the relation between the Dharmakâya and Nirmânakâya, the latter being similar to the notion of God incarnate or to that of Avatara. Inasmuch as the Dharmakâya does not exist outside the triple world but in it as the raison d'être of its existence, all beings must be considered a partial manifestation of it; and in this sense Buddhists sometimes call themselves Bodhisattvas, that is, beings of intelligence, because intelligence (*Bodhi*) is the psychological aspect of the Dharmakâya as realised in sentient beings. But the conception of Sambhogakâya is altogether too mysterious to be fathomed by a limited consciousness. The fact becomes more apparent when we are told that the Sambhogakâya, Body of Bliss, is a corporeal existence and at the same time filling the universe and that there are two forms of the Body of Bliss, one for self-enjoyment and the other as a sort of religious object for the Bodhisattvas.

That the Body of Bliss is corporeal and yet infinite has already been shown by the quotations from the *Suvarna Prabhâ* and Açvaghoṣa on the preceding pages. For further confirmation of this point no less authority than Asanga and Vasubandhu will be here refered to.

In *A Comprehensive Treatise on the Mahâyana* and

in its commentary, the author Asanga and the commentator Vasubandhu endeavor to prove why the Body of Bliss cannot be the raison d'être of the Dharmakâya, instead of vice versa; and in this connection they argue that (1) the Body of Bliss consists of the five Skandhas, that is, of material form (*rûpa*), sensation (*vedanâ*), ideas (*samjñâ*), deeds (*sanskâra*), and consciousness (*vijñâna*); (2) it is subject to particularisation; (3) it reveals different virtues and characters according to the desires of Bodhisattvas; (4) even to the same individual it appears differently at different times; (5) when it manifests itself simultaneously before an assemblage of Bodhisattvas of divers characters and qualifications, it at once assumes divers forms, in order to satisfy their infinitely diversified inclinations; (6) it is a creation of the Âlayavijñâna, All-conserving Mind.

These six peculiarities of the Body of Bliss as enumerated by Asanga and Vasubandhu make it indeed entirely dependent on the Dharmakâya, but they do not place us in any better position to penetrate into the deep mystery of its nature. Its supernatural incomprehensibility remains the same forever. In a certain sense, however, the Body of Bliss may be considered to be corresponding to the Christian idea of an angel. Supernaturalness and luminosity are the two characters possessed by both, but angels are merely messengers of God communicating the latter's will to human beings. When they reveal themselves to a specially favored person, it is not of their own account. When they speak to him at all, it is by the name of the being who sent them. They do not represent him, they do not act his own will by themselves. On the contrary, the Body of Bliss is the master of its own. It is an expression of the Dharmakâya. It instructs and benefits all the creatures who come to it. It acts according to its own will and judgment. In these respects the Body of Bliss is altogether different from the Christian conception of angels. But will it be more appropriately compared to Christ in glory?

Let us make another quotation from later authorities than Asanga and his brother Vasubandhu, and let us see more convincingly what complicated notions are involved in the idea of the Body of Bliss. According to the commentators on Vasubandhu's *Vijñânamâtra Çâstra* (a treatise on the Yoga philosophy),[1] the Body of Bliss has two distinct aspects: (1) The body obtained by the Tathâgata for his self-enjoyment, by dint of his religious discipline through eons; (2) The body which the Tathâgata manifests to the

[1] This is one of the most important philosophical works of the Yogacâra school. Vasubandhu wrote the text (Nanjo, No. 1215) which consists only of thirty verses, but there appeared many commentators after the death of the author, who naturally entertained widely different views among themselves on the subject-matter, as it is too tersely treated in the text. Hsüen Tsang made selections out of the ten noted Hindu exegetists in A. D. 659 and translated them into the Chinese language. The compilation consists of ten fascicles and is known as *Discourse on the Ideality of the Universe* (a free rendering of the Chinese title *Chang wei shi lun*, Nanjo, No. 1197).

Bodhisattvas in Pure Land (*sukhâvatî*). This last body is in possession of wonderful spiritual powers, reveals the Wheel of Dharma, resolves all the religious doubts raised by the Bodhisattvas, and lets them enjoy the bliss of the Mahâyâna Dharma.

A Mere Subjective Existence.

Judging from all these characterisations, the most plausible conclusion that suggests itself to modern sceptical minds is that the Sambhogakâya must be a mere creation of an intelligent, finite mind, which is intently bent on reaching the highest reality, but, not being able, on account of its limitations, to grasp the object in its absoluteness, the finite mind fabricates all its ideals after its own fashion into a spiritual-material being, which is logically a contradiction, but religiously an object deserving veneration and worship. And this being is no more than the Body of Bliss. [1] It lies half way between the pure being of Dharmakâya and the earthly form of Nirmânakâya, the Body of Transformation. It does not belong to either, but partakes something of both. It is in a sense spiritual

[1] May I venture to say that the conception of God as entertained by most Christians is a Body of Bliss rather than the Dharmakâya itself? In some respects their God is quite spiritual, but in others he is thought of as a concrete material being like ourselves. It seems to me that the human soul is ever struggling to free itself from this paradox, though without any apparent success, while the masses are not so intellectual and reflective enough as to become aware of this eternal contradiction which is too deeply buried in their minds.

like the Dharmakâya, and yet it cannot go beyond material limitations, for it has a form, definite and determinate. When the human soul is thirsty after a pure being or an absolute which cannot be comprehended in a palpable form, it creates a hybrid, an imitation, or a reflection, and tries to be satisfied with it, just as a little girl has her innate and not yet fully developed maternity satisfied by tenderly embracing and nursing the doll, an inanimate imitation of a real living baby. And the Mahâyânists seem to have made most of this childish humanness. They produced as many sûtras as their spiritual yearnings demanded, quite regardless of historical facts, and made the Body of Bliss of the Tathâgata the author of all these works. For if the Dharmakâya of the Tathâgata never entered into Parinirvâna, why then could he not deliver sermons and cite gâthâs as often as beings of intelligence (Bodhisattvas) felt their needs? The *Suvarna Prabhâ* (fas. 2, chap. 3) again echoes this sentiment as follows:

"To illustrate by analogy, the sun or the moon does not make any conscious discrimination, nor does the water-mirror, nor the light [conceived separate from the body from which it emanates]. But when all these three are brought together, there is produced an image [of the sun or the moon in the water]. So it is with Suchness and Knowledge of Suchness. It is not possessed of any particular consciousness, but by virtue of the Spontaneous Will [inherent in the nature of Suchness, or what is the same thing, in the

Dharmakâya], the Body of Transformation or of Bliss [as a shadow of the Dharmakâya] reveals itself in response to the spiritual needs of sentient beings.

"And, again, as the water-mirror boundlessly expanding reflects in all different ways the images of âkâsa (void space) through the medium of light, while space itself is void of all particular marks, so the Dharmakâya reflects its images severally in the receiving minds of believers, and this by virtue of Spontaneous Will. The Will creates the Body of Transformation as well as the Body of Bliss in all their possible aspects, while the original, the Dharmakâya, does not suffer one whit a change on this account."

According to this, it is evident that whenever our spiritual needs become sufficiently intense there is a response from the Dharmakâya, and that this response is not always uniform as the recipient minds show different degrees of development, intellectually and spiritually. If we call this communion between sentient souls and the Dharmakâya an inspiration, all the phenomena that flow out of fulness of heart and reflect purity of soul should be called "works of inspiration"; and in this sense the Mahâyânists consider their scriptures as emanating directly from the fountainhead of the Dharmakâya.

Attitude of Modern Mahāyânists.

Modern Mahâyânists in full accordance with this interpretation of the Doctrine of Trikâya do not place much importance on the objective aspects of the Body of Bliss (*Sambhogakâya*). They consider them at best the fictitious products of an imaginative mind; they never tarry a moment to think that all these mysterious Tathâgatas or Bodhisattvas who are sometimes too extravagantly and generally too tediously described in the Mahâyâna texts are objective realities, that the Sukhâvatîs or Pure Lands [1] are decorated with such worldly stuff as gold, silver, emerald, cat's eye, pearl, and other precious stones, that pious Buddhists would be transfered after their death to these ostentatiously ornamented heavens, be seated on the pedestals of lotus-flowers, surrounded by innumerable Bodhisattvas and Buddhas, and would enjoy all the spiritual enjoyments that human mind can conceive. On the contrary, modern Buddhists look with disdain on these egotistic materialistic conceptions of religious life. For, to a fully enlightened soul, of what use could those worldly trea-

[1] The reader must not think that there is but one Pure Land which is elaborately described in the *Sukhâvatî Vyûha Sûtra* as the abode of the Tathâgata Amitâbha, situated innumerable leagues away in the West. On the contrary, the Mahâyâna texts admit the existence of as innumerable pure lands as there are Tathâgatas and Bodhisattvas, and every single one of these holy regions has no boundary and is coexistent with the universe, and, therefore, their spheres necessarily intercrossing and overlapping one another. It would look to every intelligent mind that those innumerable Buddha-countries existing in such a mysterious and incomprehensible manner cannot be anything else than our own subjective creation.

sures be? What happiness, earthly or heavenly, does such a soul dream of, outside the bliss of embracing the will of the Dharmakâya as his own?

Recapitulation.

To sum up, the Buddha in the Pâli scriptures was a human being, though occasionally he is credited to have achieved things supernatural and superhuman. His historical career began with the abandonment of a royal life, then the wandering in the wilderness, and a long earnest meditation on the great problems of birth-and-death, and his final enlightenment under the Bodhi tree, then his fifty years' religious peregrination along the valleys of the Ganges, and the establishment of a religious system known as Buddhism, and finally his eternal entrance into the "Parinirvâna that leaves nothing behind" (*anupadhiçeṣanirvâna*). And as far as plain historical facts are concerned, these seem to exhaust the life of Çâkyamuni on earth. But the deep reverence which was felt by his disciples could not be satisfied with this prosaic humanness of their master and made him something more than a mortal soul. So even the Pâli tradition gives him a supramundane life besides the earthly one. He is supposed to have been a Bodhisattva in the Tuṣita heaven before his entrance into the womb of Mâyâdevî. The honor of Bodhisattvahood was acceded to him on account of his deeds of self-sacrifice which were praised throughout his innumerable past incarnations. While he was walking among us in the flesh, he was glorified with the thirty-two major and eighty minor excellent characteristics of a great man. [1] But he was not the first Buddha that walked on earth to teach the Dharma, for there were already seven Buddhas before him, nor was he the last one that would appear among us, for

[1] For a description of these marks see the *Dharmasangraha*, pp. 53 ff. A process of mystifying or deifying the person of Buddha seems to have been going on immediately after the death of the Master; and the Mahâyânistic conception of Nirmânakâya and Sambhogakâya is merely the consummation of this process. Southern Buddhists who are sometimes supposed to represent a more "primitive" form of Buddhism describe just as much as Mahâyânism the thirty-two major and eighty minor exellent physical marks of a great man as having been possessed by Çâkyamuni, (for instance, see the *Milindapañha*, *S.B.E.* Vol. XXXV. p. 116). But any person with common sense will at once see the absurdity of representing any human being with those physical peculiarities. And this seems to have inspired more rational Mahâyânists to abandon the traditional way of portraying the human Buddha with those mysterious signs. They transfered them through the doctrine of Trikâya to the characterisation of the Sambhogakâya Buddha, that is, to the Buddha enjoying in a celestial abode the fruit of his virtuous earthly life. The Buddha who walked in the flesh as the son of King Suddhodana was, however, no more than an ordinary human being like ourselves, because he appeared to us in a form of Nirmânakâya, i. e. as a Body of Transformation, devoid of any such physical peculiarities known as thirty-two or eighty lakṣanas. Southern Buddhists, so called, seem, however, to have overlooked the ridiculousness of attributing these fantastic signs to the human Buddha; and this fact explains that as soon as the memory of the personal disciples of Buddha about his person vanished among the later followers, intense speculation and resourceful imagination were constantly exercised until the divers schools settled the question each in its own way.

a Bodhisattva by the name of Maitreya is now in heaven and making preparations for the attainment of Buddhahood in time to come. But here stopped the Pâli writers, they did not venture to make any further speculation on the nature of Buddhahood. Their religious yearnings did not spur them to a higher flight of the imagination. They recited simple sûtras or gâthâs, observed the çîlas (moral precepts) as strictly and literally as they could, and thought the spirit of their Master still alive in these instructions; — let alone the personality of the Tathâgata.

But there was at the same time another group of the disciples of the Buddha, whose religious and intellectual inclinations were not of the same type as their fellow-believers; and on that account a simple faith in the Buddha as present in his teachings did not quite satisfy them. They perhaps reasoned in this fashion: "If there were seven Buddhas before the advent of the Great Muni of Çakya and there would be one more who is to come, where, let us ask, did they derive their authority and knowledge to preach? How is it that there cannot be any more Buddhas, that they do not come to us much oftener? If they were human beings like ourselves, why not we ourselves be Buddhas?" These questions, when logically carried out, naturally led them to the theory of Dharmakâya, that all the past Buddhas, and those to come, and even we ordinary mortals made of clay and doomed to die soon, owe the raison d'être of their existence to the Dharmakâya, which alone is immortal in us as well as in Buddhas The first religious effort we have to make is, therefore, to recognise this archetype of all Buddhas and all beings. But the Dharmakâya as such is too abstract for the average mind to become the object of its religious consciousness; so they personified or rather materialised it. In other words, they idealised Çâkyamuni, endowed him not only with the physical signs (*lakṣas*) of greatness as in the Pâli scriptures, but with those of celestial transfiguration, and called him a Body of Bliss of the Tathâgata; while the historical human Buddha was called a Body of Transformation and all sentient beings Bodhisattvas, that is, beings of intelligence destined to become Buddhas.

This idealised Buddha, or, what is the same thing, a personified Dharmakâya, according to the Mahâyâna Buddhists, not only revealed himself in the particular person of Siddhârtha Gautama in Central Asia a few thousand years ago, but is revealing himself in all times and all places. There is no specially favored spot on the earth where only the Buddha makes his appearance; from the zenith of Akaniṣta heaven down to the bottom of Nâraka, he is manifesting uninterruptedly and unintermittently and is working out his ideas, of which, however, our limited understanding is unable to have an adequate knowledge. The *Avatamsaka Sûtra* (Buddhabhadra's translation, fas. 45, chap. 34) describes how the Buddha works out his scheme of salvation in all possible ways. (See also the *Saddharma pundarîka*, Kern's translation, chap. 2, p. 30 et seq., and also pp. 413-411.)

"In this wise the Buddha teaches and delivers all sentient beings through his religious teachings whose number is innumerable as atoms. He may reveal sometimes in the world of devas, sometimes in that of Nâgas, Yakṣas, Gandharvas, Asuras, Garudas, Kinnaras, Mahoragas, etc., sometimes in the world of Brahmans, sometimes in the world of human beings, sometimes in the palace of Yâmarâja (king of death), sometimes in the underworld of damned spirits, ghosts, and beasts. His all-swaying compassion, intelligence, and will would not rest until all beings had been brought under his shelter through all possible means of salvation. He may achieve his work of redemption sometimes by means of his name, sometimes by means of memory, sometimes of voice, sometimes of perfect illumination, sometimes of the net of illumination. Whenever and wherever conditions are ripe for his appearance, he would never fail to present himself before sentient beings and also to manifest views of grandeur and splendor.

"The Buddha does not depart from his own region, he does not depart from his seat in the tower; yet he reveals himself in all the ten quarters of the globe. He would sometimes emanate from his own body the clouds of Nirmânakâyas, or sometimes reveal himself in an undivided personality, and itinerating in all quarters would teach and deliver all sentient beings. He may assume sometimes the form of a Çrâvaka, sometimes that of a Brahmadeva, sometimes that of an ascetic, sometimes that of a good physician, sometimes that of a tradesman, sometimes that of a Bhikṣu [or honest worker], sometimes that of an artist, sometimes that of a deva. Again, he may reveal himself sometimes in all the forms of art and industry, sometimes in all the places of congregation, such as towns, cities, villages, etc. And whatever his subjects for salvation may be, and whatever his surroundings, he will accommodate himself to all possible conditions and achieve his work of enlightenment and salvation" [1] ....

The practical sequence of this doctrine of Trikâya is apparent; it has ever more broadened the spirit of tolerance in Buddhists. As the Dharmakâya universally responds to the spiritual needs of all sentient beings in all times and in all places and at any stage of their spiritual development, Buddhists consider all spiritual leaders, whatever their nationality and personality, as the expressions of the one omnipotent Dharmakâya. And as the Dharmakâya always manifests itself for the best interests of sentient creatures, even those doctrines and their authors that are apparently against the teachings of Buddhism are tolerated through the conviction that they are all moving according to the Spontaneous Will that pervades everywhere and works all the time. Though, superficially, they may appear as evils, their central and final aim is goodness and harmony which are destined by the Will of the Dharmakâya to overcome this world of tribulations and

[1] Cf. I Cor. xi. 19 et seq.

contradictions. The general intellectual tendency of Buddhism has done a great deal towards cultivating a tolerant spirit in its believers, and we must say that the doctrine of Trinity which appears sometimes too radical in its pantheistic spirit has contributed much to this cause.

CHAPTER XI.

THE BODHISATTVA.

NEXT to the conception of Buddha, what is important in Mahâyâna Buddhism is that of Bodhisattva (intelligence-being) and of that which constitutes its essence, Bodhicitta, intelligence-heart. As stated above, the followers of Mahâyânism do not call themselves Çrâvakas or Pratyekabuddhas or Arhats as do those of Hînayânism; but they distinguish themselves by the title of Bodhisattva. What this means will be the subject-matter of this chapter.

Let us begin with a quotation from the *Saddharma-pundarîka Sûtra*, in which a well-defined distinction between the Çrâvakas and the Pratyekabuddhas and the Bodhisattvas is given.[1]

The Three Yânas.

"Now, Çâriputra, the beings who have become wise, have faith in the Tathâgata, the father of the world, and consequently apply themselves to his commandments.

"Amongst them there are some who, wishing to follow the dictate of an authoritative voice, apply themselves to the commandment of the Tathâgata to

[1] Kern's English translation (*S.B.E.* Vol. XXI), Chap. III, p. 80.

acquire the knowledge of the Four Great Truths, for the sake of their own complete Nirvana. These, one may say, to be those who, seeking the vehicle of the Çrâvaka, fly from the triple world.....

"Other beings desirous of the unconditioned knowledge, of self-restraint and tranquillity, apply themselves to the commandment of the Tathâgata to learn to understand the Twelve Chains of Dependence, for the sake of their own complete Nirvana. These, one may say, to be those who, seeking the vehicle of the Pratyekabuddha, fly from the triple world.....

"Other beings again desirous of omniscience, Buddha-knowledge, absolute knowledge, unconditioned knowledge, apply themselves to the commandment of the Tathâgata and to learn to understand the knowledge, powers, and conviction of the Tathâgata, for the sake of the common weal and happiness, out of compassion to the world, for the benefit, weal and happiness of the world at large, of both gods and men, for the sake of the complete Nirvana of all beings. These, one may say, to be those who seeking the Great Vehicle (*Mahâyâna*) fly from the triple world. Therefore, they are called Bodhisattva-mahâsattvas.".....

This characterisation of the Bodhisattvas as distinct from the Çrâvakas and Pratyekabuddhas constitutes one of the most significant features of Mahâyâna Buddhism. Here the Bodhisattva does not exert himself in religious discipline for the sake of his own weal, but for the sake of the spiritual benefit of all his fellow-creatures. If he will, he could, like the Çrâvakas and Pratyekabuddhas, enter into eternal Nirvana that never slides back; he could enjoy the celestial bliss of undisturbed tranquillity in which all our worldly tribulations are forever buried; he could seclude himself from the hurly-burly of the world, and, sitting cross-legged in a lonely cave, quietly contemplate on the evanescence of human interests and the frivolity of earthly affairs, and then self-contentedly await the time of final absorption into the absolute All, as streams and rivers finally run into one great ocean and become of one taste. But, in spite of all these self-sufficient blessings, the Bodhisattva would not seek his own ease, but he would mingle himself in the turmoil of worldly life and devote all his energy to the salvation of the masses of people, who, on account of their ignorance and infatuation, are forever transmigrating in the triple world, without making any progress towards the final goal of humanity.

Along this Bodhisattvaic devotion, however, there was another current of religious thought and practice running among the followers of Buddha. By this I mean the attitude of the Çrâvakas and the Pratyekabuddhas. Both of them sought peace of mind in asceticism and cold philosophical speculation. Both of them were intently inclined to gain Nirvana which may be likened unto an extinguished fire. It was not theirs to think of the common weal of all beings, and, therefore, when they attained their own redemption from earthly sins and passions, their religious discipline was completed, and no further attempt was made by them to extend the bliss of their personal enlightenment to their fellow-creatures.[1] They recoiled from mingling themselves among vulgar people lest their holy life should get contaminated. They did not have confidence enough in their own power to help the masses to break the iron yoke of ignorance and misery. Moreover, everybody was supposed to exert himself for his own emancipation, however unbearable his pain was for others could not do anything to alleviate it. Sympathy was of no avail; because the reward of his own karma good or evil could be suffered by himself alone, nor could it be avoidable even by the doer himself. Things done were done

[1] It should be noted here that the idea of universal salvation was lacking altogether in the followers of Hînayânism. But what distinguished it so markedly from Mahâyânism is that the former did not extend the idea wide enough, but confined it to Buddhahood only. Buddha attained omniscience in order that he might deliver the world, but we, ordinary mortals, are too ignorant and too helpless to aspire for Buddhahood; let us be contented with paying homage to Buddha and faithfully observing his precepts as laid down by him for our spiritual edification. Our knowledge and energy are too limited to cope with such a gigantic task as to achieve a universal salvation of mankind; let a Buddha or Bodhisattva attempt it while we may rest with a profound confidence in him and in his work. Thoughts somewhat like these must have been going about in the minds of the Hînayânists, when their Mahâyâna brethren were making bold to strive after Buddhahood themselves. The difference between the two schools of Buddhism, when most concisely expressed, is this: While one has a most submissive confidence in the Buddha, the other endeavors to follow his example by placing himself in his position. The following quotation ("the Story of Sumedha,"

once for all, and their karma made an indelible mark on the pages of his destiny. Even Buddha who was supposed to have attained that exalted position by practising innumerable pious deeds in all his former lives, could not escape the fruit of evil karma which was quite unwittingly commited by him. This iron arm of karma seizes everybody in person and does not allow any substitute whatever. Those who wish to give a halt to the working of karma could do so only by applying a counter-force to it, and this with no other hand than his own. The Mahâyânist conception of Bodhisattvahood may be considered an effort somewhat to mitigate this ruthless mechanical rigidity of the law of karma.

a Jâtaka tale, from Warren's *Buddhism*, p. 14) in which Sumedha, one of the Buddha's former incarnations, expresses his resolve to be a Buddha, may just as well be considered as that of a Mahâyânist himself, while the Hînayânists would not dare to make this wish their own:

"Or why should I, valorous man,
The ocean seek to cross alone?
Omniscience first will I achieve,
And men and gods convey across.

"Since now I make this earnest wish,
In presence of this Best of Men,
Omniscience sometime I'll achieve,
And multitude convey across.

"I'll rebirth' circling stream arrest,
Destroy existence's three modes;
I'll climb the sides of Doctrine's ship,
And men and gods convey across."

Strict Individualism.

The Buddhism of the Çrâvakas and the Pratyeka-buddhas is the most unscrupulous application to our ethico-religious life of the individualistic theory of karma. All things done are done by oneself; all things left undone are left undone by oneself. They would say: "Your salvation is exclusively your own business, and whatever sympathy I may have is of no avail. All that I can do toward helping you is to let you see intellectually the way to emancipation. If you do not follow it, you have but to suffer the fruition of your folly. I am helpless with all my enlightenment, even with my Nirvana, to emancipate you from the misery of perpetual metempsychosis." But with the Buddhism of the Mahâyâna Bodhisattvas the case is entirely different. It is all-sympathy, it is all-compassion, it is all-love. A Bodhisattva would not seclude himself into the absolute tranquillity of Nirvana, simply because he wishes to emancipate his fellow-creatures also from the bondage of ignorance and infatuation. Whatever rewards he may get for his self-enjoyment as the karma of his virtuous deeds, he would turn them over (*parivarta*) towards the uplifting of the suffering masses. And this self-sacrifice, this unselfish devotion to the welfare of his fellow-beings constitutes the essence of Bodhisattvahood. The ideal Bodhisattva, therefore, is thought to be no more than an incarnation of Intelligence and Love, of Prajñâ and Karunâ.

The irrefragability of karma seems to be satisfactory

from the intellectual and individualistic standpoint, for the intellect demands a thorough application of logic, and individualism does not allow the transfering of responsibility from one person to another. From this viewpoint, therefore, a rigorous enforcement as demanded by Hînayânism of the principle of self-emancipation does not show any logical fault; divine grace must be suspended as the curse of karma produced by ignorance tenaciously clings to our soul. But when viewed from the religious side of the question, this inflexibility of karma is more than poor mortals can endure. They want something more elastic and pliable that yields to the supplication of the feeling. When individuals are considered nothing but isolated, disconnected atoms, between which there is no unifying bond which is the feeling, they are too weak to resist and overcome the ever-threatening force of evil, whose reality as long as a world of particulars exists cannot be contradicted. This religious necessity felt in our inmost consciousness may explain the reason why Mahâyâna Buddhism proposed the doctrine of parivarta (turning over) founded on the oneness of Dharmakâyâ.

The Doctrine of Parivarta.

The doctrine of turning over (*parivarta*) of one's own merits to others is a great departure from that which seems to have been the teaching of "primitive Buddhism." In fact, it is more than a departure, it is even in opposition to the latter in some measure. Because while individualism is a predominant feature in the religious practice of the Çrâvakas and the Pratyekabuddhas, universalism or supra-individualism, if I am allowed to use these terms, is the principle advocated by the Bodhisattvas. The latter believe that all beings, being a manifestation of the Dharmakâya, are in their essence of one nature; that individual existences are real so far as subjective ignorance is concerned; and that virtues and merits issuing directly from the Dharmakâya which is intelligence and love, cannot fail to produce universal benefit and to effect final emancipation of all beings. Thus, the religion of the Bodhisattvas proposes to achieve what was thought impossible by the Çrâvakas and the Pratyekabuddhas, that is, the turning over of one's own merits to the service of others

It is in this spirit that the Bodhisattvas conceive the seriousness of the significance of life; it is in this spirit that, pondering over the reason of their existence on earth, they come to the following view of life:

"All ignorant beings are daily and nightly performing evil deeds in innumerable ways; and, on this account, their suffering beggars description. They do not recognise the Tathâgata, do not listen to his teachings, do not pay homage to the congregation of holy men. And this evil karma will surely bring them a heavy crop of misery. This reflection fills the heart of a Bodhisattva with gloomy feelings, which in turn gives rise to the immovable resolution, that he himself will carry all the burdens for ignorant beings and help them to reach the final goal of Nirvana. Inestimably heavy as these burdens are, he will not swerve nor yield under their weight. He will not rest until all ignorant beings are freed from the entangling meshes of desire and sin, until they are uplifted above the darkening veil of ignorance and infatuation; and this his marvelous spiritual energy defies the narrow limitations of time and space, and will extend even to eternity when the whole system of worlds comes to a conclusion. Therefore, all the innumerable meritorious deeds practised by the Bodhisattvas are dedicated to the emancipation of ignorant beings.

"The Bodhisattvas do not feel, however, that they are being compelled by any external force to devote their lives to the edification and uplifting of the masses. They do not recognise any outward authority, the violation of which may react upon them in the form of a punishment. They have already passed beyond this stage of world-conception which implies a dualism; they are on the contrary moving in a much wider and higher sphere of thought. All that is done by them springs from their spontaneous will, from the free activity of the Bodhicitta, which constitutes their reason of existence; and thus there is nothing compulsory in their thoughts and movements. [To use Laotzean terminology, they are practising non-action, *wu wei*, and whatever may appear to the ignorant and unenlightened as a strenuous and restless life, is merely a natural overflow from the inexhaustible fount of energy called Bodhicitta, heart of intelligence!"[1]

Bodhisattva in "Primitive" Buddhism.

The notion of Bodhisattva was not entirely absent in "primitive" Buddhism, only it did not have such a wide signification. All Buddhas were Bodhisattvas in their former lives. The Jâtaka stories minutely describe what self-sacrificing deeds were done by them and how by the karma of these merits they finally attained Buddhahood. Çâkyamuni was not the only Buddha, but there had already been seven or twenty-four Buddhas prior to him, and the coming Buddha to be known as Maitreya is believed to be disciplining himself in the Tuṣita heaven and going through the stages of Bodhisattvahood. The one who is thus destined to be the future Buddha must be extraordinarily gifted in spiritual energy. He must pass through eons of self-discipline, must practise deeds of non-atman with unflinching courage and fortitude through innumerable existences.

The following quotation from the Jâtaka tales will be sufficient to see what ponderous and exacting conditions were conceived by the so-called Hînayânists to be necessary for a human being to become a fully qualified Buddha.[2]

[1] This is a very rough summary of the doctrine that is known as Parivarta and expounded in the *Avatamsaka Sûtra*, fas. 21-22 where ten forms of Parivarta are distinguished and explained at length.

[2] Warren's *Buddhism in Translations*, the "Story of Sumedha," pp. 14—15.

"Of men it is he, and only he, who is in a fit condition by the attainment of saintship in that same existence, that can successfully make a wish to be a Buddha. Of those in a fit condition it is only he who makes the wish in the presence of a living Buddha that succeeds in his wish; after the death of a Buddha a wish made at a relic shrine, or at the foot of a Bo-tree, will not be successful. Of those who make the wish in the presence of a Buddha it is he and only he who has retired from the world that can successfully make the wish, and not one who is a layman. Of those who have retired from the world it is only he who is possessed of the Five High Powers and is master of the Eight Attainments that can successfully make the wish, and no one can do so who is lacking in these excellences. Of those, even, who possess these excellences, it is he, and only he, who has such firm resolve that he is ready to sacrifice his life for the Buddhas that can successfully make the wish, but no other. Of those who possess this resolve it is he, and only he, who has great zeal, determination, strenuousness, and endeavor in striving for the qualities that make a Buddha that is successful. The following comparisons will show the intensity of the zeal. If he is such a one as to think: "The man who, it all within the rim of the world were to become water, would be ready to swim across it with his own arms and get further shore,—he is the one to attain the Buddhaship: or, in case all within the rim of the world were to become a jungle of bamboo, would be ready to elbow and trample his way through it and get to the further side,—he is the one to attain the Buddhaship; or, in case all within the rim of the world were to become a *terra firma* of thick-set javelins, would be ready to tread on them and go afoot to the further side,—he is the one to attain the Buddhaship; or, in case all within the rim of the world were to become live coals, would be ready to tread on them and so get to the further side,—he is the one to attain the Buddhaship,'—if he deems not even one of these feats too hard for himself but has such great zeal, determination, strenuousness, and power of endeavor that he would perform these feats in order to attain the Buddhaship, then, but not otherwise, will his wish succeed."

From this it is apparent that everybody could not become a Buddha in "primitive" Buddhism; the highest aspiration that could be cherished by him was to believe in the teachings of Buddha, to follow the precepts laid down by him, and to attain at most to Arhatship. The idea of Arhatship, however, was considered by Mahâyânists cold, impassionate, and hard-hearted, for the saint calmly reviews the sight of the suffering masses; and therefore Arhatship was altogether unsatisfactory to be the object for the Bodhisattvas of their high religious aspirations.

The Mahâyânists wanted to go even beyond the attainment of Arhatship, however exalted its spirituality may be. They wanted to make every humble soul a being like Çâkyamuni, they wanted lavishly to distribute the bliss of enlightenment; they wanted to remove all the barriers that were supposed to lie between Buddhahood and the common humanity. But how could they do this when the iron hands of karma held tight the fate of each individual! How was it possible for him to identify his being with the ideal of mankind? Perhaps this serious problem could not very well be solved by Buddhists, when their memory of the majestic personality of Çâkyamuni was still vivid before their mental eyes. It was probably no easy task for them to overcome the feeling of awe and reverence which was so deeply engraved in their hearts, and to raise themselves to such a height as reached by their Master, even ideally. This was certainly an act of sacrilege. But, as time advances, the personal recollection of the Master would naturally wane and would not play so much influence as their own religious consciousness which is ever fresh and active. Generally speaking, all great historical characters that command the reverence and awe of posterity do so only when their words or acts or both unravel the deepest secrets of the human heart. And this feeling of awe and reverence and even of worship is not due so much to the great characters themselves as to the worshiper's own religious consciousness. History passes, but the heart persists. An individual called Çâkyamuni may be forgotten in the course of time, but the sacred chord in the inmost heart struck by him reverberates through eternity. So with the Mahâyâna Buddhists, the religious sentiment at last asserted itself in spite of the personal recollection and reverential feeling for the Master. And perhaps in the following way was the reasoning then advanced by them relative to the great problem of Buddhahood.

We are all Bodhisattvas.

As Çâkyamuni was a Bodhisattva in his former lives destined to become a Buddha, so we are all Bodhisattvas and even Buddhas in a certain sense, when we understand that all sentient beings, the Buddha not excepted, are one in the Dharmakâya. The Dharmakâya manifests in us as Bodhi which is the essence of Buddhas as well as of Bodhisattvas. This Bodhi can suffer no change whatever in quantity even when the Bodhisattva attains finally to the highest human perfection as Çâkyamuni Buddha. In this spirit, therefore, the Buddha exclaimed when he obtained enlightenment, "It is marvelous indeed that all beings animate and inanimate universally partake of the nature of Tathâgatahood." The only difference between a Buddha and the ignorant masses is that the latter do not make manifest in them the glory of Bodhi.

They only are not Bodhisattvas who, enveloped in the divine rays of light in a celestial abode, philosophically review the world of tribulations. Even we mortals made of dust are Bodhisattvas, incarnates of the Bodhi, capable of being united in the all-embracing love of the Dharmakâya and also of obliterating the individual curse of karma in the eternal and absolute intelligence of the Dharmakâya. As soon as we come to live in this love and intelligence, individual existences are no hindrance to the turning over (*parivarta*) of one's spiritual merits (*punya*) to the service of others. Let us only have an insight into the spirituality of our existence and we are all Bodhisattvas and Buddhas. Let us abandon the selfish thought of entering into Nirvana that is conceived to extinguish the fire of heart and leave only the cold ashes of intellect. Let us have sympathy for all suffering beings and turn over all our merits, however small, to their benefit and happiness. For in this way we are all made the Bodhisattvas.[1]

The Buddha's Life.

This spirit of universal love prevails in all Mahâyâna literature, and the Bodhisattvas are everywhere represented as exercising it with utmost energy. The Mahâyânists, therefore, could not rest satisfied with a simple, prosaic, and earthly account of Çâkyamuni,

[1] It may be interesting to Christian readers to note in this connection that modern Buddhists do not reject altogether the idea of vicarious atonement, for their religious conviction as seen here admits the parivarta of a Bodhisattva's merits to the spiritual welfare of his fellow-creatures. But they will object to the Christian interpretation that Jesus was sent down on earth by his heavenly father for the special mission to atone for the original sin through the shedding of his innocent blood, for this is altogether too puerile and materialistic.

they wanted to make it as ideal and poetic as possible, illustrating the gospel of love, as was conceived by them, in every phase of the life of the Buddha.

The Mahâyânists first placed the Buddha in the Tuṣita heaven before his birth, (as was done by the Hînayânists,) made him feel pity for the distressed world below, made him resolve to deliver it from "the ocean of misery which throws up sickness as its foam, tossing with the waves of old age, and rushing with the dreadful onflow of death," and after his Parinirvana, they made him abide forever on the peak of the Mount Vulture delivering the sermon of immortality to a great assemblage of spiritual beings. In this wise, they explained the significance of the appearance of Çâkyamuni on earth, which was nothing but a practical demonstration of the "Great Loving Heart" (*mahâkarunâcitta*).

The Bodhisattva and Love.

Nâgârjuna in his work on the *Bodhicitta*[1] elucidates the Mahâyânist notion of Bodhisattvahood as follows:

"Thus the essential nature of all Bodhisattvas is a great loving heart (*mahâkarunâcitta*), and all sentient beings constitute the object of its love. Therefore, all the Bodhisattvas do not cling to the blissful taste

[1] The full title of the work is *A Treatise on the Transcendentality of Bodhicitta* (Nanjo, No. 1304). It is a little book consisting of seven or eight sheets in big Chinese type. It was translated into Chinese by Dânapâla (Shih Hu) during the tenth century of the Christian Era.

that is produced by the divers modes of mental tranquilisation (*dhyâna*), do not covet the fruit of their meritorious deeds, which may heighten their own happiness.

"Their spiritual state is higher than that of the Çrâvakas, for they do not leave all sentient beings behind them [as the Çrâvakas do]. They practise altruism, they seek the fruit of Buddha-knowledge [instead of Çrâvaka-knowledge].

"With a great loving heart they look upon the sufferings of all beings, who are diversely tortured in Avici Hell in consequence of their sins — a hell whose limits are infinite and where an endless round of misery is made possible on account of all sorts of karma [committed by sentient creatures]. The Bodhisattvas filled with pity and love desire to suffer themselves for the sake of those miserable beings.

"But they are well acquainted with the truth that all those diverse sufferings causing diverse states of misery are in one sense apparitional and unreal, while in another sense they are not so. They know also that those who have an intellectual insight into the emptiness (*çûnyatâ*) of all existences, thoroughly understand why those rewards of karma are brought forth in such and such ways [through ignorance and infatuation].

"Therefore, all Bodhisattvas, in order to emancipate sentient beings from misery, are inspired with great spiritual energy and mingle themselves in the filth of birth and death. Though thus they make themselves subject to the laws of birth and death, their hearts are free from sins and attachments. They are like unto those immaculate, undefiled lotus-flowers which grow out of mire, yet are not contaminated by it.

"Their great hearts of sympathy which constitute the essence of their being never leave suffering creatures behind [in their journey towards enlightenment]. Their spiritual insight is in the emptiness (*çûnyatâ*) of things, but [their work of salvation] is never outside the world of sins and sufferings."

The Meaning of Bodhi and Bodhicitta.

What is the meaning of the word "Bodhisattva"? It is a Sanskrit term consisting of two words, "Bodhi," and "sattva." *Bodhi* which comes from the root *budh* meaning "to wake," is generally rendered "knowledge" or "intelligence." *Sattva* (*sat-tva*) literally means "state of being"; thus "existence," "creature," or "that which is," being its English equivalent. "Bodhisattva" as one word means "a being of intelligence," or "a being whose essence is intelligence." Why the Mahâyânists came to adopt this word in contradistinction to Çrâvaka is easily understood, when we see what special significance they attached to the conception of Bodhi in their philosophy. When Bodhi was used by the Çrâvakas in the simple sense of knowledge, it did not bear any particular import. But as soon as it came to express some metaphysical relation to the conception of Dharmakâya, it ceased to be used in its generally accepted sense.

Bodhi, according to the Mahâyânists, is an expression of the Dharmakâya in the human consciousness. Philosophically speaking, Suchness or Bhûtatathâtâ is an ontological term, and Dharmakâya or Tathâgata or Buddha bears a religious significance; while all these three, Bodhi, Bhûtatathâtâ, and Dharmakâya, and their synonyms are nothing but different aspects of one and the same reality refracting through the several defective lenses of a finite intellect.

Bodhi, though essentially an epistemological term, assumes a psychological sense when it is used in conjunction with citta, i.e. heart or soul. Bodhicitta, or Bodhihṛdaya which means the same thing, is more generally used than Bodhi singly in the Mahâyâna texts, especially when its religious import is emphasised above its intellectual one. Bodhicitta, viz. intelligence-heart is a reflex in the human heart of its religious archetype, the Dharmakâya.

Bodhicitta when further amplified is called anuttara-samyak-sambodhicitta, that is, "intelligence-heart that is supreme and most perfect."

It will be easily understood now that what constitutes the essence of the Bodhicitta is the very same thing that makes up the Dharmakâya. For the former is nothing but an expression of the latter, though finitely, fragmentarily, imperfectly realised in us. The citta is an image and the Dharmakâya the prototype, yet one is just as real as the other, only the two must not be conceived dualistically. There is a Dharmakâya, there is a human heart, and the former reflects itself in the latter much after the fashion of the lunar reflection in the water:—to think in this wise is not perfectly correct; because the fundamental teaching of Buddhism is to view all these three conceptions, the Dharmakâya, human heart, and the reflections of the former in the latter, as different forms of one and the same activity.

Love and Karunâ.

The Bodhicitta or Intelligence-heart, therefore, like the Dharmakâya is essentially love and intelligence, or, to use Sanskrit terms, *karunâ* and *prajñâ*. Here some may object to the use of the term "love" for karunâ, perhaps on the ground that karunâ does not exactly correspond to the Christian notion of love, as it savors more of the sense of commiseration. But if we understand by love a sacrifice of the self for the sake of others (and it cannot be more than that), then karunâ can correctly be rendered love, even in the Christian sense. Is not the Bodhisattva willing to abandon his own Nirvanic peace for the interests of suffering creatures? Is he not willing to dedicate the karma of his meritorious deeds performed in his successive existences to the general welfare of his fellow-beings? Is not his one fundamental motive that governs all his activities in life directed towards a universal emancipation of all sentient beings? Is he not perfectly willing to forsake all the thoughts and passions that arise from egoism and to embrace the will of the Dharmakâya? If this be the case, then there is no reason why karunâ should not be rendered by love. Christians say that without love we are become sounding brass or a tinkling cymbal; and Buddhists would declare that without karunâ we are like unto a dead vine hanging over a frozen boulder, or like unto the cold ashes left after a blazing fire.

Some may say, however, that the Buddhist sympathy or commiseration somewhat betrays a sense of passive contemplation of evils. When Christians say that God loves his creatures, the love implies activity and shows God's willingness to do whatever for the actual benefits of his subject-beings. Quite true. Yet when the Buddha is stated to have declared that all sentient beings in the triple world are his own children or that he will not enter into his final Nirvana unless all beings in the three thousand great chiliocosms, not a single soul excepted, are emancipated from the misery of birth and death, his self-sacrificing love must be considered to be all-comprehensive and at the same time full of energy and activity. Whatever objections there may be, we do not see any sufficient reason against speaking of the love-essence of the Dharmakâya and the Bodhicitta.

Nâgârjuna and Sthiramati on the Bodhicitta.

Says Nâgârjuna in his *Discourse on the Transcendentality of the Bodhicitta*: "The Bodhicitta is free from all determinations, that is, it is not included in the categories of the five skandhas, the twelve âyatanas, and the eighteen dhâtus. It is not a particular existence which is palpable. It is non-atmanic, universal. It is uncreate and its self-essence is void [*çûnya*, immaterial, or transcendental].

"One who understands the nature of the Bodhicitta sees everything with a loving heart, for love is the essence of the Bodhicitta.

"The Bodhicitta is the highest essence.

"Therefore, all Bodhisattvas find their raison d'être of existence in this great loving heart.

"The Bodhicitta, abiding in the heart of sameness (*samatâ*) creates individual means of salvation (*upaya*). [1]

[1] Upaya, meaning "expedient," "stratagem," "device," or "craft," has a technical sense in Buddhism. It is used in contrast to intelligence (*prajñâ*) and is synonymous with love (*karunâ*). So, Vimalakîrti says in the sûtra bearing his name (chap. 8, verses 1—4): "Prajñâ is the mother of the Bodhisattva and Upaya his father; there is no leader of humanity who is not born of them.". Intelligence (*prajnâ*) is the one, the universal, representing the principle of sameness (*samatâ*). while Upaya is the many, being the principle of manifoldness (*nânâtvâ*). From the standpoint of pure intelligence, the Bodhisattvas do not see any particular suffering existences, for there is nothing that is not of the Dharmakâya: but when they see the universe from the standpoint of their love-essence, they recognise everywhere the conditions of misery and sin that arise from clinging to the forms of particularity. To remove these, they devise all possible means that are directed towards the attainment of the final aim of existence. There is only one religion, religion of truth, but there are many ways, many means, many upayas, all issuing from the all-embracing love of the Dharmakâya and equally efficient to lead the masses to supreme enlightenment and universal good. Therefore, ontologically speaking, this universe, the Buddhists would say, is nothing but a grand display of Upayas by the Dharmakaya that desires thereby to lead all sentient beings to the ultimate

One who understands this heart becomes emancipated from the dualistic view of birth and death and performs such acts as are beneficial both to oneself and to others."

Sthiramati advocates in his *Discourse on the Mahâyâna-Dharmadhâtu* [1] the same view as Nâgârjuna's on the nature of the Bodhicitta, which I summarise here: "Nirvâna, Dharmakâya, Tathâgata, Tathâgata-garbha, Paramârtha, Buddha, Bodhicitta, or Bhûtatathâtâ,—all these terms signify merely so many different aspects of one and the same reality; and Bodhicitta is the name given to a form of the Dharmakâya or Bhûtatathâtâ as it manifests itself in the human heart, and its perfection, or negatively its liberation from all egoistic impurities, constitutes the state of Nirvana."

Being a reflex of the Dharmakâya, the Bodhicitta is practically the same as the original in all its characteristics; so continues Sthiramati: "It is free from compulsive activities; it has no beginning, it has no end; it cannot be defiled by impurities, it cannot be obscured by egoistic individualistic prejudices; it is incorporeal, it is the spiritual essence of Buddhas,

realisation of Buddhahood. In many cases, thus, it is extremely difficult to render upaya by any of its English equivalents and yet to retain its original technical sense unsuffered. This is also the case with many other Buddhist terms, among which we may mention Bodhi, Dharmakâya, Prajñâ, Citta, Parivarta, etc. The Chinese translators have *fang p'ien* for upaya which means "means-accommodation."

[1] Its full title is *A Discourse on the Non-duality of the Mahâyâna-Dharmadhâtu*. It consists of less than a dozen pages in ordinary Chinese large print. It was translated by Devaprajñâ and others in the year 691 A. D.

it is the source of all virtues earthly as well as transcendental; it is constantly becoming, yet its original purity is never lost.

"It may be likened unto the ever-shining sunlight which may temporarily be hidden behind the clouds. All the modes of passion and sin arising from egoism may sometimes darken the light of the Bodhicitta, but the Citta itself forever remains free from these external impurities. It may again be likened unto all-comprehending space which remains eternally identical, whatever happenings and changes may occur in things enveloped therein. When the Bodhicitta manifests itself in a relative world, it looks as if being subject to constant becoming, but in reality it transcends all determinations, it is above the reach of birth and death (*samsâra*).

"So long as it remains buried under innumerable sins arising from ignorance and egoism, it is productive of no earthly or heavenly benefit. Like the lotus-flower whose petals are yet unfolded, like the gold that is deeply entombed under the débris of dung and dirt, or like the light of the full moon eclipsed by Açura; the Bodhicitta, when blindfolded by the clouds of passion, avarice, ignorance, and folly, does not reveal its intrinsic spiritual worth.

"Destroy at once with your might and main all those entanglements; then like the full-bloomed lotus-flower, like genuine gold purified from dirt and dust, like the moon in a cloudless sky, like the sun in its full glory, like mother earth producing all kinds of cereals, like the ocean containing innumerable treasures, the eternal bliss of the Bodhicitta will be upon all sentient beings. All sentient beings are then emancipated from the misery of ignorance and folly, their hearts are filled with love and sympathy and free from the clinging to things worthless.

"However defiled and obscured the Bodhicitta may find itself in profane hearts, it is essentially the same as that in all Buddhas. Therefore, says the Muni of Çakya: 'O Câriputra, the world of sentient beings is not different from the Dharmakâya; the Dharmakâya is not different from the world of sentient beings. What constitutes the Dharmakâya is the world of sentient beings; and what constitutes the world of sentient beings is the Dharmakâya.'

"As far as the Dharmakâya or the Bodhicitta is concerned, there is no radical distinction to be made between profane hearts and the Buddha's heart; yet when observed from the human standpoint [that is, from the phenomenal side of existence] the following general classification can be made:

"(1) The heart hopelessly distorted by numberless egoistic sins and condemned to an eternal transmigration of birth and death which began in the timeless past, is said to be in the state of profanity.

"(2) The heart that, loathing the misery of wandering in birth and death and taking leave of all sinful and depraved conditions, seeks the Bodhi in the ten virtues of perfection (*pâramitâ*) and 84.000 Buddhadharmas and disciplines itself in all meritorious deeds, is said to be the [spiritual] state of a Bodhisattva.

"(3) The state in which the heart is emancipated from the obscuration of all passions, has distanced all sufferings, has eternally effaced the stain of all sins and corruptions, is pure, purer, and purest, abides in the essence of Dharma, has reached the height from which the states of all sentient beings are surveyed, has attained the consummation of all knowledges, has realised the highest type of manhood, has gained the power of spiritual spontaneity which frees one from attachment and hesitation, — this spiritual state is that of the fully, perfectly, enlightened Tathâgata".

The Awakening of the Bodhicitta.

The Bodhicitta is present in the hearts of all sentient beings. Only in Buddhas it is fully awakened and active with its immaculate virility, while in ordinary mortals it is dormant and miserably crippled by its unenlightened intercourse with the world of sensuality. One of the most favorite parables told by the Mahâyânists to illustrate this point is to compare the Bodhicitta to the moonlight in the heavens. When the moon shines with her silvery light in the clear, cloudless skies, she is reflected in every drop and in every mass of water on thé earth. The crystal dews on the quivering leaves reflect her like so many pearls hung on the branches. Every little water-pool; probably formed temporarily by heavy showers in the daytime, reflects her like so many stars descended on earth. Perhaps some of the pools are muddy and others even filthy, but the moonlight does not refuse to reflect her immaculate image in them. The image is just as perfect there as in a clear, undisturbed, transparent lake, where cows quench their thirst and swans bathe their taintless feathers. Wherever there is the least trace of water, there is seen a heavenly image of the goddess of night. Even so with the Bodhicitta: where there exists a little warmth of the heart, there it unfailingly glorifies itself in its best as circumstances permit.

Now, the question is: How should this dormant Bodhicitta in our hearts be awakened to its full sense? This is answered more or less definitely in almost all the Mahâyâna writings, and we may here recite the words of Vasubandhu from his *Discourse on the Awakening of the Bodhicitta*,[1] for they give us a somewhat systematic statement of those conditions which tend to awaken the Bodhicitta from its lethargic inactivity. (Chap. II.)

The Bodhicitta or Intelligence-heart is awakened in us (1) by thinking of the Buddhas, (2) by reflecting on the faults of material existence, (3) by observing the deplorable state in which sentient beings are living, and finally (4) by aspiring after those virtues which are acquired by a Tathâgata in the highest enlightenment.

[1] This work was translated by Kumârajîva into Chinese at the beginning of the fifth century A. D. It is divided into two fascicles, each consisting of about one score of Chinese pages.

To describe these conditions more definitely:

(1) *By thinking of the Buddhas.* "All Buddhas in the ten quarters, of the past, of the future, and of the present, when first started on their way to enlightenment, were not quite free from passions and sins (*kleça*) any more than we are at present; but they finally succeeded in attaining the highest enlightenment and became the noblest beings.

"All the Buddhas, by strength of their inflexible spiritual energy, were capable of attaining perfect enlightenment. If enlightenment is attainable at all, why should we not attain it?

"All the Buddhas, erecting high the torch of wisdom through the darkness of ignorance and keeping awake an excellent heart, submitted themselves to penance and mortification, and finally emancipated themselves from the bondage of the triple world. Following their steps, we, too, could emancipate ourselves.

"All the Buddhas, the noblest type of mankind, successfully crossed the great ocean of birth and death and of passions and sins; why, then, we, being creatures of intelligence, could also cross the sea of transmigration.

"All the Buddhas manifesting great spiritual power sacrificed the possessions, body, and life, for the attainment of omniscience (*sarvajñâ*); and we, too, could follow their noble examples."

(2) *The faults of the material existence.* "This our bodily existence consisting of the five skandhas and the four mahats (elements) is a perpetuator of innu-

merable evil deeds; and therefore it should be cast aside. This our bodily existence constantly secretes from its nine orifices filths and impurities which are truly loathsome; and therefore it should be cast aside. This our bodily existence, harboring within itself anger, avarice, and infatuation, and other innumerable evil passions, consumes a good heart; and therefore it should be destroyed. This our bodily existence is like a bubble, like a spatter, and is decaying every minute. It is an undesirable possession and should be abandoned. This our bodily existence engulfed in ignorance is creating evil karma all the time, which throws us into the whirlpool of transmigration through the six gatis."

(3) *The miserable conditions of sentient beings which arouse the sympathy of the Bodhisattvas.* "All sentient beings are under the bondage of ignorance. Spell-bound by folly and infatuation, they are suffering the severest pain Not believing in the law of karma, they are accumulating evils; going astray from the path of righteousness, they are following false doctrines; sinking deeper in the whirlpool of passions, they are being drowned in the four waters of sin.

"They are being tortured with all sorts of pain. They are needlessly haunted by the fear of birth and death and old age, and do not seek the path of emancipation. Mortified with grief, anxiety, tribulation, they do not refrain from committing further foul deeds. Clinging to their beloved ones and being always afraid of separation, they do not understand that there is no individual reality, that individual existences are not worth clinging to. Trying to shun enmity, hatred, pain, they cherish more hatred." ....

(4) *The virtues of the Tathâgata.* "All the Tathâgatas, by virtue of their discipline, have acquired a noble, dignified mien which aspires every beholder with the thought that dispels pain and woe. The Dharmakâya of all the Tathâgatas is immortal and pure and free from evil attachments. All the Tathâgatas are possessed of moral discipline, tranquillity, intelligence, and emancipation. They are not hampered by intellectual prejudices and have become the sanctuary of immaculate virtues. They have the ten bâlas (powers), four abhayas (fearlessness), great compassion, and the three smṛtyupasthânas (contemplations). They are omniscient, and their love for suffering beings knows no bounds and brings all creatures back to the path of righteousness, who have gone astray on account of ignorance."

* * *

In short, the Intelligence-heart or Bodhicitta is awakened in us either when love for suffering creatures (which is innate in us) is called forth, or when our intellect aspires after the highest enlightenment, or when these two psychical activities are set astir under some favorable circumstances. As the Bodhicitta is a manifestation of the Dharmakâya in our limited conscious mind, it constantly longs for a unification with its archetype, in spite of the curse of ignorance heavily weighing upon it. When this unification is not effected for any reason, the heart (*citta*) shows its dissatisfaction in some way or other. The dissatisfaction may take sometimes a morbid course, and may result in pessimism, or misanthropy, or suicide, or asceticism, or some other kindred eccentric practices. But if properly guided and naturally developed, the more intense the dissatisfaction, the more energetic will be the spiritual activity of a Bodhisattva.

The Bodhisattva's Pranidhâna.

Having awakened his Bodhicitta from its unconscious slumber, a Bodhisattva will now proceed to make his vows.

Let me remark here, however, that "vow" is not a very appropriate term to express the meaning of the Sanskrit *pranidhâna.* Pranidhâna is a strong wish, aspiration, prayer, or an inflexible determination to carry out one's will even through an infinite series of rebirths. Buddhists have such a supreme belief in the power of will or spirit that, whatever material limitations, the will is sure to triumph over them and gain its final aim. So, every Bodhisattva is considered to have his own particular pranidhânas in order to perform his share in the work of universal salvation. His corporeal shadow may vanish as its karma is exhausted, but his pranidhâna survives and takes on a new garment, which procedure being necessary to keep it ever effective. All that is needed for a Bodhisattva to do this is to make himself a perfect incarnation of his own aspirations, putting everything external and foreign under their controlling spiritual power. Buddhists are so thoroughly idealistic and their faith in ideas and ideals is so unshakable that they firmly believe that whatever they aspire to will come out finally as real fact; and, therefore, the more intense and permanent and born of the inmost needs of humanity, the more certain are our yearnings to be satisfied. (This belief, by the way, will help to explain the popular belief among the Buddhists that any strong passion possessed by a man will survive him and take a form, animate or inanimate, which will best achieve its end.)

According to Vasubandhu whom we have quoted several times, the Bodhisattvas generally are supposed to make the following ten pranidhânas, which naturally spring from a great loving heart now awakened in them: [1]

(1) "Would that all the merits I have accumulated in the past as well as in the present be distributed among all sentient beings and make them all aspire after supreme knowledge, and also that this my pranidhâna be constantly growing in strength and sustain me throughout my rebirths.

(2) "Would that, through the merits of my work,

[1] The above is a liberal rendering of the first part of the Chapter III, in Vasubandhu's *Bodhicitta*.

I may, wherever I am born, come in the presence of all Buddhas and pay them homage.

(3) "Would that I be allowed all the time to be near Buddhas like shadow following object, and never to be away from them.

(4) "Would that all Buddhas instruct me in religious truths as best suited to my intelligence and let me finally attain the five spiritual powers of the Bodhisattva.

(5) "Would that I be thoroughly conversant with scientific knowledge as well as the first principle of religion and gain an insight into the truth of the Good Law.

(6) "Would that I be able to preach untiringly the truth to all beings, and gladden them, and benefit them, and make them intelligent.

(7) "Would that, through the divine power of the Buddha, I be allowed to travel all over the ten quarters of the world, pay respect to all the Buddhas, listen to their instructions in the Doctrine, and universally benefit all sentient beings.

(8) "Would that, by causing the wheel of immaculate Dharma to revolve, all sentient beings in the ten quarters of the universe who may listen to my teachings or hear my name, be freed from all passions and awaken in them the Bodhicitta.

(9) "Would that I all the time accompany and protect all sentient beings and remove for them things which are not beneficial to them and give them innumerable blessings, and also that through the sacrifice

of my body, life, and possessions I embrace all creatures and thereby practise the Right Doctrine.

(10) "Would that, though practising the Doctrine in person, my heart be free from the consciousness of compulsion and unnaturalness, as all the Bodhisattvas practise the Doctrine in such a way as not practising it yet leaving nothing unpractised; for they have made their pranidhânas for the sake of all sentient beings."

CHAPTER XII.

TEN STAGES OF BODHISATTVAHOOD

Gradation in our Spiritual Life.

THEORETICALLY speaking, as we have seen above, the Bodhi or Bodhicitta is in every sentient being, and in this sense he is a Bodhisattva. In profane hearts it may be found enveloped in ignorance and egoism, but it can never be altogether annulled. For the Bodhi, when viewed from its absolute aspect, transcends the realm of birth and death (*samsâra*), is beyond the world of toil and trouble and is not subject to any form of defilement. But when it assumes a relative existence and is only partially manifested under the cover of ignorance, there appear various stages of actualisation or of perfection. In some beings it may attain a more meaningful expression than in others, while there may be even those who apparently fail on account of their accursed karma to show the evidence of its presence. This latter class is usually called "Icchantika," that is, people who are completely overwhelmed by the passions. They are morally and religiously a mere corpse which even a great spiritual physician finds it almost impossible to resuscitate. But, philosophically considered, the glory of the Bodhi must be admitted to be shining even in these dark, ignorant souls. Such souls, perhaps, will have to go round many a cycle of transmigration, before their karma loses its poignancy and becomes susceptible to a moral influence with which they may come in contact.

This accursed force of karma is not the same in all beings, it admits of all possible degrees of strength, and causes some to suffer more intensely than others. But there is no human heart or soul that is absolutely free from the shackle of karma and ignorance, because this very existence of a phenomenal world is a product of ignorance, though this fact does not prove that this life is evil. The only heart that transcends the influence of karma and ignorance and is all-purity, all-love, and all-intelligence, is the Dharmakâya or the absolute Bodhi itself. The life of a Bodhisattva and indeed the end of our religious aspiration is to unfold, realise, and identify ourselves with the love and intelligence of that ideal and yet real Dharmakâya.

The awakening of the Bodhicitta (or intelligence-heart) marks the first step towards the highest good of human life. This awakening must pass through several stages of religious discipline before it attains perfection. These stages are generally estimated by the Mahâyânists at ten. They appear, however, to our modern sceptical minds to be of no significant consequence, nor can we detect any very practical and well-defined distinction between successive stages. We fail to understand what religious necessity impelled the Hindu Buddhists to establish such apparently unimportant stages one after another in our religious life. We can see, however, that the first awakening of the Bodhicitta does not transform us all at once to Buddhahood; we have yet to overcome with strenuous efforts the baneful influence of karma and ignorance which asserts itself too readily in our practical life. But the marking of stages as in the gradation of the Daçabhûmî in our spiritual progress seems to be altogether too artificial. Nevertheless I here take pains as an historical survey to enumerate the ten stages and to give some features supposed to be most characteristic of each Bhûmî (stage as expounded in the *Avatamsaka Sutra*. Probably they will help us to understand what moral conceptions and what religious aspirations were working in the establishment of the doctrine of Daçabhûmî, for it elaborately describes what was considered by the Mahâyânists to be the essential constituents of Bodhisattvahood, and also shows what spiritual routine a Buddhist was expected to pursue.

The ten stages are: (1) Pramuditâ, (2) Vimalâ, (3) Prabhâkarî, (4) Arcismatî, (5) Sudurjayâ, (6) Abhimukhî, (7) Dûrangamâ, (8) Acalâ, (9) Sâdhumatî, (10) Dharmameghâ.

(1) *The Pramuditâ.*

Pramuditâ means "delight" or "joy" and marks the first stage of Bodhisattvahood, at which the Buddhists emerge from a cold, self-sufficing, and almost nihilistic contemplation of Nirvâna as fostered by the Çrâvakas and Pratyekabuddhas. This spiritual emergence and emancipation is psychologically accompanied by an intense feeling of joy, as that which is experienced by a person when he unexpectedly recognises the most familiar face in a faraway land of strangers. For this reason the first stage is called "joy."

Even in the midst of perfect tranquillity of Nirvâna in which all passions are alleged to have died away as declared by ascetics or solitary philosophers, the inmost voice in the heart of the Bodhisattva moans in a sort of dissatisfaction or uneasiness, which, though undefined and seemingly of no significance, yet refuses to be eternally buried in the silent grave of annihilation. He vainly gropes in the darkness; he vainly seeks consolation in the samâdhi of non-resistance or non-activity; he vainly finds eternal peace in the gospel of self-negation; his soul is still troubled, not exactly knowing the reason why. But as soon as the Bodhicitta (intelligence-heart) is awakened from its somnolence, as soon as the warmth of love (*mahâkarunâ*) penetrates into the coldest cell of asceticism, as soon as the light of supreme enlightenment (*mahâprajñâ*) dawns upon the darkest recesses of ignorance, the Bodhisattva sees at once that the world is not made for self-seclusion nor for self-negation, that the Dharmakâya is the source of "universal effulgence," that Nirvâna if relatively viewed in contrast to birth-and-death is nothing but sham and just as unreal as any worldly existence; and these insights finally lead him to feel that he cannot rest quiet until all sentient beings are emancipated from the snarl of ignorance and elevated to the same position as now occupied by himself.

(2) *The Vimalâ.*

Vimalâ means "freedom from defilement," or, affirmatively, "purity." When the Bodhisattva attains, through the spiritual insight gained at the first stage, to rectitude and purity of heart, he reaches the second stage. His heart is now thoroughly spotless, it is filled with tenderness, he fosters no anger, no malice. He is free from all the thoughts of killing any animate beings. Being contented with what belongs to himself, he casts no covetous eyes on things not his own. Faithful to his own betrothed, he does not harbor any evil thoughts on others. His words are always true, faithful, kind, and considerate. He likes truth, honesty, and never flatters.

(3) *The Prabhâkarî.*

Prabhâkarî means "brightness," that is, of the intellect. This predominantly characterises the spiritual condition of the Bodhisattva at this stage. Here he gains the most penetrating insight into the nature of things. He recognises that all things that are created are not permanent, are conducive to misery, have no abiding selfhood (*âtman*), are destitute of purity, and subject to final decay. He recognises also that the real nature of things, however, is neither created nor subject to destruction, it is eternally abiding in the selfsame essence, and transcends the limits of time and space. Ignorant beings not seeing this truth are always worrying over things transient and worthless, and constantly consuming their spiritual energy with the fire of avarice, anger, and infatuation, which in turn accumulates for their future existences the ashes of misery and suffering. This wretched condition of sentient beings further stimulates the loving heart of the Bodhisattva to seek the highest intelligence of Buddha, which, giving him great spiritual energy, enables him to prosecute the gigantic task of universal emancipation. His desire for the Buddha-intelligence and his faith in it are of such immense strength that he would not falter even for a moment, if he is only assured of the attainment of the priceless treasure, to plunge himself into the smeltering fire of a volcano.

(4) *The Arciṣmatî.*

Arciṣmatî, meaning "inflammation," is the name given to the fourth stage, at which the Bodhisattva consumes all the sediments of ignorance and evil passions in the fiery crucible of the purifying Bodhi. He practises here most strenuously the thirty-seven virtues called Bodhipâkṣikas which are conducive to the perfection of the Bodhi. These virtues consist of seven categories:

(I) Four Contemplations (*smṛtyusthâna*): 1. On the impurity of the body; 2. On the evils of sensuality; 3. On the evanescence of the wordly interests; 4. On the non-existence of âtman in things composite.

(II) Four Righteous Efforts (*samyakprahâna*): 1. To

prevent evils from arising; 2. To suppress evils already existing; 3. To produce good not yet in existence; 4. To preserve good already in existence.

(III) Four Forces of the Will (*ṛddhipâda*): 1. The determination to accomplish what is willed; 2. The energy to concentrate the mind on the object in view; 3. The power of retaining the object in memory; 4. The intelligence that perceives the way to Nirvâna.

(IV) Five Powers (*indrya*), from which all moral good is produced: 1. Faith; 2. Energy; 3. Circumspection; 4. Equillibrium, or tranquillity of mind; 5 Intelligence.

(V) Five Functions (*bala*): Same as the above.[1]

(VI) Seven Constituents of the Bodhi (*bodhyanga*): 1. The retentive power; 2. Discrimination; 3. Energy; 4. Contentment; 5. Modesty; 6. The balanced mind; 7. Large-heartedness.

(VII) The Eightfold Noble Path (*âryamârga*): 1. Right view; 2. Right resolve; 3. Right speech; 4. Right conduct; 5. Right livelihood; 6 Right recollection; 8 Right tranquilisation, or contemplation.

[1] The distinction between the five indriyas and the five balas seems to be rather redundant. But the Hindu philosophers usually distinguish actor from action, agent from function or operation. Thus the sense-organs are distinguished from sensations or sense-consciousnesses, and the manovijñâna (mind) from its functions such as thinking, attention, memory, etc. The âtman has thus come to be considered the central agent that controls all the sensuous and intellectual activities. Though the Buddhists do not recognise this differentiation of actor and action in reality, they sometimes loosely follow the popular usage.

(5) *The Sudurjayâ.*

Sudurjayâ means "very difficult to conquer." The Bodhisattva reaches this stage when he, completely armed with the thirty-seven Bodhipâkṣikas and guided by the beacon-light of Bodhi, undauntedly breaks through the column of evil passions. Provided with the two spiritual provisions, love and wisdom, and being benefitted by the spirits of all the Buddhas of the past, present, and future, the Bodhisattva has developed an intellectual power to penetrate deep into the system of existence. He perceives the Fourfold Noble Truth in its true light; he perceives the highest reality in the Tathâgata; he also perceives that the highest reality, though absolutely one in its essence, manifests itself in a world of particulars, that relative knowledge (*samvrtti*) and absolute knowledge (*paramârtha*) are two aspects of one and the same truth, that when subjectivity is disturbed there appears particularity, and that when it is not disturbed there shines only the eternal light of Tathâgatajñâ (Tathâgata-knowledge).

(6) *The Abhimukhî.*

Abhimukhî means "showing one's face," that is, the presentation of intelligence (*prajñâ*) before the Bodhisattva at this stage.

The Bodhisattva enters upon this stage by reflecting on the essence of all dharmas which are throughout of one nature. When he perceives the truth, his heart is filled with great love, he serenely contemplates on the life of ignorant beings who are constantly going astray yielding themselves to evil temptations, clinging to the false conception of egoism, and thus making themselves the prey of eternal damnation. He then proceeds to contemplate the development of evils generally. There is ignorance, there is karma; and in this fertile soil of blind activity the seeds of consciousness are sown; the moisture of desire thoroughly soaks them, to which the water of egoism or individuation is poured on. The bed for all forms of particularity is well prepared, and the buds of nâmarûpas (name-and-form) most vigorously thrive here. From these we have the flowers of sense-organs, and which come in contact with other existences and produce impressions, feel agreeable sensations, and tenaciously cling to them. From this clinging or the will to live as the principle of individuation or as the principle of bhâva as is called in the Twelve Nidânas, another body consisting of the five skandhas comes into existence, and, passing through all the phases of transformation, dissolves and disappears. All sentient beings are thus kept in a perpetual oscillation of combination and separation, of pleasure and pain, birth and death. But the insight of the Bodhisattva has gone deeply into the inmost essence of things, which forever remains the same and in which there is no production and dissolution.

(7) *The Dûrangamâ.*

Dûrangamâ means "going far away." The Bodhisattva enters upon this stage by attaining the so-called

Upâyajñâ, i e. the knowledge that enables him to produce any means or expediency suitable for his work of salvation. He himself abides in the principles of *çûnyatâ* (transcendentality), *animitta* (non-individuality), and *apranihita* (desirelessness), but his loving-kindness keeps him busily engaged among sentient beings. He knows that Buddhas are not creatures radically and essentially different from himself, but he does not stop tendering them due homage. He is always contemplating on the nature of the Absolute, but he does not abandon the practice of accumulating merits. He is no more encumbered with worldly thoughts, yet he does not disdain managing secular affairs. He keeps himself perfectly aloof from the consuming fire of passsion, but he plans all possible means for the sake of sentient beings to quench the enraging flames of avarice (*lobha*), anger (*dveṣa*), and infatuation (*moha*). He knows that all individual existences are like dream, mirage, or the reflection of the moon in the water, but he works and toils in the world of particulars and submits himself to the domination of karma. He is well aware of the transcendental nature of Pure Land (*sukhâvatî*), but he describes it with material colors for the sake of unenlightened masses. He knows that the Dharmakâya of all the Buddhas is not a material existence, but he does not refuse to dignify himself with the thirty-two major and eighty minor excellent features of a great man or god (*mahâpuruṣa*). He knows that the language of all the Buddhas does not fall within the ken of human comprehension, but he endeavors with all contrivances (*upâya*) to make it intelligible enough to the understanding of people. He knows that all the Buddhas perceive the past, present, and future in the twinkling of an eye, but he adapts himself to divers conditions of the material world and endeavors to help sentient beings to understand the significance of the Bodhi according to their destinies and dispositions. In short, the Bodhisattva himself lives on a higher plane of spirituality far removed from the defilements of worldliness; but he does not withdraw himself to this serene, unmolested subjectivity; he boldly sets out in the world of particulars and senses; and, placing himself on the level of ignorant beings, he works like them, he toils like them, and suffers like them; and he never fails all these times to practise the gospel of lovingkindness and to turn over (*parivarta*) all his merits towards the emancipation and spiritual edification of the masses, that is, he never gets tired of practising the ten virtues of perfection (*pâramitâ*).

That is to say, (1) the Bodhisattva practises the virtue of charity (*dâna*) by freely giving away to all sentient creatures all the merits that he has acquired by following the path of Buddhas. (2) He practises the virtue of good conduct (*çîla*) by destroying all the evil passions that disturb serenity of mind. (3) He practises the virtue of patience (*kṣânti*), for he never gets irritated or excited over what is done to him by ignorant beings. (4) He practises the virtue of strenuousuess (*vriya*), for he never gets tired of accumulating merits and of promoting good-will among his fellow-creatures. (5) He practises the virtue of calmness (*dhyâna*), for his mind is never distracted in steadily pursuing his way to supreme knowledge. (6) He practises the virtue of intelligence (*prajñâ*), for he always restrains his thoughts from wandering away from the path of absolute truth. (7) He practises the virtue of tactfulness (*upâya*), for he has an inexhaustible mine of expediencies ready at his command for the work of universal salvation. (8) He practises the virtue of will-to-do (*pranidhâna*) by determinedly following the dictates of the highest intelligence. (9) He practises the virtue of strength (*bala*), for no evil influences, no heretical thoughts can ever frustrate or slacken his efforts for the general welfare of people. (10) Finally, he practises the virtue of knowledge, (*jñâna*), by truthfully comprehending and expounding the ultimate nature of beings.

(8) *The Acalâ.*

Acalâ, "immovable," is the name for the eighth stage of Bodhisattvahood. When a Bodhisattva, transcending all forms of discursive or deliberate knowledge, acquires the highest, perfect knowledge called *anutpattikadharmakṣânti*, he is said to have gone beyond the seventh stage. Anutpattikadharmakṣânti literally means "not-created-being-forbearance"; and the Buddhists use the term in the sense of keeping one's thoughts in conformity to the views that nothing in this world has ever been created, that things are such as they are, i. e. they are Suchness itself. This knowledge is also called non-conscious or non-deliberate knowledge in contradistinction to relative knowledge that constitutes all our logical and demonstrative knowledge. Strictly speaking, this so-called knowledge is not knowledge in its ordinary signification, it is a sort of unconscious or subconscious intelligence, or immediate knowledge as some call it, in which not only willing and acting, but also knowing and willing are one single, undivided exhibition of activity, all logical or natural transition from one to the other being altogether absent. Here indeed knowledge is will and will is action; "Let there be light," and there is light, and the light is good; it is the state of a divine mind.

At this stage of perfection, the Bodhisattva's spiritual condition is compared to that of a person who, attempting when in a dreamy state to cross deep waters, musters all his energy, plans all schemes, and, while at last at the point of starting on the journey, suddenly wakes up and finds all his elaborate preparations to no purpose. The Bodhisattva hitherto showed untiring spiritual efforts to attain the highest knowledge, steadily practised all virtues tending to the acquirement of Nirvâna, and heroically endeavored to exterminate all evil passions, and at the culmination of all these exercises, he enters all of a sudden upon the stage of Acalâ and finds the previous elaboration mysteriously vanished from his conscious mind. He cherishes now no desire for Buddhahood, Nirvâna, or Bodhicitta, much less after worldliness, egoism, or the satisfaction of evil passions. The conscious striving that distinguished all his former course has now given way to a state of spontaneous activity, of saintly innocence, and of divine playfulness. He wills and it is done. He aspires and it is actualised. He is nature herself, for there is no trace in his activity that betrays any artificial lucubration, any voluntary or compulsory restraint. This state of perfect ideal freedom may be called esthetical, which characterises the work of a genius. There is here no trace of consciously following some prescribed laws, no pains of elaborately conforming to the formula. To put this poetically, the inner life of the Bodhisattva at this stage is like the lilies of the field whose glory is greater than that of Solomon in all his human magnificence.

Kant's remarks on this point are very suggestive, and I will quote the following from his *Kritik der Urteilskraft* (Reclam edition, p. 173):

"Also muss die Zweckmässigkeit im Produkte der schönen Kunst, ob sie zwar absichtlich ist, doch nicht absichtlich scheinen: d. i., schöne Kunst muss als Natur anzusehen sein, ob man sich ihrer zwar als Kunst bewusst ist. Als Natur aber erscheint ein Produkt der Kunst dadurch, dass zwar alle Pünktlichkeit in der Uebereinkunst mit Regeln, nach denen allein das Produkt das werden kann, was es soll sein, angetroffen wird, aber ohne Peinlichkeit, d. i., ohne eine Spur zu zeigen, dass die Regel dem Künstler vor Augen geschwebt und seinen Gemüthskräften Fesseln angelegt haben." [1]

(9) *The Sâdhumatî.*

Sâdhumatî, meaning "good intelligence," is the name given to the ninth stage of Bodhisattvahood. All the Bodhisattvas are said to have reached here, when sentient beings are benefitted by the Bodhisattva's attainment of the highest perfect knowledge, which is unfathomable by the ordinary human intelligence. The knowledge leads them to the Dharma of the deepest mystery, to the Samâdhi of perfect spirituality, to the Dhâranî of divine spontaneity, to Love of absolute purity, to the Will of utmost freedom.

The Bodhisattva will acquire at this stage the four Pratisamvids (comprehensive knowledge), which are (1) Dharmapratisamvid, (2) Arthapratisamvid, (3) Niruktipratisamvid, (4) Pratibhanapratisamvid. By the Dharmapratisamvid, the Bodhisattvas understand the

[1] In this connection it is very interesting also to note that Carlyle expresses the same sentiment about the greatness of Shakespeare in his *Hero Worship.* "If I say that Shakspeare is the greatest of Intellects, I have said all concerning him. But there is more in Shakspeare's intellect than we have yet seen It is what I call an unconscious intellect; there is more virtue in it that he himself is aware of. Novalis beautifully remarks of him, that those dramas of his are Products of Nature too, as deep as Nature herself. I find a great truth in this saying, Shakspeare's Art is not Artifice; the noblest worth of it is not there by plan or precontrivance. It grows from the deeps of Nature, through this noble sincere soul, who is a voice of Nature."

self-essence (*svabhâva*) of all beings; by the Artha-pratisamvid, their individual attributes; by the Nirukti-pratisamvid, their indestructibility; by the Pratibhana-pratisamvid, their eternal order. Again, by the first intelligence they understand that all individual dharmas have no absolute reality; by the second, that they are all subject to the law of constant becoming; by the third, that they are no more than mere names; by the fourth, that even mere names as such are of some value. Again, by the first intelligence, they comprehend that all dharmas are of one reality which is indestructible; by the second, that this one reality differentiating itself becomes subject to the law of causation; by the third, that by virtue of a superior understanding all Buddhas become the object of admiration and the haven of all sentient beings; by the fourth, that in the one body of truth all Buddhas preach infinite lights of the Dharma

(10) *The Dharmameghâ.*

Dharmameghâ, "clouds of dharma," is the name of the tenth and final stage of Bodhisattvahood. The Bodhisattvas have now practised all virtues of purity, accumulated all the constituents of Bodhi, are fortified with great power and intelligence, universally practise the principle of great love and sympathy, have deeply penetrated into the mystery of individual existences, fathomed the inmost depths of sentiency, followed step by step the walk of all the Tathâgatas. Every thought cherished by the Bodhisattva now dwells in all the Tathâgatas' abode of eternal tranquillity, and every deed practised by him is directed towards the ten balas (power), [1] four vaiçâradyas (conviction), [2] and eighteen avenikas (unique characteristics), [3] of the Buddha. By these virtues the Bodhisattva has now acquired the knowledge of all things (*sarvajñâ*), is dwelling in the sanctum sanctorum of all dhâraṇîs and samâdhis, have arrived at the summit of all activities.

[1] The ten powers of the Buddha are: (1) The mental power which discriminates between right and wrong, (2) The knowledge of the retribution of karma, (3) The knowledge of all the different stages of creation, (4) The knowledge of all the different forms of deliverance, (5) The knowledge of all the different dispositions of sentient beings, (6) The knowledge of the final destination of all deeds, (7) The knowledge of all the different practices of meditation, deliverance, and tranquilisation, (8) The knowledge of former existences, (9) The unlimited power of divination, (10) The knowledge of the complete subjection of evil desires (*âçrava*).

[2] The four convictions (*vaiçâradyas*) of the Buddha are: (1) That he has attained the highest enlightenment, (2) That he has destroyed all evil desires, (3) That he has rightly described the obstacles that lie in the way to a life of righteousness, (4) That he has truthfully taught the way of salvation.

[3] The eighteen unique characteristics which distinguish the Buddha from the rest of mankind are: (1) He commits no errors. Since time out of mind, he has disciplined himself in morality, meditation, intelligence, and lovingkindness, and as the result his present life is without faults and free from all evil thoughts. (2) He is faultless in his speeches. Whatever he speaks comes from his transcendental eloquence and leads the audience to a higher conception of life. (3) His mind is faultless. As he has trained himself in samâdhi, he is always calm, serene, and contented. (4) He retains his sameness of heart (*samâhitacitta*), that is, his love for sentient beings is

The Bodhisattva at this stage is a personification of love and sympathy, which freely issue from the fount of his inner will. He gathers the clouds of virtue and wisdom, in which he manifests himself in manifold figures; he produces the lightnings of Buddhi, Vidyâs, and Vaiçâradyas; and shaking the whole world with the thunder of Dharma he crushes all the evil ones; and pouring forth the showers of Good Law he quenches the burning flames of ignorance

universal and not discriminative. (5) His mind is free from thoughts of particularity (*nânâtvasamjñâ*), that is, it is abiding in truth transcendental, his thoughts are not distracted by objects of the senses. (6) Resignation (*upekṣâ*). The Buddha knows everything, yet he is calmly resigned. (7) His aspiration is unfathomable, that is, his desire to save all beings from the sufferings of ignorance knows no bounds. (8) His energy is inexhaustible, which he applies with utmost vigor to the salvation of benighted souls. (9) His mentation (*smṛti*) is inexhaustible, that is, he is ever conscious of all the good doctrines taught by all the Buddhas of the past, present, and future. (10) His intelligence (*prajñâ*) is inexhaustible, that is, being in possession of all-intelligence which knows no limits, he preaches for the benefits of all beings. (11) His deliverance (*vimukti*) is permanent, that is, he has eternally distanced all evil passions and sinful attachments. (12) His knowledge of deliverance (*vimuktijñâna*) is perfect, that is, his intellectual insight into all states of deliverance is without a flaw. (13) He possesses a wisdom which directs all his bodily movements towards the benefit and enlightenment of sentient beings. (14) He possesses a wisdom which directs all his speeches toward the edification and conversion of his fellow-creatures. (15) He possesses a wisdom which reflects in his clear mind all the turbulent states of ignorant souls, from which he removes the dark veil of nescience and folly. (16) He knows all the past. (17) He knows all the future. (18) He knows all the present.

and passion in which all sentient creatures are being consumed.

* * *

The above presentation of the Daçabhûmî[1] of Bodhisattvahood allows us to see what ideal life is held out by the Mahâyânists before their own eyes and in what respect it differs from that of the Çrâvakas and Pratyekabuddhas as well as from that of other religious followers. Mahâyânism is not contented to make us mere transmitters or "hearers" of the teachings of the Buddha, it wants to inspire with all the religious and ethical motives that stirred the noblest heart of Çâkyamuni to its inmost depths. It fully recognises the intrinsic worth of the human soul; and, holding up its high ideals and noble aspirations, it endeavors to develop all the possibilities of our soul-life, which by our strenuous efforts and all-defying courage will one day be realised even on this earth of impermanence. We as individual existences are nothing but shadows which will vanish as soon as the conditions disappear that make them possible; we as mortal beings are no more than the

[1] For an elaborate exposition of the Daçabhûmî, see the *Avatamsaka* (sixty volume edition, fas. 24-27), the *Çûrangama*, Vasubandhu's Commentary on Asanga's *Comprehensive Treatise on Mahâyanism* (fas. 10—11), the *Vijnânamâtra Çâstra* (fas. 9), etc., and for a special treatment of the subject consult the sûtra bearing the name, which by the way exists in a Sanskrit version and whose brief sketch is given by Rajendra Mitra in his *Nepalese Buddhist Literature*, p. 81 et seq.

thousands of dusty particles that are haphazardly and powerlessly scattered about before the cyclone of karma; but when we are united in the love and intelligence of the Dharmakâya in which we have our being, we are Bodhisattvas, and we can immovably stand against the tempest of birth and death, against the overwhelming blast of ignorance. Then even an apparently insignificant act of lovingkindness will lead finally to the eternal abode of bliss, not the actor alone, but the whole community to which he belongs. Because a stream of love spontaneously flows from the lake of Intelligence-heart (*Bodhicitta*) which is fed by the inexhaustible spring of the Dharmakâya, while ignorance leads only to egoism, hatred, avarice, disturbance, and universal misery.

CHAPTER XIII.

NIRVÂNA.

NIRVÂNA, according to Mahâyâna Buddhism, is not understood in its nihilistic sense. Even with the Çrâvakas or Hînayânists, Nirvâna in this sense is not so much the object of their religious life as the recognition of the Fourfold Noble Truth, or the practise of the Eightfold Path, or emancipation from the yoke of egoism. It is mostly due, as far as I can see, to non-Buddhist critics that the conception of Nirvâna has been selected among others as one of the most fundamental teachings of Buddha, declaring it at the same time to consist in the annihilation of all human passions and aspirations, noble as well as worthless.

In fact, Nirvâna literally means "extinction" or "dissolution" of the five skandhas, and therefore it may be said that the entering into Nirvâna is tantamount to the annihilation of the material existence and of all the passions. Catholic Buddhists, however, do not understand Nirvâna in the sense of emptiness, for they say that Buddhism is not a religion of death nor for the dead, but that it teaches how to attain eternal life, how to gain an insight into the real nature of things, and how to regulate our conduct in accordance with the highest truth. Therefore, Buddhism, when rightly understood in the spirit of its founder, is something quite different from what it is commonly supposed to be by the general public.

I will endeavor in the following pages to point out that Nirvâna in the sense of a total annihilation of human activities, is by no means the primary and sole object of Buddhists, and then proceed to elucidate in what signification it is understood in the Mahâyâna Buddhism and see what relative position Nirvâna in its Mahâyânistic sense occupies in the body of Buddhism.

Nihilistic Nirvâna not the First Object.

In order to see the true signification of Nirvâna, it is necessary first to observe in what direction Buddha himself ploughed the waves in his religious cruise and upon what shore he finally debarked. This will show us whether or not Nirvâna as nihilistic nothingness is the primary and sole object of Buddhism, to which every spiritual effort of its devotees is directed.

If the attainment of negativistic Nirvâna were the sole aim of Buddhism, we should naturally expect Buddha's farewell address to be chiefly dealing with that subject. In his last sermon, however, Buddha did not teach his disciples to concentrate all their moral efforts on the attainment of Nirvânic quietude disregarding all the forms of activity that exhibit themselves in life. Far from it. He told them, according to the *Mahânibbâna sutta* (the Book of the Great decease, *S. B. E.* Vol. XI. p. 114) that "Decay is inherent in all component things! Work out your salvation with diligence!" This exhortation of the strenuous life is quite in harmony with the last words of Buddha as recorded in Açvaghoṣa's *Buddhacarita* (Chinese translation, Chap. xxvi). They were:

"Even if I lived a kalpa longer,
Separation would be an inevitable end.
A body composed of various aggregates,
Its nature is not to abide forever.

"Having finished benefiting oneself and others,
Why live I longer to no purpose?
Of gods and men that should be saved,
Each and all had been delivered.

"O ye, my disciples!
Without interruption transmit the Good Dharma!
Know ye that things are destined to decay!
Never again abandon yourselves to grief!

"But pursue the Way with diligence,
And arrive at the Home of No-separation!
I have lit the Lamp of Intelligence,
That shining dispels the darkness of the world.

"Know ye that the world endureth not!
As ye should feel happy [when ye see]
The parents suffering a mortal disease
Are released by a treatment from pain;

"So with me, I now give up the vessel of misery,
Transcend [1] the current of birth and death,

[1] Literally, "to advance against."

And am eternally released from all pain and suffe ring.
This too must be deemed blest.

"Ye should well guard yourselves!
Never give yourselves up to indulgence!
All that exists finally comes to an end!
I now enter into Nirvâna." [1]

In this we find Buddha's characteristic admonition to his disciples not to waste time but to work out their salvation with diligence and rigor, but we fail to find the gospel of annihilation, the supposedly fundamental teaching of Buddhism.

Did then Buddha start in his religious discipline to attain the absolute annihilation of all human aspirations and after a long meditation reach the conclusion that contradicted his premises? Far from it. His first and last ambition was nothing else than the emancipation of all beings from ignorance, misery, and suffering through enlightenment, knowledge, and truth. When Mâra the evil one was exhausting all his evil powers upon the destruction of the Buddha in the beginning of his career, the good gods in the heavens exclaimed to the evil one: [2]

"Take not on thyself, O Mâra, this vain fatigue,—throw aside thy malevolence and retire to thy home. This sage cannot be shaken by thee any more than the mighty mountain Meru by the wind.

[1] Cf. Beal's translation in the *S. B. E.* Vol XIX. pp. 306–307, vs. 2095—2101. Beal utterly misunderstands the Chinese original.

[2] The *Buddhacarita*, Cowell's translation in the *S. B. E.* Vol. ILIX. p. 145.

"Even fire might lose its hot nature, water its fluidity, earth its steadiness, but never will he abandon his resolution, who has acquired his merit by a long course of actions through unnumbered eons.

"Such is the purpose of his, that heroic effort, that glorious strength, that compassion for all beings,—until he attains the highest wisdom [or suchness, *tattva*], he will never rise from his seat, just as the sun does not rise without dispelling the darkness.

"Pitying the world lying distressed amidst diseases and passions, he, the great physician, ought not to be hindered, who undergoes all his labors for the sake of the remedy-knowledge.

"He, who, when he beholds the world drowned in the great flood of existence and unable to reach the further shore, strives to bring them safely across,—would any right-minded soul offer him wrong?

"The tree of knowledge, whose roots go deep in firmness, and whose fibres are patience,—whose flowers are moral actions and whose branches are memory and thought,—and which gives out the Dharma as its fruit,—surely when it is growing it should not be cut down."

These words of the good gods in the heavens truthfully echo the motive that stirred Çâkyamuni to take up his gigantic task of universal salvation, and we are unable here as before to perceive a particle of the nihilistic speculation which is supposed to characterise Nirvâna. The Buddha from the very first of his religious course searched after the light that will illuminate the whole universe and dispel the darkness of nescience.

What enlightenment, then, did the Buddha, pursuing his first object, finally gain? What truth was it that he is said to have discovered under the Bodhi tree after six years' penance and deep meditation? As is universally recognised, it was no more than the Fourfold Noble Truth and the Twelve Chains of Dependence, which are acknowledged by the Mahâyânists as well as by the Hînayânists as the essentially original teachings of the Buddha. What then was his subjective state when he discovered these truths? How did he feel in his inmost being after this intellectual triumph over egoistic thoughts and passions? According to the Southern tradition, the famous Hymn of Victory is said to be his utterance on this occasion. It reads (The *Dharmapada*, 153):

> "Many a life to transmigrate,
> Long quest, no rest, hath been my fate,
> Tent-designer inquisitive for;
> Painful birth from state to state.
>
> "Tent-designer, I know thee now;
> Never again to build art thou;
> Quite out are all thy joyful fires,
> Rafter broken and roof-tree gone;
> Into the vast my heart goes on,
> Gains Eternity—dead desires." [1]

In this Hymn of Victory, the "tent-designer" means

[1] From A. J. Edmunds's translation of *Dhammapada*.

the ego that is supposed to be a subtle existence behind our mental experiences. As was pointed out elsewhere the negative phase of Buddhism consists in the eradication of this ego-substratum or the "designer" of eternal transmigration. The Buddha now finds out that this ego-soul is a fantasmagoria and has no final existence; and with this insight his ego-centric desires that troubled him so long are eternally dead; he feels the breaking up of their limitations; he is absorbed in the Eternal Vast, in which we all live and move and have our being. No shadow is perceptible here that suggests anything of an absolute nothingness supposed to be the attribute of Nirvâna.

Before proceeding further, let us see what the Mahâyâna tradition says concerning this point. The tradition varies in this case as in many others. According to Beal's *Romantic History of Buddha*, which is a translation of a Chinese version of the *Buddhacarita* (*Fo pen hing ching*),[1] Buddha is reported to have exclaimed this:

"Through ages past have I acquired continual merit,
That which my heart desired have I now attained,
How quickly have I arrived at the ever-constant condition,
And landed on the very shore of Nirvâna.
The sorrows and opposition of the world,
The Lord of the Kâmalokas, Mâra Pisuna,
These are unable now to affect, they are wholly destroyed;
By the power of religious merit and of wisdom are they cast away.

[1] P. 225. Beal's translation is not always reliable, and I would have my own if the Chinese original were at all accessible.

Let a man but persevere with unflinching resolution,
And seek Supreme Wisdom, it will not be hard to acquire it;
When once obtained, then farewell to all sorrows,
All sin and guilt are forever done away." [1]

Viewing the significance of Buddhism in this light, it is evident that Buddha did not emphasise so much the doctrine of Nirvâna in the sense of a total abnegation of human aspirations as the abandonment of egoism and the practical regulation of our daily life in accordance with this view. Nirvâna in which all the passions noble and base are supposed to have been "blown out like a lamp" was not the most coveted object of Buddhist life. On the contrary, Buddhism advises all its followers to exercise most strenuously all their spiritual energy to attain perfect freedom from the bondage of ignorance and egoism; because that is the only way in which we can conquer the vanity of worldliness and enjoy the bliss of eternal life. The following verse from the *Visuddhi Magga* (XXI) prac-

[1] The gâthâs supposed to be the first utterance of the Buddha after his enlightenment, according to Rockhill's *Life of the Buddha* (p. 33) compiled from Tibetan sources, give an inkling of nihilism, though I am inclined to think that the original Tibetan will allow a different interpretation when examined by some one who is better acquainted with the spirit of Buddhism than Rockhill. Rockhill betrays in not a few cases his insufficient knowledge of the subject he treats. His translation of the gâthâs is as follows:

> "All the pleasures of the worldly joys,
> All which are known among the gods,
> Compared with the joy of ending existence,
> Are not as its sixteenth part.

tically sums up the teaching of Buddhism as far as its negative and individual phase is concerned:

"Behold how empty is the world,
Mogharâja! In thoughtfulness
Let one remove belief in self,
And pass beyond the realm of death.
The king of death will never find
The man who thus the world beholds." [2]

Nirvâna is Positive.

It is not my intention here to investigate the historical side of this question; we are not concerned with the problem of how the followers of Buddha gradually developed the positive aspect of Nirvâna in connection with the practical application of his moral and religious

"Sorry is he whose burden is heavy,
And happy he who has cast it down;
When once he has cast off his burden,
He will seek to be burthened no more.

"When all existences are put away,
When all notions are at an end,
When all things are perfectly known,
Then no more will craving come back."

In the *Udâna*, II., 2, we have a stanza corresponding to the first gâthâ here cited, but the *Udâna* does not say "the joy of ending existence," but "the destruction of desire."

According to the *Lalita Vistara*, the Buddha's utterance of victory is (Râjendra Mitra's Edition p. 448):

"Cinna vartmopaçânta rajâh çuṣkâ âçravâ na punaḥ çravanti. Chinne vartmani varttate duḥkhasyaiṣonta ucyate."

[2] Warren's *Buddhism in Translations*, p. 376.

teachings; nor are we engaged in tracing the process of evolution through which Buddha's noble resolution to save all sentient beings from ignorance and misery was brought out most conspicuously by his later devotees. What I wish to state here about the positive conception of Nirvâna and its development is this: The Mahâyâna Buddhism was the first religious teaching in India that contradicted the doctrine of Nirvâna as conceived by other Hindu thinkers who saw in it a complete annihilation of being, for they thought that existence is evil, and evil is misery, and the only way to escape misery is to destroy the root of existence, which is nothing less than the total cessation of human desires and activities in Nirvânic unconsciousness The Yoga taught self-forgetfulness in deep meditation; the Samkhya, the absolute separation of Puruṣa from Prakṛti, which means undisturbed self-contemplation; the Vedânta, absorption in the Brahma, which is the total suppression of all particulars; and thus all of them considered emancipation from human desires and aspirations a heavenly bliss, that is, Nirvâna. Metaphysically speaking, they might have been correct each in its own way, but, ethically considered, their views had little significance in our practical life and showed a sad deficiency in dealing with problems of morality.

The Buddha was keenly aware of this flaw in their doctrines. He taught, therefore, that Nirvâna does not consist in the complete stoppage of existence, but in the practise of the Eightfold Path. This moral practise leads to the unalloyed joy of Nirvâna, not as the tranquillisation of human aspirations, but as the fulfilment or unfolding of human life. The word Nirvâna in the sense of annihilation was in existence prior to Buddha, but it was he who gave a new significance to it and made it worthy of attainment by men of moral character. All the doctrinal aspects of Nirvâna are later additions or rather development made by Buddhist scholars, according to whom their arguments are solidly based on some canonical passages. Whatever the case may be, my conviction is that those who developed the positive significance of Nirvâna are more consistent with the spirit of the founder than those who emphasised another aspect of it. In the *Udâna* we read (IV., 9):

> "He whom life torments not,
> Who sorrows not at the approach of death,
> If such a one is resolute and has seen Nirvâna,
> In the midst of grief, he is griefless.
> The tranquil-minded Bhikkhu, who has uprooted the
> thirst for existence,
> By him the succession of births is ended,
> He is born no more." [1]

According to the Mahâyânistic conception Nirvâna is not the annihilation of the world and the putting an end to life; but it is to live in the whirlpool of birth and death and yet to be above it. It is affirmation and fulfilment, and this is done not blindly and egoistically, for Nirvâna is enlightenment. Let us see how this is.

[1] General D. M. Strong's translation, p. 64.

The Mahâyânistic Conception of Nirvâna.

While the conception of Nirvâna seems to have remained indefinite and confused as far as Hînayânism goes, the Mahâyâna Buddhists have attached several definite shades of meaning to Nirvâna and tried to give each of them some special, distinctive character. When it is used in its most comprehensive metaphysical sense, it becomes synonymous with Suchness (*tattva*) or with the Dharmakâya. When we speak of Buddha 's entrance into Nirvâna, it means the end of material existence, i. e., death. When it is used in contrast to birth and death (*samsâra*) or to passion and sin (*kleça*), it signifies in the former case an eternal life or a state of immortality, and in the latter case a state of consciousness that follows from the recognition of the presence of the Dharmakâya in individual existences. Nirvâna has thus become a very comprehensive term, and this fact adds much to the confusion and misunderstanding with which it has been treated ever since Buddhism became known to the Occident. The so-called "primitive Buddhism" is not altogether unfamiliar with all these meanings given to Nirvâna, though in some cases they might have been but faintly foreshadowed. Most of European missionaries and scholars have ignored this fact and wanted to see in Nirvâna but one definite, stereotyped sense which will loosen or untie all the difficult knots connected with its use, One scholar would select a certain passage in a certain sûtra, where the meaning is tolerably distinct, and taking this as the key endeavor to solve all the rest; while another scholar would do the same thing with another passage from the scriptures and refute other fellow-workers. The majority of them, however, have found for missionary purposes to be advantageous to hold one meaning prominently above all the others that may be considered possibly the meaning of Nirvâna This one meaning that has been made specially conspicuous is its negativistic interpretation.

According to the *Vijñânamâtra çâstra* (Chinese version Vol. X.), the Mahâyâna Buddhists distinguish four forms of Nirvâna. They are:

(1) *Absolute Nirvâna*, as a synonym of the Dharmakâya. It is eternally immaculate in its essence and constitutes the truth and reality of all existences. Though it manifests itself in the world of defilement and relativity, its essence forever remains undefiled. While it embraces in itself innumerable incomprehensible spiritual virtues, it is absolutely simple and immortal; its perfect tranquillity may be likened unto space in which every conceivable motion is possible, but which remains in itself the same. It is universally present in all beings whether animate or inanimate [1] and makes their existence real. In one respect it can be identified with them, that is, it can be pantheistically viewed; but in the other respect it is transcen-

[1] The text does not expressly say "animate or inanimate", but this is the author's own interpretation according to the general spirit of Mahâyânism.

dental, for every being as it is is not Nirvâna. This spiritual significance is, however, beyond the ken of ordinary human understanding and can be grasped only by the highest intelligence of Buddha.

(2) *Upadhiçeṣa Nirvâna*, or Nirvâna that has some residue. This is a state of enlightenment which can be attained by Buddhists in their lifetime. The Dharmakâya which was dormant in them is now awakened and freed from the "affective obstacles,"[1] but they are yet under the bondage of birth and death; and thus they are not yet absolutely free from the misery of life: something still remains in them that makes them suffer pain.

(3) *Anupadhiçeṣa Nirvâna*, or Nirvâna that has no residue. This is attained when the Tathâgata-essence (the Dharmakâya) is released from the pain of birth and death as well as from the curse of passion and sin. This form of Nirvâna seems to be what is generally understood by Occidental missionary-scholars as the Nirvâna of Buddhists. While in lifetime, they have been emancipated from the egoistic conception of the soul, they have practised the Eightfold Path, and they

[1] There are two obstacles to final emancipation: (1) affective, and (2) intellectual. The former is our unenlightened affective or emotional or subjective life and the latter our intellectual prejudice. Buddhists should not only be pure in heart but be perfect in intelligence. Pious men are of course saved from transmigration, but to attain perfect Buddhahood they must have a clear, penetrating intellectual insight into the significance of life and existence and the destiny of the universe. This emphasising of the rational element in religion is one of the most characteristic points of Buddhism.

have destroyed all the roots of karma that makes possible their metempsychosis in the world of birth and death (*samsâra*), though as the inevitable sequence of their previous karma they have yet to suffer all the evils inherent in the material existence. But at last they have had even this mortal coil dissolved away, and have returned to the original Absolute from which by virtue of ignorance they had come out and gone through a cycle of births and deaths. This state of supramundane bliss in the realm of the Absolute is Anupadiçeṣa Nirvâna, that is, Nirvâna that has no residue.

(4) *The Nirvâna that has no abode.* In this, the Buddha-essence has not only been freed from the curse of passion and sin (*kleça*), but from the intellectual prejudice, which most tenaciously clings to the mind. The Buddha-essence or the Dharmakâya is revealed here in its perfect purity. All-embracing love and all-knowing intelligence illuminate the path. He who has attained to this state of subjective enlightenment is said to have no abode, no dwelling place, that is to say, he is no more subject to the transmigration of birth and death (*samsâra*), nor does he cling to Nirvâna as the abode of complete rest; in short, he is above Samsâra and Nirvâna. His sole object in life is to benefit all sentient beings to the end of time; but this he proposes to do not by his human conscious elaboration and striving Simply actuated by his all-embracing love which is of the Dharmakâya, he wishes to deliver all his fellow-creatures from misery, he does

not seek his own emancipation from the turmoil of life. He is fully aware of the transitoriness of worldly interests, but on this account he desires not to shun them. With his all-knowing intelligence he gains a spiritual insight into the ultimate nature of things and the final course of existence. He is one of those religious men "that weep, as though they wept not; that rejoice as though they rejoiced not; that buy, as though they possessed not; that use this world, as not abusing it; for the fashion of this world passes away." Nay, he is in one sense more than this; his life is full of positive activity, because his heart and soul are devoted to the leading of all beings to final emancipation and supreme bliss. When a man attains to this stage of spiritual life, he is said to be in the Nirvâna that has no abode.

A commentator on the *Vijñânamâtra Çâstra* adds that of these four forms of Nirvâna the first is possessed by every sentient being, whether it is actualised in its human perfection or lying dormant *in posse* and miserably obscured by ignorance; that the second and third are attained by all the Çrâvakas and Pratyekabuddhas, while it is a Buddha alone that is in possession of all the four forms of Nirvâna.

Nirvâna as the Dharmakâya.

It is manifest from the above statement that in Mahâyânism Nirvâna has acquired several shades of meaning psychological and ontological. This apparent confusion, however, is due to the purely idealistic tendency of Mahâyânism, which ignores the distinction usually made between being and thought, object and subject, the perceived and the perceiving. Nirvâna is not only a subjective state of enlightenment but an objective power through whose operation this beatific state becomes attainable. It does not simply mean a total absorption in the Absolute or of emancipation from earthly desires in lifetime as exemplified in the life of the Arhat. Mahâyânists perceive in Nirvâna not only this, but also its identity with the Dharmakâya, or Suchness, and recognise its universal spiritual presence in all sentient beings.

When Nâgârjuna says in his *Mâdhyamika Çâstra*[1] that: "That is called Nirvâna which is not wanting, is not acquired, is not intermittent, is not non-intermittent, is not subject to destruction, and is not created;" he evidently speaks of Nirvâna as a synonym of Dharmakâya, that is, in its first sense as above described. Chandra Kîrti, therefore, rightly comments that Nirvâna is *sarva-kalpanâ-kṣaya-rûpam*,[2] i. e., that which transcends all the forms of determination.

[1] This is one of the most important philosophical texts of Mahâyânism. Its original Sanskrit with the commentary of Chandra Kîrti has been edited by Satis Chandra Acharya and published by the Buddhist Text Society of India. The original lines run as follows (p. 193):

"Aprahînam, asamprâptam, anucchinnam, açâçvatam,
Aniruddham, anutpannam, evam nirvânam ucyate."

[2] Literally, that which is characterised by the absence of all characterisation.

Nirvâna is an absolute, it is above the relativity of existence (*bhâva*) and non-existence (*abhâva*).[1]

Nirvâna is sometimes spoken of as possessing four attributes; (1) eternal (*nitya*), (2) blissful (*sukha*), (3) self-acting (*âtman*), and (4) pure (*çuçi*). Judging from these qualities thus ascribed to Nirvâna as its essential features, Nirvâna is here again identified with the highest reality of Buddhism, that is, with the Dharmakâya. It is eternal because it is immaterial; it is blissful because it is above all sufferings; it is self-acting because it knows no compulsion; it is pure because it is not defiled by passion and error.[2]

[1] Cf. the following from the *Mâdhyamika*:
"Bhaved abbâvo bhâvaç ca nirvânam ubhayam katham:
Asamskṛtam ca nirvânam bhâvâbhavâi ca samskṛtam."
Or, "Tasmânna bhâvo nâbhâvo nirvânamiti yujyate"

[2] In the *Visuddhi-Magga* XXI. (Warren's translation, p. 376 et seq.), we read that there are three starting points of deliverance arising from the consideration of the three predominant qualities of the constituents of being: 1. The consideration of their beginnings and ends leads the thoughts to the unconditioned; 2. The insight into their miserableness agitates the mind and leads the thoughts to the desireless; 3. The consideration of the constituents of being as not having an ego leads the thoughts to the empty. And these three, we are told, constitute the three aspects of Nirvâna as unconditioned, desireless, and empty. Here we have an instance in the so-called Southern "primitive" Buddhism of viewing Nirvâna in the Mahâyânistic light which I have here explained at length.

En passant, let us remark that as Buddha did not leave any document himself embodying his whole system, there sprang up soon after his departure several schools explaining

Nirvâna in its Fourth Sense.

No further elucidation is needed for the first signification of Nirvâna, for we have treated it already when explaining the nature of the Dharmakâya. Nor is it necessary for us to dwell upon the second and the third phases of it. The Occidental missionary-scholars and Orientalists, however one-sided and often biased, have almost exhaustively investigated these points from the Pâli sources. What remains for us now is to analyse the Mahâyânistic conception of Nirvâna which was stated above as its fourth signification.

Nirvâna, briefly speaking, is a realisation in this life of the all-embracing love and all-knowing intelligence of Dharmakâya. It is the unfolding of the reason of existence, which in the ordinary human life remains more or less eclipsed by the shadow of ignorance and egoism. It does not consist in the mere observance of the moral precepts laid down by Buddha, nor in the blind following of the Eightfold Path, nor in retirement from the world and absorption in abstract meditation The Mahâyânistic Nirvâna is full of energy and activity which issues from the all-embracing love of the Dharmakâya. There is no passivity in it, nor a keeping aloof from the hurly-burly of worldliness.

the Master's view in divers ways, each claiming the legitimate interpretation; that in view of this fact it is illogical to conclude that Southern Buddhism is the authoritative representation par excellence of original Buddhism, while the Eastern or the Northern is a mere degeneration.

He who is in this Nirvâna does not seek a rest in the annihilation of human aspirations, does not flinch in the face of endless transmigration. On the contrary, he plunges himself into the ever-rushing current of Samsâra and sacrifices himself to save his fellow-creatures from being eternally drowned in it.

Though thus the Mahâyâna Nirvâna is realised only in the mire of passions and errors, it is never contaminated by the filth of ignorance. Therefore, he that is abiding in Nirvâna, even in the whirlpool of egoism and in the darkness of sin, does not lose his all-seeing insight that penetrates deep into the ultimate nature of being. He is aware of the transitoriness of things. He knows that this life is a mere passing moment in the eternal manifestation of the Dharmakâya, whose work can be realised only in boundless space and endless time. As he is fully awake to this knowledge, he never gets engrossed in the world of sin. He lives in the world like unto the lotus-flower, the emblem of immaculacy, which grows out of the mire and yet shares not its defilement. He is also like unto a bird flying in the air that does not leave any trace behind it. He may again be likened unto the clouds that spontaneously gather around the mountain peak, and, soaring high as the wind blows, vanish away to the region where nobody knows. In short, he is living in, and yet beyond, the realm of Samsâra and Nirvâna.

We read in the *Vimalakirti Sûtra* (chap. VIII.):

"Vimalakirti asks Mañjuçri: 'How is it that you

declare all [human] passions and errors are the seeds of Buddhahood?'

"Mañjuçri replies: 'O son of good family! Those who cling to the view of non-activity [*asamskṛita*] and dwell in a state of eternal annihilation do not awaken in them supremely perfect knowledge [*anuttara-samyak-sambodhi*]. Only the Bodhisattvas, who dwell in the midst of passions and errors, and who, passing through the [ten] stages, rightly contemplate the ultimate nature of things, are able to awaken and attain intelligence [*prajñâ*].

"'Just as the lotus-flowers do not grow in the dry land, but in the dark-colored, waterly mire, O son of good family, it is even so [with intelligence (*prajñâ* or *bodhi*)]. In non-activity and eternal annihilation which are cherished by the Çrâvakas and the Pratyekabuddhas, there is no opportunity for the seeds and sprouts of Buddhahood to grow. Intelligence can grow only in the mire and dirt of passion and sin. It is by virtue of passion and sin that the seeds and sprouts of Buddhahood are able to grow.

"'O son of good family! Just as no seeds can grow in the air, but in the filthy, muddy soil,—and there even luxuriously,—O son of good family, it is even so [with the Bodhi]. It does not grow out of non-activity and eternal annihilation. It is only out of the mountainous masses of egoistic, selfish thoughts that Intelligence is awakened and grows to the incomprehensible wisdom of Buddha-seeds.

"'O son of good family! Just as we cannot obtain priceless pearls unless we dive into the depths of the four great oceans, O son of good family, it is even so [with Intelligence]. If we do not dive deep into the mighty ocean of passion and sin, how could we get hold of the precious gem of Buddha-essence? Let it therefore be understood that the primordial seeds of Intelligence draw their vitality from the midst of passion and sin.' " In a Pauline epistle we read, "From the foulness of the soil, the beauty of new life grows." And Emerson sings:

> "Let me go where'er I will,
> I hear a sky-born music still.
> 'Tis not in the high stars alone,
> Nor in the cup of budding flowers,
> Nor in the redbreast's mellow tone,
> Nor in the bow that smiles in showers,
> But in the mud and scum of things.
> There always, always, something sings"

Do we not see here a most explicit statement of the Mahâyânistic sentiment?

Nirvâna and Samsâra are One.

The most remarkable feature in the Mahâyânistic conception of Nirvâna is expressed in this formula: "Yas kleças so bodhi, yas samsâras tat nirvânam." What is sin or passion, that is Intelligence, what is birth and death (or transmigration), that is Nirvâna. This is a rather bold and revolutionising proposition in the dogmatic history of Buddhism. But it is no more than the natural development of the spirit that was breathed by its founder.

In the *Viçeṣacinta-brahma-paripṛccha Sûtra,*[1] it is said that (chap. II):

"Samsâra is Nirvâna, because there is, when viewed from the ultimate nature of the Dharmakâya, nothing going out of, nor coming into, existence, [samsâra being only apparent]: Nirvâna is samsâra, when it is coveted and adhered to."

In another place (*op. cit.*) the idea is expressed in much plainer terms: "The essence of all things is in truth free from attachment, attributes, and desires; therefore, they are pure, and, as they are pure, we know that what is the essence of birth and death that is the essence of Nirvâna, and that what is the essence of Nirvâna that is the essence of birth and death (*samsâra*). In other words, Nirvâna is not to be sought outside of this world, which, though transient, is in reality no more than Nirvâna itself. Because it is contrary to our reason to imagine that there is Nirvâna and there is birth and death (*samsâra,*) and that the one lies outside the pale of the other, and, therefore, that we can attain Nirvâna only after we have annihilated or escaped the world of birth and death. If we are not hampered by our confused subjectivity, this our worldly life is an activity of Nirvâna itself."

Nâgârjuna repeats the same sentiment in his *Mâdhyamika Çâstra*, when he says:

[1] There are three Chinese translations of this Mahâyâna text, by Dharmarakṣa, Kumârajîva, and Bodhiruci, between 265 and 517 A. D.

"Samsâra is in no way to be distinguished from Nirvâna:
Nirvâna is in no way to be distinguished from Samsâra."[1]

Or,

"The sphere of Nirvâna is the sphere of Samsâra:
Not the slightest distinction exists between them."[2]

Asanga goes a step further and boldly declares that all the Buddha-dharmas, of which Nirvâna or Dharmakâya forms the foundation, are characterised with the passions, errors, and sins of vulgar minds. He says in *Mahâyâna-Sangraha Çâstra* (the Chinese Tripitaka, Japanese edition of 1881, *wang* VIII., p. 84):

"(1) All Buddha-dharmas are characterised with eternality, for the Dharmakâya is eternal.

"(2) All Buddha-dharmas are characterised with an extinguishing power, for they extinguish all the obstacles for final emancipation.

"(3) All Buddha-dharmas are characterised with regeneration, for the Nirmânakâya [Body of Transformation] constantly regenerates.

"(4) All Buddha-dharmas are characterised with the power of attainment, for by the attainment [of truth] they subjugate innumerable evil passions as cherished by ignorant beings.

"(5) All Buddha-dharmas are characterised with the desire to gain, ill humor, folly, and all the other

[1] Samsârasya ca nirvânât kincid asti viçeṣaṇam:
Na nirvâṇasya samsârât kincid asti viçesaṇam.

[2] Nirvâṇasya ca yâ kotiḥ kotiḥ samsârasya ca,
Vidyâdanantaraṃ kincit susuksnaṃ vidyate.

passions of vulgar minds, for it is through the Buddha's love that those depraved souls are saved.

"(6) All Buddha-dharmas are characterised with non-attachment and non-defilement, for Suchness which is made perfect by these virtues cannot be defiled by any evil powers.

"(7) All Buddha-dharmas are above attachment and defilement, for though all Buddhas reveal themselves in the world, worldliness cannot defile them." [1]

Buddha-dharma means any thing, or any virtue, or any faculty, that belongs to Buddhahood. Non-attachment is a Buddha-dharma, love is a Buddha-dharma, wisdom is a Buddha-dharma, and in fact anything is a Buddha-dharma which is an attribute of the Perfect One, not to mention the Dharmakâya or Nirvâna which constitutes the very essence of Buddhahood. Therefore, the conclusion which is to be drawn from those seven propositions of Asanga as above quoted is this: Not only is this world of constant transformation as a whole Nirvâna, but its apparent errors and sins and evils are also the various phases of the manifestation of Nirvâna.

The above being the Mahâyânistic view of Nirvâna, it is evident that Nirvâna is not something transcendental or that which stands above this world of birth

[1] Concerning the similarity in meaning of this statement to the one just preceding, a commentator says that the sixth is the statical view of Suchness (or Dharmakâya) and the seventh its dynamical view. One explains what the highest reality of Buddhism is and the other what it does or works.

and death, joy and sorrow, love and hate, peace and struggle. Nirvâna is not to be sought in the heavens nor after a departure from this earthly life nor in the annihilation of human passions and aspirations. On the contrary, it must be sought in the midst of worldliness, as life with all its thrills of pain and pleasure is no more than Nirvâna itself. Extinguish your life and seek Nirvâna in anchoretism, and your Nirvâna is forever lost. Consign your aspirations, hopes, pleasures, and woes, and everything that makes up a life to the eternal silence of the grave, and you bury Nirvâna never to be recovered. In asceticism, or in meditation, or in ritualism, or even in metaphysics, the more impetuously you pursue Nirvâna, the further away it flies from you. It was the most serious mistake ever committed by any religious thinkers to imagine that Nirvâna which is the complete satisfaction of our religious feeling could be gained by laying aside all human desires, ambitions, hopes, pains, and pleasures. Have your own Bodhi (intelligence) thoroughly enlightened through love and knowledge, and everything that was thought sinful and filthy turns out to be of divine purity. It is the same human heart, formerly the fount of ignorance and egoism, now the abode of eternal beatitude — Nirvâna shining in its intrinsic magnificence.

Suppose a torch light is taken into a dark cell, which people had hitherto imagined to be the abode of hideous, uncanny goblins, and which on that account they wanted to have completely destroyed to the ground. The bright light now ushered in at once disperses the darkness, and every nook and corner therein is perfectly illumined. Everything in it now assumes its proper aspect. And to their surprise people find that those figures which they formerly considered to be uncanny and horrible are nothing but huge precious stones, and they further learn that every one of those stones can be used in some way for the great benefit of their fellow-creatures. The dark cell is the human heart before the enlightenment of Nirvâna, the torch light is love and intelligence. When love warms and intelligence brightens, the heart finds every passion and sinful desire that was the cause of unbearable anguish now turned into a divine aspiration. The heart itself, however, remains the same just as much as the cell, whose identity was never affected either by darkness or by brightness. This parable nicely illustrates the Mahâyânistic doctrine of the identity of Nirvâna and Samsâra, and of the Bodhi and Kleça, that is, of intelligence and passion.

Therefore, it is said:

"All sins transformed into the constituents of enlightenment!
The vicissitudes of Samsâra transformed into the beatitude of Nirvâna!
All these come from the exercise of the great religious discipline (*upâya*);
Beyond our understanding, indeed, is the mystery of all Buddhas."[1]

[1] *The Discourse on Buddha-essence* by Vasubandhu. The Japanese Tripitaka edition of 1881, fas. II., p. 84, where the stanza is quoted from the *Sûtra on the Incomprehensible.*

The Middle Course.

In one sense the Buddha always showed an eclectic, conciliatory, synthetic spirit in his teachings. He refused to listen to any extreme doctrine which elevates one end too high at the expense of the other and culminates in the collapse of the whole edifice. When the Buddha left his seat of enlightenment under the Bodhi tree, he made it his mission to avoid both extremes, asceticism and hedonism. He proved throughout his life to be a calm, dignified, thoughtful, well-disciplined person, and at no time irritable in character, — in this latter respect being so different from the sage of Nazareth, who in anger cast out all the tradesmen in the temple and overthrew the tables of the money-changers, and who cursed the fig tree on which he could not find any fruit but leaves unfit to appease his hunger. The doctrine of the Middle Path (*Mâdhyamârga*), whatever it may mean morally and intellectually, always characterised the life and doctrine of Buddha as well as the later development of his teachings. His followers, however different in their individual views, professed as a rule to pursue steadily the Middle Path as paved by the Master. Even when Nâgârjuna proclaimed his celebrated doctrine of Eight No's which seems to superficial critics nothing but an absolute nihilism, he said that the Middle Path could be found only in those eight no's.[1]

[1] This is expressed in the first verse of the *Mâdhyamika Çâstra*, which runs as follows:

Mahâyânism has certainly applied this synthetic method of Buddha to its theory of Nirvâna and ennobled it by fully developing its immanent signification. In the *Discourse on Buddha-essence*, Vasubandhu quotes the following passage from the *Çrimala Sûtra*, which plainly shows the path along which the Mahâyânists traveled before they reached their final conclusion: "Those who see only the transitoriness of existence are called nihilists, and those who see only the eternality of Nirvâna are called eternalists. Both views are incorrect." Vasubandhu then proceeds to say: "Therefore, the Dharmakâya of the Tathâgata is free from both extremes, and on that account it is called the Great Eternal Perfection. When viewed from this absolute standpoint of Suchness, the logical distinction between Nirvâna and Samsâra cannot in reality be maintained, and hereby we enter upon the realm of non-duality." And this realm of non-duality is the Middle Path of Nirvâna, not in its nihilistic, but in its Mahâyânistic, significance.

How to Realise Nirvâna.

How can we attain the Middle Path of Nirvâna? How can we realise a life that is neither pessimistic asceticism nor materialistic hedonism? How can we steer through the whirlpools of Samsâra without being

"Anirodham anutpâdam anucchedam açâçvatam
Anekârtham anânârtham anâgamam anirgamam."

Literally translated these lines read:

"No annihilation, no production, no destruction, no persistence,
No unity, no plurality, no coming in, no going out."

swallowed up and yet braving their turbulent gyration? The answer to this can readily be given, when we understand, as repeatedly stated above, that this life is the manifestation of the Dharmakâya, and that the ideal of human existence is to realise within the possibilities of his mind and body all that he can conceive of the Dharmakâya. And this we have found to be all-embracing love and all-seeing intelligence. Destroy then your ignorance at one blow and be done with your egoism, and there springs forth an eternal stream of love and wisdom.

Says Vasubandhu: "By virtue of Prajñâ [intelligence or wisdom], our egoistic thoughts are destroyed: by virtue of Karuṇâ [love], altruistic thoughts are cherished. By virtue of Prajñâ, the [affective] attachment inherent in vulgar minds is abolished; by virtue of Karuṇâ, the [intellectual] attachment as possessed by the Çrâvakas and Pratyekabuddhas is abolished. By virtue of Prajñâ, Nirvâna [in its transcendental sense] is not rejected; by virtue of Karuṇâ, Samsâra [with its changes and transmigrations] is not rejected. By virtue of Prajñâ the truth of Buddhism is attained; by virtue of Karuṇâ, all sentient beings are matured [for salvation]."

The practical life of a Buddhist runs in two opposite, though not antagonistic, directions, one upward and the other downward, and the two are synthesised in the Middle Path of Nirvâna. The upward direction points to the intellectual comprehension of the truth, while the downward one to a realisation of all-embracing love among his fellow-creatures. One is complemented by the other. When the intellectual side is too much emphasised at the expense of the emotional, we have a Pratyekabuddha, a solitary thinker, whose fountain of tears is dry and does not flow over the sufferings of his fellow-beings. When the emotional side alone is asserted to the extreme, love acquires the egoistic tint that colors everything coming in contact with it. Because it does not discriminate and takes sensuality for spirituality. If it does not turn out sentimentalism, it will assume a hedonistic form. How many superstitious, or foul, or even atrocious deeds in the history of religion have been committed under the beautiful name of religion, or love of God and mankind! It makes the blood run cold when we think how religious fanatics burned alive their rivals or opponents at the stake, cruelly butchered thousands of human lives within a day, brought desolation and ruin throughout the land of their enemies, — and all these works of the Devil executed for sheer love of God! Therefore, says Devala, the author of the *Discourse on the Mahâpuruṣa* (Great Man): "The wise do not approve lovingkindness without intelligence, nor do they approve intelligence without lovingkindness; because one without the other prevents us from reaching the highest path." Knowledge is the eye, love is the limb. Directed by the eye, the limb knows how to move; furnished with the limb, the eye can attain what it perceives. Love alone is blind, knowledge alone is lame. It is only when one is supplemented by the other that we have a perfect, complete man.

In Buddha as the ideal human being we recognise the perfection of love and intelligence; for it was in him that the Dharmakâya found its perfect realisation in the flesh. But as far as the Bodhisattvas are concerned, their natural endowments are so diversified and their temperament is so uneven that in some the intellectual elements are more predominant while in others the emotional side is more pronounced, that while some are more prone to practicality others preferably look toward intellectualism. Thus, as a matter of course, some Bodhisattvas will be more of philosophers than of religious seers. They may tend in some cases to emphasise the intellectual side of religion more than its emotional side and uphold the importance of prajñâ (intelligence) above that of karuṇâ (love). But the Middle Path of Nirvâna lies in the true harmonisation of prajñâ and karuṇâ, of bodhi and upâya, of knowledge and love, of intellect and feeling.

Love Awakens Intelligence

But if we have to choose between the two, let us first have all-embracing love, the Buddhists would say; for it is love that awakens in us an intense desire to find the way of emancipating the masses from perpetual sufferings and eternal transmigration. The intellect will now endeavor to realise its highest possibilities; the Bodhi will exhibit its fullest strength. When it is found out that this life is an expression of the Dharmakâya which is one and eternal, that individual existences have no selfhood (*âtman* or *svabhâva*) as far as they are due to the particularisation of subjective ignorance, and, therefore, that we are true and real only when we are conceived as one in the absolute Dharmakâya, the Bodhisattva's love which caused him to search after the highest truth will now unfold its fullest significance.

This love, or faith in the Mahâyâna, as it is sometimes called, is felt rather vaguely at the first awakening of the religious consciousness, and agitates the mind of the aspirant, whose life has hitherto been engrossed in every form of egocentric thought and desire. He no more finds an unalloyed satisfaction, as the Çrâvakas or the Pratyekabuddhas do, in his individual emancipation from the curse of Samsâra. However sweet the taste of release from the bond of ignoranee, it is lacking something that makes the freedom perfectly agreeable to the Bodhisattva who thinks more of others than of himself; to be sweet as well as acceptable, it must be highly savored with lovingkindness which embraces all his fellow-beings as his own children. The emancipation of the Çrâvaka or of the Prayekabuddha is like a delicious food which is wanting in saline taste, for it is no more than a dry, formal philosophical emancipation. Love is that which stimulates a man to go beyond his own interests. It is the mother of all Buddhas and Bodhisattvas. The sacred motive that induces them to renounce a life of Nirvânic self-complacency, is nothing but their boundless love for all beings. They do not wish to rest in their individual emancipation, they want to have all sentient creatures without a single exception emancipated and blest in paradisiacal happiness. Love, therefore, bestows on us two spiritual benefits: (1) It saves all beings from misery and (2) awakens in us the Buddha-intelligence.

The following passages quoted at random from Devala's *Mahâpuruṣa* will help our readers to understand the true signification of Nirvâna and the value of love (*karuṇâ*) as estimated by the Mahâyânists.

"Those who are afraid of transmigration and seek their own benefits and happiness in final emancipation, are not at all comparable to those Bodhisattvas, who rejoice when they come to assume a material existence once again, for it affords them another opportunity to benefit others. Those who are only capable of feeling their own selfish sufferings may enter into Nirvâna [and not trouble themselves with the sufferings of other creatures like themselves]; but the Bodhisattva who feels in himself all the sufferings of his fellow-beings as his own, how can he bear the thought of leaving others behind while he is on his way to final emancipation, and when he himself is resting in Nirvânic quietude?..... Nirvâna in truth consists in rejoicing at other's being made happy, and Samsâra in not so feeling. He who feels a universal love for his fellow-creatures will rejoice in distributing blessings among them and find his Nirvâna in so doing.[1]

[1] Compare this Buddhist sentiment of universal love with that of the Christian religion and we shall see the truth that

"Suffering really consists in pursuing one's egotistic happiness, while Nirvâna is found in sacrificing one's welfare for the sake of others. People generally think that it is an emancipation when they are released from their own pain, but a man with loving heart finds it in rescuing others from misery.

"With people who are not kindhearted, there is no sin that will not be committed by them. They are called the most wicked whose hearts are not softened at the sight of others, misfortune and suffering.

"When all beings are tortured by avarice, passion, ill humor, infatuation, and folly, and are constantly threatened by the misery of birth and death, disease and decay..... how can the Bodhisattva live among them and not feel pity for them?

"Of all good virtues, lovingkindness stands foremost.... It is the source of all merit.... It is the

all religions are one at the bottom. We read in Thomas à Kempis's *Imitation of Christ* (ch. XIII): "My son, I descended from heaven for thy salvation; I took upon me thy sorrows, not necessity but love drawing me thereto; that thou thyself mightest learn patience and bear temporal sufferings without repining For from the hour of my birth, even until my death on the cross, I was not without suffering of grief." This is exactly the sentiment that stimulates the Bodhisattvas to their gigantic task of universal salvation. Those who are free from sectarian biases will admit without hesitation that there is but one true religion which may assume various forms according to circumstances. "Many are the roads to the summit, but when reached there we have but one universal moonlight."

mother of all Buddhas. . . . It induces others to take refuge in the incomparable Bodhi.

"The loving heart of a Bodhisattva is annoyed by one thing, that all beings are constantly tortured and threatened by all sorts of pain."

Let us quote another interesting passage from a Mahâyâna sûtra.

When Vimalakirti was asked why he did not feel well, he made the following reply, which is full of religious significance: "From ignorance there arises desire and that is the cause of my illness. As all sentient beings are ill, so am I ill. When all sentient beings are healed of their illness, I shall be healed of my illness, too. Why? The Bodhisattva suffers birth and death because of sentient beings. As there is birth and death, so there is illness. When sentient beings are delivered from illness, the Bodhisattvas will suffer no more illness. When an only son in a good family is sick, the parents feel sick too: when he is recovered they are well again. So it is with the Bodhisattva. He loves all sentient beings as his own children. When they are sick, he is sick too. When they are recovered, he is well again. Do you wish to know whence this [sympathetic] illness is? The illness of the Bodhisattva comes from his all-embracing love (*mahâkarunâ*")).

This gospel of universal love is the consummation of all religious emotions whatever their origin. Without this, there is no religion — that is, no religion that is animated with life and spirit. For it is in the fact and nature of things that we are not moved by mere contemplation or mere philosophising. Every religion may have its own way of intellectually interpreting this fact, but the practical result remains the same everywhere, viz. that it cannot survive without the animating energy of love. Whatever sound and fine reasoning there may be in the doctrine of the Çrâvaka and the Pratyekabuddha, the force that is destined to conquer the world and to deliver us from misery is not intellection, but the will, i. e. the pûrvapranidhâna of the Dharmakâya.

Conclusion.

We now conclude. What is most evident from what we have seen above is that the Mahâyâna Nirvâna is not the annihilation of life but its enlightenment, that it is not the nullification of human passions and aspirations but their purification and ennoblement. This world of eternal transmigration is not a place which should be shunned as the playground of evils, but should be regarded as the place of ever-present opportunities given to us for the purpose of unfolding all our spiritual possibilities and powers for the sake of the universal welfare. There is no need for us to shrink, like the snail into his cozy shelter, before the duties and burdens of life. The Bodhisattva, on the contrary, finds Nirvâna in a concatenation of births and deaths and boldly faces the problem of evil and solves it by purifying the Bodhi from subjective ignorance.

His rule of conduct is:

> "Sabba pâpassa akaranam,
> Kusalassa upasampada,
> Sacitta pariyodapanam;
> Etam buddhânu sâsanam." [1]

His aspirations are solemnly expressed in this, which we hear daily recited in the Mahâyâna Buddhist temples and monasteries and seminaries:

> "Sentient beings, however innumerable, I take vow to save;
> Evil passions, however inextinguishable, I take vow to destroy;
> The avenues of truth, however numberless, I take vow to study;
> The way of the Enlightened, however unsurpassable, I take vow to attain."

And an indefatigable pursuit of these noble aims will finally lead to the heaven of the Buddhists, Nirvâna, which is not a state of eternal quietude, but the source of energy and intelligence.

By way of summary, and to avoid all misconceptions, let me repeat once more that Nirvâna is thus no negation of life, nor is it an idle contemplation on the misery of existence. The life of a Buddhist consists by no means in the monotonous repetition of reciting the sûtras and going his rounds for meals. Far from that. He enters into all the forms of life-activity, for he does not believe that universal emanci-

[1] The *Dharmapada*, XIV. 5. Mr. A. J. Edmunds's translation is,

> "Ceasing to do all wrong,
> Initiation into goodness,
> Cleansing the heart:
> This the religion of the Buddhas."

ipation is achieved by imprisoning himself in the cloister.

Theoretically speaking, Nirvâna is the dispersion of the clouds of ignorance hovering around the light of Bodhi. Morally, it is the suppression of egoism and the awakening of love (*karunâ*). Religiously, it is the absolute surrender of the self to the will of the Dharmakâya. When the clouds of ignorance are dispersing, our intellectual horizon gets clearer and wider; we perceive that our individual existences are like bubbles and lightnings, but that thay obtain reality in their oneness with the Body of Dharma. This conviction compels us to eternally abandon our old egoistic conception of life. The ego finds its significance only when it is conceived in relation to the not-ego, that is, to the *alter*; in other words, self-love has no meaning whatever unless it is purified by love for others. But this love for others must not remain blind and unenlightened, it must be in harmony with the will of the Dharmakâya which is the norm of existence and the reason of being. The mission of love is ennobled and fulfilled in its true sense when we come to the faith that says "thy will be done." Love without this resignation to the divine ordinance is merely another form of egoism: the root is already rotten, how can its trunk, stems, leaves, and flowers make a veritable growth?

Let us then conclude with the following reflections of the Bodhisattva, in which we read the whole signification of Buddhism.

"Having practised all the six virtues of perfection (*pâramitâ*) and innumerable other meritorious deeds, the Bodhisattva reflects in this wise:

" 'All the good deeds practised by me are for the benefit of all sentient beings, for their ultimate purification [from sin]. By the merit of these good deeds I pray that all sentient beings be released from the innumerable sufferings suffered by them in their various abodes of existence. By the turning over (*parivarta*) of these deeds I would be a haven for all beings and deliver them from their miserable existences; I would be a great beacon-light to all beings and dispel the darkness of ignorance and make the light of intelligence shine.'

"He reflects again in this wise:

" 'All sentient beings are creating evil karma in innumerable ways, and by reason of this karma they suffer innumerable sufferings. They do not recognise the Tathâgata, do not listen to the Good Law, do not pay homage to the congregration of holy men. All these beings carry an innumerable amount of great evil karma and are destined to suffer in innumerable ways. For their sake I will in the midst of the three evil creations suffer all their sufferings and deliver every one of them. Painful as these sufferings are, I will not retreat, I will not be frightened. I will not be negligent, I will not forsake my fellow-beings. Why? Because it is the will [of the Dharmakâya] that all sentient beings should be universally emancipated.'

"He reflects again in this wise:

" 'My conduct will be like the sun-god who with his universal illumination seeks not any reward, who ceases not on account of one unrighteous person to make a great display of his magnificent glory, who on account of one unrighteous person abandons not the salvation of all beings. Through the dedication (*parivarta*) of all my merits I would make every one of my fellow-creatures happy and joyous.' " (The *Avatamsaka Sûtra*, fas XIV).

APPENDIX

HYMNS OF MAHÂYÂNA FAITH.

DHARMAKÂYA (TATHÂGATA).[1]

In all beings there abideth the Dharmakâya;
With all virtues dissolved in it, it liveth in eternal
calmness.
It knoweth nor birth nor death, coming nor going;
Not one, not two; not being, not becoming;
Yet present everywhere in worlds of beings:
This is what is perceived by all Tathâgatas.
All virtues, material and immaterial,
Dependent on the Dharmakâya, are eternally pure in it.

Like unto the sky is the ultimate nature of the Dharmakâya;
Far away from the six dusts, it is defilement-free.
Of no form and devoid of all attributes is the Dharmakâya,
In which are void both actor and action:
The Dharmakâya of all Buddhas, thus beyond comprehension,
Quells all the struggles of sophistry and dialectics,
Distances all the efforts of intellection,
Thoughts all are dead in it, and suchness alone abideth.

THE DHARMAKÂYA OF TATHÂGATA.[2]

In all the worlds over the ten quarters,
O ye, sentient creatures living there,
Behold the most venerable of men and gods,
Whose spiritual Dharma-body is immaculate and pure.

As through the power of one mind,
A host of thoughts is evolved:
So from one Dharma-body of Tathâgata,
Are produced all the Buddha-bodies.

In Bodhi nothing dual there existeth,
Nor is any thought of self present:
The Dharma-body, undefiled and non-dual,
In its full splendor manifesteth itself everywhere.

Its ultimate reality is like unto the vastness of space;
Its manifested forms are like unto magic shows;
Its virtues excellent are inexhaustible,
This, indeed, the spiritual state of Buddhas only.

All the Buddhas of the present, past, and future,
Each one of them is an issue of the Dharma-body immaculate and pure;
Responding to the needs of sentient creatures,
They manifest themselves everywhere, assuming corporeality which is beautiful.

They never made the premeditation
That they would manifest in such and such forms.
Separated are they from all desire and anxiety,
And free and self-acting are their responses.

They do not negate the phenomenality of dharmas,
Nor do they affirm the world of individuals:
But manifesting themselves in all forms,
They teach and convert all sentient creatures.

The Dharma-body is not changeable,
Neither is it unchangeable;
All dharmas [in essence] are without change,
But manifestations are changeable.

The Sambodhi knoweth no bounds,
Extending as far as the limits of the Dharmaloka itself;
Its depths are bottomless, and its extent limitless;
Words and speeches are powerless to describe it.

Of all the ways that lead to Enlightenment
The Tathâgata knoweth the true significance;
Wandering freely all over the worlds,
Obstacles he encountereth nowhere.

THE TATHÂGATA. (1)[3]

The Tathâgata appeared not on earth,
Nor did he enter into Nirvana;
By the supreme power of his inmost will,
He reveals himself freely as he wills.[4]

This fact is beyond comprehension,
Belongs not to the sphere of a limited consciousness,
Only an intelligence perfect and gone beyond
Is able to have an insight into the realm of Buddhas.

The material body is not the Tathâgata,
Nor is the voice, nor the sound :
Yet he is not beyond the visible and the audible:
The Buddha has indeed a power miraculous.

People of little faith are unable to know
The inmost adytum of Buddhahood.
It is by the perfecting of primordial karma-intelligence
That the realm of all Buddhas is revealed.

All Buddhas come from nowhere,
And depart for nowhere:
The Body of Dharma that is pure, immaculate, and
 incomprehensible,
Is invested with a power miraculously free.

In infinity of worlds,
Revealing itself in the body of Tathâgata,
It universally preaches the Law supremely excellent,
And in its heart no attachment lingers.

An intellect that knows no limits or bounds
Perceives no obstacles in all dharmas,
And penetrates into the depths of the Dharmaloka,
Revealing itself with a power miraculously divine.

All sentient beings and all creatures,
It understandeth thoroughly without difficulty:
Its Bodies of Transformation are innumerable,
And universally revealed in all the worlds.

Those who seek after All-knowledge
May in course of time attain perfect enlightenment;
Let them above all purify the heart
And complete their discipline in Bodhisattvahood.

And then they will see the Tathâgata's
Immeasurable power that comes from his free will;
Devoid of all doubts they are, and accompanied
With sages whose virtue is unsurpassable.

THE TATHÂGATA (2).[5]

The Tathâgata, in pure golden color,
And in person resplendent and majestic,
In innumerable ages past,
All merits hath accumulated.

With bliss and wisdom all in perfection,
And the highest enlightenment attaining.
And with great loving heart animated,
He now appeareth in this world of endurance.

Men and devas and the eight hosts of demons,
All pay him homage most reverent,
Who, from his inmost self-being,
Preacheth the deepest spiritual Dharma.

Which is so unfathomably deep,
That Buddha alone can understand it:
Multitudes of beings, ignorant and blind,
Listening to it, are unable to comprehend.

The Tathâgata is the great leader of beings;
With skill that is excellent and marvellous,
Guiding all those ignorant souls,
By degrees bringeth them to Enlightenment.

The heart of all beings is miraculously bright,
And eternally calm in its being.
Pure and immaculate and defilement-free,
It is replenished with all merits.

Its essence is like unto the sky:
Devoid of all liminations,
Knoweth neither birth nor death,
And there is neither coming nor departing.

Eternally abiding in the Dharma-essence,
It is immovable as the Mount Sumeru;
The oneness in it of all beings
Is indeed beyond finite knowledge.

Vulgar minds from time immemorial,
Blindly clinging to all passions,
Are thrown deep into the ocean of pain,
And know not how to escape.

The most profound doctrine of Tathâgata,
Full of meaning, spiritual and transcendental,
With recipient intellects in all degrees,
In harmony unfoldeth he the Law.

A shower of one taste from above
Covering all the ten quarters,
Grasses and trees, woods and forests,
Roots and trunks, large and small,

Of all growing on this vast earth,
Nothing is there that thereby itself benefiteth not.
The Law delivered by the Tathâgata
May even be likened unto it.

With one voice which is wondrous,
He giveth utterance to thoughts innumerable,
That are received by audience of all sort,
Each understanding them in his own way.

In this wise among the assemblage,
None is there but that enters upon Buddha-knowledge
Such is Buddha's miraculous power,
Truly called "Incomprehensible."

REPENTANCE. [6]

Those who repent as prescribed by the Dharma,
Altogether their earthly sins uproot;
As fire on doomsday the world will consume,
With its mountain peaks and infinite seas.

Repentance burns up of earthly desires the fuel;
Repentance to heaven the sinners is leading;
Repentance the bliss of the four Dhyânas imparteth;
Repentance brings showers of jewels and gems;

Repentance a holy life renders firm as a diamond;
Repentance transports to the palace of bliss everlasting;
Repentance from the triple world's prison releases;
Repentance makes blossom the bloom of the Bodhi.

ALL BEINGS ARE MOTHERS AND FATHERS.

All senient beings in transmigration travel through the six gatis,
Like unto a wheel revolving without beginning and end,
Becoming in turn fathers and mothers, men and women:
Generations and generations, each owes something to others.

Ye should then regard all beings as fathers and mothers;
Though this truth is too hidden to be recognised without
the aid of Holy Knowledge,
All men are your fathers,
All women are your mothers.

While not yet requiting their love received in your prior lives,
Why should ye, thinking otherwise, harbor enmity?
Ever thinking of love, endeavor ye to benefit one another;
And provoke ye not hostility, quarreling and insulting.

THE TEN PÂRAMITÂS.

O ye, sons of Buddha, in the Holy Way trained,
With the Heart of Highest Intelligence awakened,
And living in seclusion at the Aranyaka,
Should practice the ten pâramitâs.

At daily meal think ye first of almsgiving,
And also distribute among beings the Treasure of Law;
When the three rings [7] are pure, it is called true charity;
Through this practice perfected are the merits of discipline.

Would ye understand the merits of almsgiving?
Know ye that it comes from the heart pure, and not from the wealth given;
A precious treasure with a heart unclean,
Is surpassed by a mite with a heart clean.

Wealth giving is a dâna-pâramitâ,
And there are other dâna-pâramitâs:
To give away one's life, wife, or children,
This is called blood-giving.

Should a man of good family come and ask for the Law
Let him have all the Mahâyâna sûtras explained,
And awaken in him the Heart of Highest Intelligence;
This is called a true pâramitâ.

With sympathy and pure faith and conscience,
Embrace ye all beings and befree them from greed,
That they might attain to the highest intelligence of the Tathâgata:
The giving of wealth and of the Law is the first pâramitâ.

Firmly observing the three sets of the Bodhisattva-çîlas,[8]
O ye, evolve the Bodhi, distance birth-and-death,
Guard the Law of Buddha and make it long live in the world,
Repent the violation of the çîlas, and be always mindful of the true ones.

Subdue ye anger and hate and cultivate in your heart love and sympathy;
Mindful of the karma past, harbor ye not evil thoughts against offenders;
Be not reluctant for the sake of all beings to sacrifice life:
This is called the pâramitâ of meekness.

In practicing what is hard to practice, hesitate ye not awhile;
With ever-increasing energy through three asankheya kalpas,
Defile not yourselves, but always discipline the heart;
And for the sake of all creatures seek ye salvation.

Entering into and rising from the Samâdhi, spiritual freedom
is obtained:
Transforming yourselves and travelling in all the ten quarters,
Have for all beings the cause of evil desire removed,
And let them seek deliverance in the doctrine of Samâdhi.

Would ye desire to attain to True Intelligence?
Friendly approach Bodhisattvas and Tathâgatas;
Gladly listening to the doctrine transcendental and sublime,
Attain ye the three disciplines [9] and remove the two obstacles [10].

Recognising difference in the disposition of beings,
Apply the medicine proper for each disease:
Love and sympathy, skill and expediency, each fitting the case,
Try the proper means for the benefit of the multitudes.

Would ye know the true meaning of existence?
The middle path lies in non-attachment, neither "yea"
nor "nay";
Intelligence pure is unfathomable and unites in Suchness;
Identify mine with thine, embracing the whole.

By the force of intellect, grasping the nature of beings,
Teach the masses each in accord with his capacity;
The force of intellect penetrating through the heart of all
beings,
Destroys the root of transmigration in birth and death.

Intelligently judging between black and white,
Conscientiously take hold of one and put the other aside,
and let each rest in its place;
Samsâra and Nirvâna are but one in their essence;
Fulfilling the meaning of existence, cherish ye not self-conceit.

These ten deeds of excellence
Comprise all eighty-four thousand virtues;
Each in its class excels all the others,
And is called the Pâramitâ of Bodhisattva.

Eighty-four thousand samâdhis
Becalm the disturbant mind of all beings;
Eighty-four thousand dhâranîs
Keep away all the prejudices and evil influences.

The Great Sage, King of Dharma, with marvellous skill,
Teacheth the Law in three ways and converteth all beings;
Casting the net of the Doctrine in the ocean of birth and death,
He draweth out men and gods to the abode of bliss.

THE BODHI. [11]

All things are of the Bodhi,
The Bodhi is in all things;
The Bodhi and all things are one:
Who knoweth this is called the World-honored.

NIRVANA AND THE THREE EVILS.

Greed is Nirvana;
So is hate, and folly;
In these three passions
There dwells a Buddha-dharma inexpressible.

Who severalises, thinking,
"There's greed, and hate, and folly,"
He is as far from Buddha,
As heaven from earth.

The Bodhi and greed,
They're one, not two:
Out of one Dharma-gate cometh all;
Here's sameness, no diversity.

This hearing, the vulgar stand aghast;
Far from the Buddha-path are they.
The heart, when innocent of greed, [12]
Is never troubled.

In whose mind self is lurking still,
And who imagines that something he has,
Greedy is this man called,
And he is bound for hell.

What is the true nature of greed,
That is the nature of Buddha-dharma;
What is the nature of Buddha-dharma,
That is the nature of greed. [13]

These two are of one nature;
That is, of no-nature;
Who knoweth this truth,
Would be the world-leader.

NON-ATMAN AND PREJUDICE. [14]

There once was an ignorant man;
So afraid of the sky was he
That piteously crying he wandered away.
Of its sudden collapse he was fearful.
But the sky has no boundary,
And to nobody 't will be harmful.
It was due to his ignorance
That he trembled so fitfully.
With the Bhikshus and Brahmans
It is even so, who are prejudiced.
Learning that empty is the world,
Alarmed are they at heart;
And wrongly imagine that if empty were the nature of Âtman
Nothingness would be the end of all work.

NON-ACTION.

As the vacuity of sky,
Being so clear and free of cloud and fog,
Upon the earth below,
Betrays no signs a shower to give:
So the enlightened
Betray no learning, no intelligence:
And we, sentient beings,
Can trace no efforts in their deliverance of the Law. [15]

SELF-DELUSION.

There lived once a painter,
Who such a monstrous Yaksha painted
That he himself was terrified
And losing all his senses on the ground he fell:
'Tis even so with vulgar minds;
Infatuated, self-deluded by the senses,
Of their own error they are unaware,
And go from birth to birth without an end.

ALL IN ONE.

As all the waters in the valley
Are emptied in the ocean
Which is of one and the same taste:
So the enlightened,
Whatever is
Good and beneficial,
Turn over to the Bodhi
And to that Reality
In which all things become of one and the same taste.

NIHILISM.

The vast vacuity of space,
How limitless and measureless!
But in the midst of the void
How could a farmer sow his seeds?
'Tis even so with Nihilism:
The past is gone forever,
The future's not here yet,
And in the present no Buddha-seeds have they.

THE NIHILIST.

A man who suffers from a disease incurable,
However excellent his treatment be,
Impossible he will find his health to gain,
For his defies all means of remedy.
'Tis even so with them who walk in the way of emptiness;
No matter whereso'er they be,
How blindly they are clinging unto it!
Such I declare to be incurable.

THE BUDDHA'S DHARMA (I)

As in its oneness the element earth
Embraces diversities of objects,
And discriminates not this or that;
Even so is it with all the Buddha's Dharma.

As in its oneness the element fire
Burns everything on earth,
And discriminates not in its nature;
Even so is it with all the Buddha's Dharma.

As waters in the vast ocean,
Absorbing hundreds of streams,
Are of the same taste forever;
Even so is it with all the Buddha's Dharma.

As the dragon-god with thunder and lightning
Brings showers on the earth all over,
And the rain-drops discriminate not;
Even so is it with all the Buddha's Dharma.

THE BUDDHA'S DHARMA. (2)

As in her oneness mother earth
Creates diversities of seeds
And in her inmost no discrimination knows;
E'en so is it with all the Buddha's Dharma.

As in the cloudless sky the sun
O'er the ten quarters all illuminates,
And in its brightness shows no difference;
E'en so is it with all the Buddha's Dharma.

As high up in the heavens is the moon
Beheld by all beings on earth,
And there's nowhere her glory reaches not;
E'en so is it with all the Buddha's Dharma.

The Brahma-râja great
In thousands of worlds himself all manifests
And knows in his being no diversities;
E'en so is it with all the Buddha's Dharma.

THE PASSIONS AND WISDOM.

Only in the filthiness of soil,
Could the seed be sown and grow;
Even so in the mire of passion
Cherished by all sentient beings
All over the world,
If by the sons of Buddha well attended to,
There will grow the seed of Buddha-dharma.

Just as in filth and mud
The lotus grows and blooms,
Even so in a heart defiled with evil karma
The seeds of Buddha-dharma are growing.

IGNORANCE AND ENLIGHTENMENT. (1)

A mansion there was once which was a hundred thousand years of age;
No occupant was there, nor doors nor windows;
Devas and men, all of a sudden,
There came and burned a lamp;
And the darkness that dwelt so long
Departed instantly without a word.
The inky darkness that the mansion filled
Resisted not, "I've lived here for ages,
And I'll never be removed from here."
Even with karma-consciousness and the horde of passions in the heart,
The analogy holds true.
Though there abiding many hundred thousand kalpas,
Their ultimate nature is not true nor real.
When a traveler, day or night,
Enters upon the truthful path,
The lamp of wisdom burns in its full splendor;
And the horde of evil passions
Cannot tarry there, even for a moment.

IGNORANCE AND ENLIGHTENMENT. (2)

Bright shines the lamp,
And the inky night is gone.
But with the darkness
The quarters vanish not;
Yet this illuminating lamp,
If not in the dark, nowhere doth shine:
For light and dark depend upon each other;
No selfhood having, [16] they're empty.
'Tis even so with enlightenment.
In comes enlightenment,
And out goes ignorance of its own accord.
But both are like unto the flowers in the air,
For neither by itself exists;
Impossible is one alone, either to keep or to forego.

THE BODHISATTVA AND ALL BEINGS [17]

Great Mother Earth
All creatures
Provides and nourishes,
But from none of them
She seeks a favor special, nor is she to any partial:
So is the Bodhisattva.
Since his awakening of the Heart,
Until he gains the depths of the Law
And realises the highest knowledge,
He toils to save all creatures,
Himself no favor seeking, nor to others granting any;
Regardless of friend and enemy,
Embracing all with single heart,
He fashions one and all for Bodhi.

* * *

The element Water
All permeating
Makes herbs and trees
In luxury grow,
Yet any favor special it nor shows nor seeks;
So is the Bodhisattva;
With a pure heart of love
All sentient beings equally embraces he;
All permeating gradually, universally,
The seeds immaculate he nourishes,
Which, breaking down all evils powerful,
Obtain the fruit of Buddha-knowledge.

* * *

The element Fire
Matures and ripens all
The tender shoots of the cereals;
Yet the element fire
From those young plants
No favor seeks, nor any shows to them;
So is the Bodhisattva:
With knowledge-fire
Matures he all
The tender shoots of creatures;
Yet he from them
No favor special seeks, nor shows he any.

* * *

The element Air,
By reason of its virtue,
Pervades all over Buddha-lands;
With the Bodhisattva
'Tis even so,
Who with consummate skill
'To Buddha's children
Preaches the Doctrine Holy.

THE BODHISATTVA.

His Firmness.

As Mâra, the evil one,
Commanding his four armies,
Even by the devas in the Kâmaloka,
Cannot be overwhelmed;
So is the Bodhisattva,
Whose heart, pure and clean,
By all the hosts of Evil,
Cannot be tempted, nor confused.

His Progress.

As the new moon,
In size increasing gradually,
Becomes perfect and full in the end;
Even so the Bodhisattva,
With a heart defilement-free,
All the good dharmas seeking and performing,
In virtue gradually progresses,
And finally obtains the Law of Purity, perfect and full.

His Enlightenment.

The rising sun,
All illumining,
All forms and images in the world
In glory are revealed;
So is the Bodhisattva:
The light of knowledge emitting,
And sentient beings illumining,
Bringeth he all to wisdom.

His Fearlessness.

Lion, the king of beasts,
Majestic, overpowering,
And in the forest wandering,
Knows he no fear, no terror;
So is the Bodhisattva:
Calmly abiding in Learning,
Intelligence, and Morality,
Throughout the universe,
Wherever he wanders about,
Knows he no fear, no doubt.

His Energy.

The giant elephant,
With energy wondrous,
A burden heavy carrying,
Shows not the least fatigue;
So is the Bodhisattva:
Bearing, for the sake of the masses,
The misery of the flesh,
He shows not the least apathy.

His Purity.

The lotus-flower,
Though growing in the marshy land,
By dirt, or mire, or filth
Is not defiled;
So is the Bodhisattva:
Though living in this world,
No form of passion
Ever touches him.

His Self-sacrifice.

There lived once a man
Who craftily and skillfully
Felled the trunks of trees,
But left the roots untouched,
That after due time
They might once more be growing;
'Tis even so with the Bodhisattva:
With the upâya that is excellent,
Desires and passions down he fells,
But leaves their seed unscathed
By reason of his all-embracing love,
And thereby ever and anon comes he on earth. [18]

THE BODHISATTVA'S HOMELESS LIFE. [19]

The homeless Bodhisat regards the home life [or the world at large]
As a hurricane that abates not awhile,
Or as the moon's illusive image in water cast,
Which the imagination takes deliberately for the real.

The water in itself contains no lunar image [real];
The real moon, dependent on water clear, a shadow casts;
So are all beings unreal; only conditionally they exist;
Yet 'tis imagined by the vulgar that an Atman they have.

The Atman is the product of conditions, and real it is not;
But for a reality the imagination it takes.
Have the two prejudices [20] removed,
And we perceive Intelligence most high and peerless.

Our confused imagination is like unto a black storm,
Blowing over the woods of birth and death, stirs up the leaves of consciousness:
By the four winds of fallacy 'tis haunted all the time,
And five damnation-causes it produces,
Entwining are indeed the roots of evil, which are three,
Through birth and death doth transmigration ever onward move.

Who to the Sutras listen and in them devoutly believe,
The right view they acquire, removing all the thoughts which are fallacious,
And every instant growing are Seeds of Intelligence,
And the Samâdhi of knowledge great and of spirituality is awakened.

When well disciplined in speculation deep and subtle,
In the dark no more we grope, nor do we reap the crop of pain;
Perceiving Suchness in the ultimate nature of things,
Subject and object both gone, and vanished are all sins.

Female and male, they're attributes, and they are void essentially:
The ignorant imagine and create the two which only relatively exist.
The Buddha has destroyed permanently the cause of ignorance,
And in the ultimate reality nothing particular sees he, male or female.

The excellent fruit of wisdom, if ever attained, remains the same for aye;
The vulgar nathless imagine wrongly and see therein a thing concrete and definite.
The Buddha's features thirty-two are after all no-features;
Who sees no-features in the features, the feature true he understands.

To wander homeless, and immaculate deeds to practise,
Over the heart to watch, in solitude quietly to sit:
This is the rightful way the Bodhisattva cleanses his heart;
Erelong will he attain the fruit of enlightenment.

THE BUDDHIST. [21]

Encourage not, for your self-interests,
Heterodoxy and false doctrines;
A merciful heart for all have ye;
Remove stupidity and untruth from your minds;
Be ye Tathâgata's most faithful servants;
And teach the masses who are ignorant,
To them the Bodhi impart, on yourselves it practising;
And thereby make the Buddha's name resound on earth;
Deliver the multitudes from sin and initiate them
To the perfect enlightenment of the Buddha:
Ye by these virtues firmly stand,
And your Intelligence-heart doth never fail.

HYMN TO THE BODHISATTVA. [22]

With lovingkindness, a Great Being who saves and protects,
Regards all beings impartially as his only child;
Energetically, cheerfully, and without stint,
His life he sacrifices, uprooting pain, and bringing bliss
unspeakable.

Surely he will attain the height of truth and beauty,
Forever be freed from the entanglement of birth and death.
And erelong will he the fruit of enlightenment obtain,
Eternally peaceful, and in the Uncreate joy finding.

A VOW OF THE BODHISATTVA.[23]

For the sake of all sentient beings on earth,
I aspire for the abode of enlightenment which is most high;
In all-embracing love awakened, and with a heart steadily firm,
Even my life I will sacrifice, dear as it is.

In enlightenment no sorrows are found, no burning desires;
'Tis enjoyed by all men who are wise.
All sentient creatures from the turbulent waters of the triple world,
I'll release, and to eternal pease them I'll lead.

THE TRUE HOMELESS ONE.[24]

Though not wearing the yellow robe,
Whose heart is free from defilement,
In the doctrine of Buddhas,
He is the true homeless one.

Though not devoid of showy ornaments,
Who has cut off all entanglements,
And in whose heart exists neither knottiness nor looseness,
He is the true homeless one.

Though not initiated by the Rules,
Whose heart is clean of all evil thoughts,
And open only to tranquillity, intelligence, and virtuous deeds,
He is the true homeless one.

Though not instructed in the Law,
Whose insight goes deep into the ultimate,
And is no more deluded by sham appearances,
He is the true homeless one.

The mind that takes no thought of the ego,
That goes beyond the illusory phenomena,
Yet sinks not into stupidity
Truly awakened to Intelligence it is.

Whose mind, awakened to Intelligence,
Sees no substantiality in the ego,
And, not seeing, yet remains firm,
This man cannot be injured.

THE BODHISATTVA'S SPIRITUAL LIFE.

Like unto the vast ocean that receives
All the waters, and yet overflows not;
Even so is the Bodhisattva,
Who knoweth no fatigue in seeking the merits of the Dharma.

Again, like unto the vast ocean that absorbs
All the streams, and yet shows no increase;
Even so is the Bodhisattva,
Who, receiving the deepest Dharma, nothing gaineth.

Again, like unto the vast ocean that refuses to take filth,
And wherein when absorbed doth foulness change to purity;
Even so is the Bodhisattva,
Whom all the filth of passion cannot tarnish.

Again, like unto the vast ocean whose bottom is unfathomable;
Even so is the Bodhisattva,
Whose virtues and wisdom are so immeasurable
That none ever knows their limits.

Again, like unto the vast ocean in which there's no diversity,
All the waters and streams pouring thereinto become of one taste alone;
Even so is the Bodhisattva,
Who listeneth to one note of Dharma.

Again, like unto the vast ocean that existeth not
For the interests of one individual;
Even so is the Bodhisattva,
Whose aspirations are for the benefit of all.

Again, like unto the vast ocean that embosoms the jewel called "all-jewel."
Of which all jewels are produced;
Even so is the jewel-treasure of the Bodhisattva,
For it is through this that all the other jewels shine.

Again, like unto the vast ocean that produces the three kinds of jewel,
And yet discriminates not between them;
Even so is the teaching of the Bodhisattva,
Who, equally delivering the three yânas, maketh not any distinction.

Again, like unto the vast ocean that by degrees becomes deeper;
Even so is the Bodhisattva,
Who, practising virtues for the sake of all,
Forever aspireth after the deepest omniscience.

Again, like unto the vast ocean that harbors not a corpse;
Even so is the Bodhisattva,
Who, with the heart of purity and the vow of Bodhi,
Harboreth not a passion, nor the thought of the Çrâvaka.

THE BODHISATTVA'S FAITH. (1) [27]

Perceiving all in one,
And one in all,
The Bodhisattva diligent in his work
Is never given up to indolence.

Pain he shunneth not, to pleasure he clingeth not,
As he is ever bent on the deliverance of all beings;
To him all Buddhas will themselves reveal,
And of their presence he is never weary.

He is in the deepest depths of the Dharma,
Where is found the inexhaustible ocean of merit.
All sentient beings in the fivefold path of existence,
He loveth as his own child;
Removing things unclean and filthy,
Supplying them with dharmas pure and immaculate.

THE BODHISATTVA'S FAITH. (2) [28]

While to the doctrine most high listening,
The Light of Pure Intelligence within me glows,
That shining over all the universe
All the enlightened ones to me reveals.

Who think there are individuals
They put themselves in the position most difficult;
Dharmas have no ego-master which is real,
For they are merely names and expressions.

The vulgar and ignorant know not
That within themselves they have a reality true and real,
That the Tathâgata is not of any particular form;
Therefore the Tathâgata they see not.

Dirt and dust obscuring their intelligence-eye,
Enlightenment perfect and true they see not;
And throughout kalpas immeasurable and innumerable,
In the stream of birth and death they go arolling.

Wandering and rolling is Samsâra,
No-more-arolling is Nirvâna;
Yet Samsâra and Nirvâna,
Absolutely, exists neither of them.

To believer in falsehood and sophistry,
Samsâra is here and Nirvâna there;
Clearly they grasp not the Dharma of ancient sages,
Nor understand the Path Incomparable.

Those who thus cling to forms individual,
Of Buddha's universal enlightenment, though they hear,
Themselves negate, and away they wander from the
right course of thought;
Therefore, they cannot see the Buddha.

Who the Dharma of Truth perceive,
Serene they are for aye, and abide in Suchness;
Enlightenment most truthful they understand,
Transcending words and all the modes of speech.

Illusory are all forms individual;
No such thing as dharma here exists:
No enlightened ones
Seek Truth in things particular.

Whose insight to the past extends,
To the future and over the present,
And who fore'er abides in serenity of Suchness,
He's said to be a Tathâgata.

THE BODHISATTVA'S FAITH. (3) [29]

I would rather suffer sufferings innumerable
That I might listen to the voices of Buddhas,
Than enjoy all sorts of pleasure
And not hear Buddhas' names.

The reason why since ages out of mind
We suffer sufferings countless
And transmigrate through birth and death,
Is that we have not heard Buddhas' names

A reality that exists in things unreal,
A perfect Intellect synthetising truth and falsehood,
And that which transcends all the modes of relativity,
This is called the Bodhi.

Buddhas of the present are not products of composite conditions,
Nor are those of the past, nor those of the future.
What is formless in all forms,
That is the true essence of Buddhas.

Who thus perceives
The deepest significance of all existences,
In innumerable Buddhas, he will see
The truth and reality of the Dharma-body.

The Dharma-body knows truth as true,
And falsehood as false,
And well understands the realm of reality;
Therefore, it is called perfect intellect.

The enlightened has nothing enlightened,
Which is the true spirituality of all Buddhas:
And in this wise they behave,
Neither to be one nor to be two.

They see the one in the many,
They see the many in the one
The Dharma has nothing to depend upon;
How could it be a product of combination?

The actor and the action,
Neither really subsists:
Who can understand this,
Seeks not reality in either of them.

And here where reality is unseekable,
Buddhas find there the resting abode
The Dharma has nothing to depend upon;
And the enlightened have nothing to cling to.

NOTES

TO THE APPENDIX

---

[1] This and the following are translations from some Mahâyâna texts in the Buddhist Tripitaka, which were rendered into the Chinese language at various times from Sanskrit mostly through the co-operation of the Hindu missionaries and Chinese scholars. A detailed analysis of these texts is most urgently needed, as they contain many informations of great importance not only concerning the history of Buddhism in India but also concerning early Hindu culture generally. A rather incomplete idea as to their contents and material and general character will be attained by the perusal of Rev. Nanjo's *Catalogue of the Chinese Tripitaka*, Oxford, 1883.

Mahâyâna-mûlajâta-hṛdayabhûmi-dhyâna Sûtra, (Nanjo, no. 955,) fas. iii.

[2] The *Avatamsaka*, fas. xiv., p. 73.

[3] *The Avatamsaka*, (Buddhabhadra's translation), fas. xiv, p. 72.

[4] To conceive the Tathâgata as a personal being who appeared on earth for a certain limited time and then eternally disappeared is not Mahâyânistic. He reveals himself constantly and of his own will in this world of particulars.

[5] *Sarvadharma-pravṛtti-nirdeça Sûtra* (Nanjo, no. 1012)

[6] *Mahâyâna-mûlajâta-hrdavabhûmi-dhyâna Sûtra* (Nanjo 955), fas. iii, p. 75.

[7] The three rings are: 1. the giver, 2. the receiver. and 3. the thing given, material or immaterial.

[8] Precepts. The three sets are: 1. one relating to good behavior, 2. to the accumulation of merit, and 3. to lovingkindness toward all beings.

[9] The mental (subjective), physical (objective), and oral.

[10] The intellectual and the affective.

[11] *Sarvadharma-pravṛtti-nirdeça Sûtra.*

[12] Literally, "when greed is neither born nor dead." This means, to live in the world as not living in it. This subjective divine innocence is thought by Buddhists the essence of the religious life. The consciousness of one's worth, or self-conceit, is a great obstacle in the path of perfect virtue. As in the case of mechanical work or physical exercise, we attain perfect skillfulness only when the work is involuntarily done, i.e., without any conscious effort on the part of the performer; so in our moral and spiritual life we attain the height of virtuousness or saintliness when we identify ourselves with the reason of our being. This is Laotze's doctrine of non-action or non-resistance, and also the teaching of the *Bhagavadgîta.* As remarked elsewhere, when a man reaches this stage of religious life, he ceases to be human, but divine, in the sense that he transcends the world of good and evil and eternally abides in the realm of the beautiful.

[13] This is a very radical statement and is enough to frighten timid moralists and "God-fearing" pietists. Therefore, it is said that "Give not that which is holy to the dogs, neither cast ye your pearls before swine." But think not that this is expounding antinomianism.

[14] This and all the following are taken from the *Kâṣyapa-Parivarta* (Nonjo, 805).

[15] This gâthâ may not be very intelligible to our readers. The sense is: Whatever is done by a Buddha or Bodhisattva does not come from logical calculation or deliberate premeditation, but immediately from his inmost heart, which, in most natural and freest manner, responds to the needs of the suffering. This response is altogether free from all human elaboration, for the Buddha shows no painful and struggling efforts in so doing. Everything he does is like the work of nature herself. His life is above the narrow sphere of human morality which is marked with a desperate struggle between good and evil. His is in the realm of the divinely beautiful.

[16] "Having no selfhood" (*svabhâva*), means that things have no independent existence, no self-nature which will eternally preserve their thingish identity. This theory has been explained in the chapter dealing with the doctrine of non-atman. To state summarily, darkness and light are conditioned by each other; apart from darkness there is no light, and conversely, without light darkness has no meaning. Even so with enlightenment and ignorance: one independent of the other, they have no existence, they cannot be conceived. They are like imaginary flowers in the air projected there by a confused subjectivity. They are nothing but our ideal fabrication. To cling to God only, forgetting that we are living in the world below, in the world of relativity, is just as much one-sided as to lose ourselves in the whirlpool of earthly pleasures without the thought of God. Life, however, is not antithetic, but synthetic. Truth is never one-sided, it is always in the middle. Therefore, seek enlightenment in ignorance and truth in error. A dualistic interpretation of the world and life is not approved by Buddhists. Compare the sentiment expressed herein with Emerson's poem as elsewhere quoted, in which these lines occur:

> "But in the mud and scum of things,
> There always, always, something sings."

[17] *The Kâṣyapaharivarta Sûtra* (Nonjo, 805.)

[18] The sense is: The Bodhisattva never desires a complete absorption in the Absolute, in which no individual existences are distinguishable. He always leaves the "Will to live" unhurt, as it were, so that he could come in this world of particulars ever and anon. What he has destroyed is the egoistic assertion of the Will, for the aim of Buddhism is not to remove the eternal principle of life, but to manifest it in its true significance. The wishes of the Bodhisattva, therefore, are never egocentric; he knows that transmigration and rebirth are painful, but as it is by rebirth alone that he could mingle himself in the world of sin and save the suffering creatures therein, he never shuns the misery of life. His work of revelation is constant and eternal.

[19] *The Mahâyâna-mûlajâti-hrdayabhûmi-dhyâna Sûtra*, fas. IV.

[20] The two prejudices or obstacles that lie in our way to enlightenment are: 1 that which arises from intellectual shortsightedness; 2. that which arises from impurity of heart.

[21] *Sûtra on Mahâkâṣyapa's Question Concerning the Absolute.*

[22] *Suvarna-Prabhâ Sûtra.*

[23] *Suvarna-Prabhâ Sûtra*, Chap. 26

[24] *Padmapani Sûtra*, Fas. 8.

[25] *The Avatamsaka Sutru.*

[26] This means that the heart of the Bodhisattva which is pure and eternal in its essential nature has nothing added externally to it by studying the Dharma; for the Dharma is nothing else than the expression of his own heart.

[27] The *Avatamsaka*, fas. IX, p. 48. This pantheistic thought of the One-All is generally considered to be Buddhistic; but the truth is that every genuine religious sentiment inevitably leads us to this final conviction. Even in the so-called transcendental monotheistic Christianity, we find the pantheistic thought boldly proclaimed and put in contrast to the idea of "our Father which art in Heaven." For instance, read the following passage from Thomas à Kempis: "He to whom all things are one, he who reduceth all things to one, and seeth all things in one, may enjoy a quiet mind, and remain at peace in God." (Chap. III.) The passage in the Gospel of John declaring that "the Father is in me and I in him," when logically carried out, comes to echo the same sentiment entertained by Buddhists, who recognise a manifestation of the Dharmakâya in all beings, animate as well as inanimate. The Christianity of to-day is that of Paul as expounded in his letters, but the future one will advance a few steps more and will be that of John.

[28] From the *Avatamsaka Sutra.*

[29] From the *Avatamsaka Sutra.*

INDEX.